Technological innovation and network evolution

Technological Innovation and Network Evolution is one of the first volumes to illuminate contemporary network innovation in advanced technologies from a historical and evolutionary perspective. By looking at the new area of digital image processing, or 'machine vision', Anders Lundgren traces the advances which have been made as the technology becomes more and more highly developed, and the way in which success – and failure – relates to different kinds of organizational forms and industrial relationships. Through an examination of key issues, including public policy, system-builders, corporate strategy and internationalization, the author highlights the unique features of networks and the reasons for their growth and decline.

In this thought-provoking volume, Anders Lundgren shows a rare appreciation of the process of generating a network, showing clearly the role of trial and error, the limits of policy, and the nature of support by constellations of producers and users. Students and researchers concerned with the management of innovation will find this of great interest, as will policy makers aiming to foster technological and industrial change.

Anders Lundgren is Assistant Professor at the Stockholm School of Economics.

Technological innovation and network evolution

Anders Lundgren

London and New York

First published 1995
by Routledge
11 New Fetter Lane, London EC4P 4EE

Simultaneously published in the USA and Canada
by Routledge
29 West 35th Street, New York, NY 10001

© 1995 Anders Lundgren

Typeset in Times by LaserScript, Mitcham, Surrey
Printed and bound in Great Britain by
Biddles Ltd, Guildford and King's Lynn

British Library Cataloguing in Publication Data
A catalogue record for this book is available from the British Library.

Library of Congress Cataloging in Publication Data
A catalogue record for this book has been requested

ISBN 0–415–08219–6

Contents

Part IV   Critical revision of the emerging pattern

Figures

Tables

Foreword

In recent years much empirical research on innovation has concentrated on the role of networks. Several attempts have been made to enumerate the formation of new networks and to analyse their activities. Much of this literature concludes that networks of innovations have increased rapidly during the last decade and that they constitute a new and more efficient form of organizing innovative activities.

However, while it is probably true that the scope of innovation networking and the number of participants have increased, especially in international networking, it is important to remember that pluralistic inputs to innovation have always been significant, even if they were less formally organized. No firm can be self-sufficient and empirical studies of innovation have consistently shown that interactions with future users, with suppliers of materials, instruments and components, with external sources of scientific and technical information and even with competitors have often been critical for success. Moreover, there were certainly numerous examples of formal networks of innovators both before and during the Second World War. Thus the largest R&D project before the Manhattan Project was the consortium of seven oil companies and plant contractors to develop the fluid bed catalytic cracking process in the 1930s, whilst many weapon systems were developed through collaborative networks of government, industrial and university laboratories. Consequently, it is not surprising that Anne Markusen and other researchers have found similarities between weapon system projects and contemporary civil networks of research collaboration in Japan and other countries.

It is therefore of interest to identify the truly novel features of contemporary networks rather than simply to enumerate them, useful though this may be.

Furthermore, it is essential to understand the evolution of networks, including the reasons for their formation, their growth, their success or their failure and also the reasons for the decline and disappearance of some networks. As with innovative firms, there are deaths as well as births. Both from a theoretical standpoint and from a policy view, this depth of historical analysis is essential.

However, a review of the literature on networks shows that there are few studies which approach them from this historical, evolutionary perspective. This study by Anders Lundgren is therefore especially welcome, all the more so because of the exceptionally thorough nature of his research. His study illuminates many aspects of contemporary industrial innovation in advanced technologies including the continuing high degree of uncertainty affecting these technologies and the future markets, the importance of interactions between science and technology and the crucial role of sophisticated users of advanced systems. His work is thought-provoking for anyone concerned with the management of innovation or with policy-making in this difficult area. Although his results are of course particularly interesting for Swedish readers, they are no less relevant for any industrial country, since the technologies and the markets are global in nature.

Lundgren distinguishes three phases in the evolution of networks: 'Genesis', 'Coalescence' and 'Dissemination'. This part of his analysis is particularly important for policy-makers in government and industry since he shows that strategies and policies which may be valuable in one phase may be irrelevant or even counter-productive in another. University research is especially important for genesis while the understanding of user needs is critical for dissemination. The participation of university researchers and of future users may be valuable at every stage of networking but the contribution of the various participants changes substantially as a network evolves. Above all, Lundgren's study confirms the systematic nature of technology and continues the traditions of the best European and American historians of technology in this respect: both French scholars such as Bertrand Gille and Americans such as Thomas P. Hughes. He brings to this older tradition new insights based on deep understanding of a new technological system.

Christopher Freeman
Science Policy Research Unit (SPRU), University of Sussex
Brighton

Preface

Jacques Loussier's *Lumières* is resounding from my portable CD-player, the coffee machine is hotter than ever before and I know that it is time to put down the pen or rather to save and quit. In the course of this inquiry into the nature of technological and social change, I have been through three technologies of writing: an ordinary ball-point pen, an electric typewriter and finally I entered the micro-electronic age and shifted to a personal computer. If these technological shifts have had any significant, positive or negative, effect upon the quality of the work I cannot tell. They have certainly increased the cost of writing and the willingness to make changes. To a large extent I have changed my way of organizing the work. I have slowly adapted to the methods of word-processing and I have moved towards more and more sophisticated technology, yet when the writing gets difficult I sometimes go back to using the ball-point pen. The outcome of the study would probably have been slightly different had I stayed with the original technology. I chose, however, to wander in the garden of writing technologies and whichever route I might have taken would have led me to a different end, from where there would be no return.

The result of my endeavour to unravel the secrets of technological and social change has been affected not only by the technology used. The outcome of one person's struggle is the result of the social settings in which he or she is implicated. To use the words of Thomas Merton: 'My successes are not my own. The way to them was prepared by others. The fruit of my labours is not my own: for I am preparing the way for the achievements of another. Nor are my failures my own. They may spring from the failures of another, but they are also compensated for by another's achievement.' During my years of seemingly endless struggles I have needed a lot of help, which has been generously offered by friends and colleagues. My first thanks must naturally go to my family: my wife Gunilla, without whom I would not have started the project in the first place, and my daughters

Josefin and Amelie who have made all of these years at least twice as dynamic.

Reflecting on the past, one cannot help but realize how important other people have been; pursuing research is really all about assuming a great social debt. As I have trod the path of technology and society, the following people have generously provided company, guidance, comments and help: Per Andersson, Lena Björklund, Rune Castenäs, Paul A. David, Lennart Elg, Torbjörn Flink, Christopher Freeman, Håkan Håkansson, Bill Harris, Claes-Fredrik Helgesson, Susanne Hertz, Staffan Hultén, Dimitrios Ioannidis, Jens Laage-Hellman, Hans Kjellberg, Svante Lindqvist, Lars-Gunnar Mattsson, Bengt Mölleryd, Anna Nyberg, Lena Nordenlöw, Susanne Östlund, Jan Ottosson, Nathan Rosenberg, Bo Sellstedt, Ivan Snehota, Magnus Söderlund, Bengt Stymne, Mats Vilgon and Alexandra Waluszewski. I owe everything to this network and to many other actors at Stockholm School of Economics and Uppsala University.

The scientists, researchers, public policy makers, and managers in the Swedish image processing network have provided invaluable insights into the nature of digital image technology. Without them there would be no image processing network to study. Business people, bank robbers and researchers go where the money is. In my case it is the Swedish National Board for Technical Development and the Swedish Council for Research in the Humanities and Social Sciences that have kept me going for all of these years.

This book was originally published as a doctoral thesis at Stockholm School of Economics. The intention was to make some marginal revisions and then publish the study. Four months were set aside to make these revisions. It took more than two years. Still the revisions are only marginal, but in my mind they reflect a totally new understanding of the problem of technological and industrial change. In a world where history and context matter, marginal change can be substantial and also marginal changes take a very long time to realize.

The technology used and the social context in which I have worked have led me down a specific path and this has made all the difference. I am now fully computerized and the small wonders of technology are constantly luring me to write more and more. At the other end sit my colleagues and friends urging me to write better and better. The quest for knowledge seems like an endless pilgrimage where the end is just a new beginning.

Anders Lundgren
Stockholm
February 1994

Introduction

Every study can be conceived as a journey into the unknown. One starts off from somewhere and hopes to end up somewhere else, having accumulated knowledge along the way. I entered this specific journey intrigued by the capacity for resurrection and change of modern society in general and Sweden in particular. New gadgets, carried by new technologies and new firms, were constantly being turned out. Some, such as cellular phones and automobiles, were extremely successful, while others such as picture phones and plastic bicycles, were less so. Yet, in all of the dynamics and changes there was an apparent stability. We could all read about the paperless, electronic office but few of us, if any, had yet experienced it. In this paradox of change and stability, I set out to study technological and industrial change. What were the needs and possibilities in developing a high-technology industry in a small country like Sweden?

This study was embarked upon through the raising of one specific issue. How could we understand the birth of a new industrial network and what were the forces propelling the birth process? Research into the nature of corporate action in industrial networks had been under way for several years. Some reports had already been published, while others were yet to be completed.[1] The main thrust of the work was that individual and corporate actions were perceived as being embedded in an economic, social and technical structure labelled 'industrial networks'. The focus was thus upon the interrelationships between firms and between the actions undertaken by these firms. The successful completion of the first research ventures and the perceived potential of the new perspective on economic organization were transformed into a substantial research program – 'Marketing and Competitiveness' – revolving around the general theme of industrial networks.

The empirical focus in the research program – as well as in the earlier studies – was on traditional Swedish industries: mechanical engineering, steel, paper and pulp, and construction. Within the steering committee of the program it was considered necessary to complement the studies of corporate action in existing networks with a study of the birth of a new network. Several possible arenas for the study were suggested. The final choice of the object of the study fell in favour of computerized image processing, which was the suggested arena least attached to traditional Swedish industries. The study of technological innovation and the birth of a new industrial network not only fitted perfectly into the research program but also was a continuation of a long tradition of inquiries into the nature of industries and into the nature of innovation or product development.[2]

Technological networks and networks of innovators are increasingly being explored in the quest for knowledge of industrial change. Since this study was initiated several other studies of innovation in networks have been reported. Nevertheless, few have focused on the evolution of technological networks. Reviewing the literature on innovation and networks Christopher Freeman claims that 'Longitudinal studies on the evolution of networks could be particularly valuable.' He continues by arguing that network evolution should be explained not in terms of costs but rather in terms of strategic behaviour, appropriability, technological complementarity and sociological factors.[3]

The story to be told – the emergence of computerized image processing in Sweden – has been structured in accordance with the gestalt theory of invention suggested by Abbott Payson Usher in his delineation of the process of cumulative synthesis.[4] The book is accordingly divided into four parts: Setting the stage, The act of insight, Novelty in thought and action: the emergence of digital image processing in Sweden, and Critical revision of the emerging pattern. The two chapters of Part I set the stage for the inquiry into the emergence of image processing in Sweden. In Chapter 1 the issues are stated and in Chapter 2 image processing and the preconditions from which it emerged are presented. Chapter 2 continues with an overview of the relationship between research and development and industrial production in Sweden.

As we endure the hardship of our journeys we encounter others, travelling in similar directions gladly sharing their experiences. Part II describes the act of theoretical insight, provided by the predecessors and contemporaries on the paths of inquiry into the nature of technological change and industrial evolution. The three chapters of Part II elucidate the general perspectives underlying this study and the particular model generated by it. Chapter 3 exhibits perspectives on technology and industry and knowledge. In Chapter 4 I argue for the necessity of setting technological change and industrial evolution in the context of time and place. This chapter is closed with a discussion of the particular method of historical analysis employed in the study. Chapter 5 outlines a network perspective on technological change and contains a framework for understanding the emergence of a new technology and a new industrial network.

Part III comprises Chapters 6–8 and is an account of the emergence and evolution of digital image technology and of the rise of an image processing network in Sweden. In Chapter 6 the genesis of digital image technology and the image processing network is presented. Chapter 7 describes the formation years and in Chapter 8 the establishing of the new technology is related. The conclusions of this journey into the unknown and the knowledge accumulated along the way is presented in Part IV. Chapter 9 features some concluding remarks on the emergence of digital image processing in Sweden. In Chapter 10 the study is taken one step further, introducing some more general themes regarding technological innovation and industrial evolution in industrial networks. The overall structure of the book is depicted in Figure 0.1.

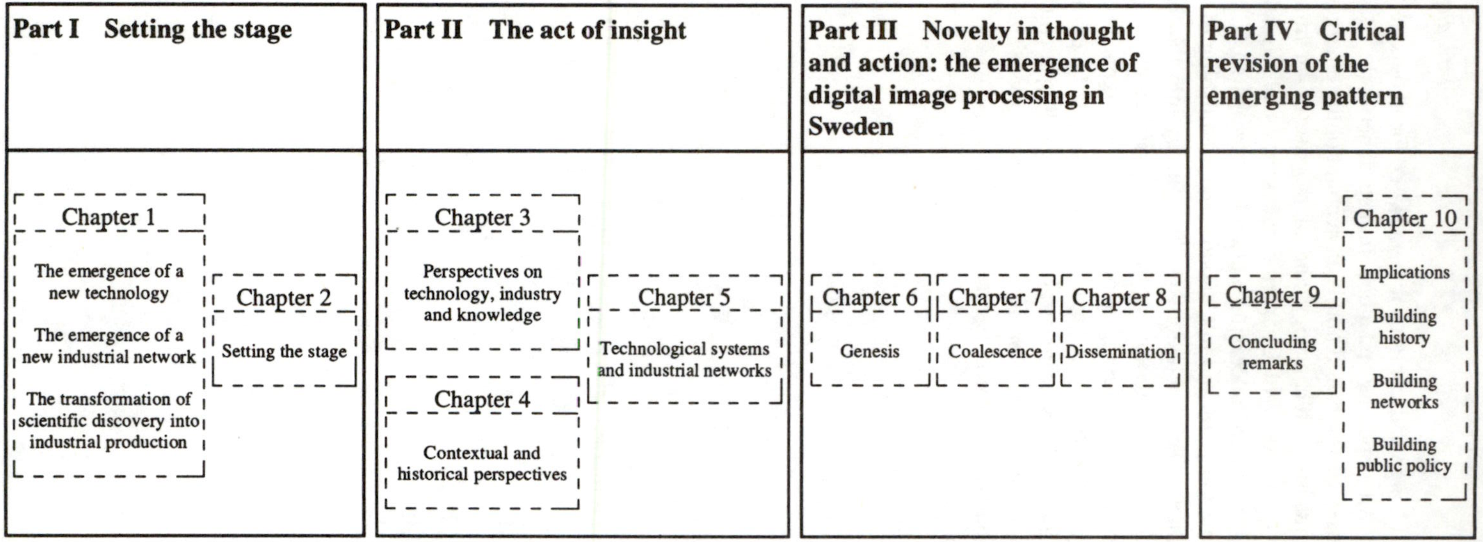

Part I Setting the stage	Part II The act of insight	Part III Novelty in thought and action: the emergence of digital image processing in Sweden	Part IV Critical revision of the emerging pattern
Chapter 1 The emergence of a new technology The emergence of a new industrial network The transformation of scientific discovery into industrial production **Chapter 2** Setting the stage	**Chapter 3** Perspectives on technology, industry and knowledge **Chapter 4** Contextual and historical perspectives **Chapter 5** Technological systems and industrial networks	**Chapter 6** Genesis **Chapter 7** Coalescence **Chapter 8** Dissemination	**Chapter 9** Concluding remarks **Chapter 10** Implications Building history Building networks Building public policy

Figure 0.1 The overall structure of the book

Part I
Setting the stage

The world was never made;
  It will change, but it will not fade.
  So let the wind range;
  For even and morn
    Ever will be
    Thro' eternity.
  Nothing was born;
  Nothing will die;
  All things will change.
               Alfred Tennyson (1809–192)

In this part the stage will be set for the study of the emergence of an image processing network in Sweden. The challenge is to set a stage where nothing is born and nothing dies, yet all things change; where new structures emerge from old ones and old structures slowly fade away. The stage setting is introduced in Chapter 1 with a discussion of the birth of a new industrial network and the formulation of the issues at hand. What are the forces behind the emergence of technologies? What are the forces provoking the emergence of a new industrial structure, a new network? What is the nature of the relationship between scientific research, technological development and economic change? Chapter 2 is a brief introduction to digital image technology and the context in which it has been developed.

1 The birth of a new industrial network

INTRODUCTION

In Great Britain the York Archaeological Trust has reproduced the face of a presumed Viking king by combining, in three dimensions, a Viking cranium and the face of a modern man. In Japan researchers have developed a robot that has the capacity both to read and to interpret musical notes and to play them on an ordinary piano. It does not require much imagination to recognize the enormous gap which exists between the reproduction of human faces and the music-playing robot and commercially viable applications. Nevertheless, digital image technology is slowly invading the prevalent structures of western technology. Digital cameras are becoming more readily available; the first Sony Mavica was presented in 1981 and lately Canon introduced a still-video camera on the consumer market. Our everyday newspapers are turning into colour magazines, exhibiting more and more colour pictures of excellent quality. An ordinary night in front of the television is filled with computer generated images. Even picture phones, first presented in the mid-1960s, are reappearing as the future of telecommunication. Digital technology is gaining headway in the battle of systems between analog and digital image technology. This technological shift can also be observed beyond the scope of our everyday lives. Radiology departments of hospitals are turning into veritable computer laboratories with CAT-scanners, magnetic resonance imaging, digital image archives and image processing computers. Computer processed satellite images are increasingly being used in the production of maps. And in industrial production robotic and machine vision is writing a new chapter in the development of industrial automation.

Digital image technology emerged in the continuation of the development of calculating machines. Groups of researchers, working independently, began to experiment, using the first generation computers to analyse data contained in images. Since then the path to image processing technology has been filled with temporary successes and failures and enclosed by futile attempts and unexplored routes. The digital image technology presently available is probably neither optimal nor conclusive.

If change results from series of activities and events, both advancements and set-backs, and if the outcome of these activities and events is not necessarily moving towards a final optimal stage, or towards a long-run equilibrium, then how can these change processes be understood? More specifically, what are the constituent forces behind the birth of new industrial networks?

THREE PATHS OF INQUIRY

A new industrial network, that is, a new economic, social and technical structure in which corporate action is embedded, does not emerge in a vacuum. Already at the outset of this study the birth of a network was associated with the development of new technologies. As scientific research seemed to be of increasing importance in the generation of new technologies, the relationship between scientific research and industrial production was considered to be critical in the birth of a new network. Thus, the birth of a new network can be perceived as being comprised of three interrelated processes: (1) the emergence of a new technology; (2) the emergence of a new industrial network; and (3) the transformation of scientific discovery into industrial production. Consequently, the journey into the birth of a new network has been pursued along three different paths of inquiry, asking three specific questions related to the development of image processing technology in Sweden. What was behind the emergence of a new technology? What was behind the emergence of new industries? What was the nature of the transformation of scientific discovery into industrial production?

Digital image processing: the emergence of a new technology

Can machines be brought to see? Vision is one of the distinctive marks of human intelligence. Can the capability of processing image information be mimicked in the development of the mechanized world? Apparently, this is the case: advances within optics and electronics, in television and computer technology have prompted a development of machine vision and computers are increasingly being used to process information contained in natural images. The first tottering attempts, in the 1950s and 1960s, to use computers to analyse image data started off the development of a new technology for computerized image processing. The new technology – machine vision, computerized image processing, digital image technology, or whatever we choose to call it – unfolded alongside the development of television and computer technology and, in the 1980s, of artefacts of the new technology; general image processing computers, robotic vision systems, digital image transmitters and others, were increasingly becoming commercially available.

Machine vision is not yet, and will perhaps never become, as general as human vision. Digital image processing is, however, a multi-purpose technology in that it stretches over several applications, from industrial automation to radiology. On the supply side digital image technology is a combination of several interrelated technologies and on the demand side it is applied in a wide variety of fields. This suggests that, instead of perceiving digital image technology, or any other technology for that matter, as an isolated, well-defined entity, we should recognize that technologies are interrelated with other technologies into technological systems. Any inquiry into the emergence of new technologies should thus be focused not upon individual innovations but on the origination and evolution of technological systems.

In Sweden the pursuit of science, research and development undertaken by both public institutions and private firms together with public policy resulted in the origination and establishment of digital image technology. Sweden has secured a remarkably prominent position in the international research and development related to digital image technology. It is remarkable considering the size of the Swedish economy and industry, and in light of the fact that digital image processing was developed at the time that the Swedish national computer industry declined. The technological achievements in digital image processing have, however, not yet been transformed into an equally successful commercialization of the technology.

The emergence and evolution of new technologies is an intriguing issue. What are the forces behind the emergence of technologies? What are the preconditions for technological innovation and how are innovations interrelated? Why has Sweden been especially successful in the development of digital image technology and why has this technological success not been transformed into a commercial success? Behind these questions lies the more intricate problem of the emergence and establishment of new technologies and industries, specifically in small or mid-size economies.

The Swedish image processing network: the emergence of a new industry structure

Technologies or technological systems are not autonomous. Behind the development of any technology lies endless human endeavour of technological innovation and social and economic organization. Prevalent technologies have thus become embedded in and inseparable from the social and economic structures fostering and sustaining them. The prevalent order has evolved over decades, revealing complex sets of flows of resources and specialized skills. The emergence of a new technology requires the development of new skills and the reorganization of the pre-existing flow of resources. Technological change and social and economic reorganization are two sides of the same coin and we cannot have one without the other. The emergence of a new technology not only requires innovators and manufacturers but also suppliers, users, distributors and others who are joined together in organized networks of functions, activities and actors. Transforming technological innovation into economic production requires the interconnection of several different industrial activities, ranging from the supply of inputs, the necessary manufacturing or assembling facilities, and distribution and marketing capabilities to the use or consumption of the new technology by the end-user. To perform these activities several different resources are required. Some of the activities and resources can be facilitated and controlled by single actors, but the performance of a full chain of activities usually calls for several actors with different skills to join forces. As they do so, a new industrial structure – a network of interrelated actors – will emerge.

Technological systems are never optimal or conclusive and the realized combinations – trials, inventions or innovations – are always far outnumbered by the possible ones. At the outset of the development of a new technological system few, if any, are even aware that pieces of different technologies one day will be put together into a system. The technological system will unfold as firms and organizations act and interact to try new combinations. The development of new technologies is thus as much a question of social construction as it is prompted by technical factors. The emergence and evolution of a new technology must therefore be accompanied or preceded by an emerging and evolving industrial structure which connects the supply and the demand sides and so facilitates the development, production and application of the new technology.

Swedish actors, acting and interacting to solve everyday problems, prompted not only the emergence of digital image technology, but also the establishment of new relationships connecting the proponents of the new technology: in other words, the moulding of a new industrial network. As the problems encountered by individual actors shifted, the actors developed relationships with other actors, resulting in changes in the emerging network.

The rise of new industrial structures is most often associated with the emergence of new technologies. Yet, apart from Schumpeter's notion that new technologies would be predominantly fostered by new entrepreneurial firms, we know little about the birth of new industries or industrial networks.

What are the forces provoking the emergence of a new institutional structure, a new industrial network? To answer this question we must study the intricate relationships between the emergence of new technologies and new industrial structures and between the micro level acts of individual inventors and entrepreneurs and the macro level social, economic and/or technological development.

Digital image technology: transforming scientific research into industrial production

The linkage between scientific research, technological development and industrial production is neither as straightforward as common logic might suggest nor as strong as it perhaps objectively should be.[1] Science and technology as they are known today did not originate from the same set of circumstances. Technological development has been motivated primarily by the solving of problems of economic production, while the growth of scientific knowledge has been motivated chiefly by non-economic factors. The linkage between science and technology has at best been weak and the evolving institutional structures for scientific research and technological development are markedly different. The relationship between science, technology and industrial innovation has, however, not remained static. Over time it has changed character, generally drifting towards increasing integration. Since World War II, the emergence and development of computer technology and biotechnology and the revitalization within telecommunications have revealed a closing of the gap between scientific discovery and industrial innovation. Science is increasingly at the service of economic production and the translation of scientific discovery into industrial innovation and economic production is a problem attracting more and more interest. Needless to say, the progress of scientific knowledge is not solely determined by economic factors.

Digital image processing carries the marks of modern technology in that it predominantly emerged, at institutions of science all over the western world, as a solution to specific problems often with no bearing at all on the economic or industrial sphere. Even though some well-established private firms took an interest in the development of automatic image analysis, the quest for the new technology was primarily pursued within military research institutions and by university based researchers. In Sweden, university based research played a critical role in the fostering of digital image technology and by establishing new firms the scientists attempted to realize the economic potential of the new technology. Translating the results from scientific research into viable industrial innovations proved, however, to be much more problematic and costly than the proponents and supporters of digital image   processing had anticipated when the first firms were established.

Transforming scientific discovery into economic productivity – in other words, bridging the gap between scientific research and industrial innovation, between two different institutional structures – seems to pose specific problems in the emergence and evolution of a new technology. Even though several authors have dedicated their lives to unravelling the secrets behind technological development and economic change, much still remains to be learned. The question to be posed is: What is the nature of the relationship between scientific research, technological development and economic change? To begin to answer this question we must first address the complexity of evolutionary processes and thus attain a better under-standing of the interdependencies of the relationships between science, technology and industry.

Progress, growth or development is not – as was assumed by the classical and neo-classical economists – universally available and achievable; hence it is not inevitable.[2] The process of growth is both problematic and painful and the sources of growth, such as technology, are unclear and their conse-quences are uncertain. To learn more about technology and its consequences we must probe into the process of growth, but the bare history of an industry, an invention, an organization, is inadequate. If we are to embrace the complex structures of growth and change, we must observe what is oc-curring in various fields simultaneously. Thus, the emergence of a new industrial network must be studied in its specific context of time and space.

STATING THE ISSUE

I have here outlined an agenda for the study of emerging technologies and industries. It is apparent that the emergence and evolution of image pro-cessing in Sweden is a complex process with many facets representing most aspects of social progress. The processes sketched above, namley the emergence of a technology, the emergence of an industrial network and the transformation of scientific discovery into industrial production, are but some of the puzzles contained in the birth of a new network.

The paths of inquiry into the emergence of computerized image pro-cessing in Sweden have generated the following broad research questions.

1 What are the forces behind the emergence of technologies?
2 What are the forces provoking the emergence of a new industrial struc-ture, a new network?
3 What is the nature of the relationship between scientific research, tech-nological development and economic change?

The questions put forward are both broad and far-reaching. It would thus seem logical to treat them in isolation since the answering of each question requires a major inquiry. Yet, the questions are interrelated: they are really complementary verses of the same song. To answer one of them we must have at least tentative answers to the other two.

The fact that we are dealing with a highly complex problem should not prevent us from venturing into the matter. Instead of trying to simplify the problem as far as we can, which would be the natural way of conducting a scientific inquiry, we should acknowledge the fact that this is a complex issue and that only by retaining some of the whole will we be able to increase our understanding of the complex problem. This implicitly suggests that some of the more important insights might arise in the interface between different facets of the problem. Scientific inquiry, however, is all about simplification and abstraction, at least when we proceed beyond pure description, but although this must be featured in the inquiry as a whole, it need not pertain to how we approach the problem.

Nevertheless, when studying the development of image processing in Sweden it is necessary to narrow the perspective to more specific problems. Using non-neoclassical economic theory, predominantly theoretical economic history, history of technology and the growing field of network studies as focusing devices, we are able to limit the analysis to a few more specific aspects of technological progress. The three parallel lines of reasoning outlined above provide us with an intriguing set of interrelated research questions. Combined, they constitute the backbone of this study of the emergence and evolution of digital image technology.

The purpose is twofold. First, there is the empirically oriented aim of providing a comprehensive picture of the development of digital image processing in Sweden. Second, there is the theoretically oriented aim of depicting the complex interplay of the emergence of technologies and industrial networks in the transformation of scientific discovery into industrial production.

It is obvious that a complex set of interrelated issues is addressed. First the emergence of digital image technology in particular will be depicted and then the emergence of technologies and industries in general will be highlighted. Given this context, two basic problems of social progress are addressed. The main problem is the relationship between technological and industrial change: the relationship between the emergence and evolution of a new technological system and the emergence and evolution of a new industrial network. Enclosed in this problem is the second enigma, that of translating scientific discovery into technological innovation and industrial production – a theme characteristic of post-Second World War industrial evolution.

The specific focus of the study is motivated partly by the potential implications for the formulation of theoretical propositions regarding technological development and industrial change and partly by the practical implications for the formulation of public and business policies towards the support and the pursuit of technological development. Despite numerous studies of technological change we are still surprised by the poor performance of research and development, when it comes to its impact upon the present state of affairs. It usually takes much longer and is much more costly to develop new technologies than was expected. This gap between the stylized facts of our knowledge of technological and industrial change and the observed outcome suggests that we still have much more to learn regarding the process of technological development and industrial change.

Knowledge of the relationship between technological and industrial change in the transformation of scientific discovery into economic production is essential in the formulation of future public policy towards the support of technological development and commercialization of new technology. This study produces insights into the crucial issue of the balance between support for every venture into technology and support for only the most prosperous ones. By relating technological innovation to industrial evolution it will be possible to discuss not only who or what should be supported and when but also to elaborate on the organization of the support. For business firms and other individual actors who are promoting or pursuing the development of new technologies, this study provides new perspectives on research and business strategies in that it connects the acts of individual actors with changes in the overall industrial structure.

2 Setting the stage for digital image technology

This chapter sets the stage on which Swedish image processing emerged. It opens with a characterization of digital image technology, followed by an inquiry into the Swedish national system of innovation. It ends with an outline of the international developments within computer technology.

DIGITAL IMAGE TECHNOLOGY

Digital image technology is a multi-purpose technology emanating from the progress within a combination of technologies, especially computer science and telecommunications. A technology may be characterized by what it does: in short, digital image technology makes automatic processing of images possible. It may be distinguished from computer graphics, its closest relative, in that it deals with natural images.[1] The technology originated in the early 1960s in the shape of optical character recognition, computer tomography, picture phones, scientific instruments and remote sensing for military intelligence. The basic problem solved at that time was the reading of images into the computer. In the 1970s special image computers were developed which were capable of processing the huge amount of data contained in images. During the 1980s commercial applications of digital image processing became more readily available. Today the most common areas where image processing is applied extensively are: remote sensing, especially for military intelligence; cartography and meteorology; industrial automation, inspection and control in automated production and robotic vision; desk top publishing, electronic darkrooms and image archives; medicine, radiology and cytology. Image processing computers are also used as general scientific instruments to analyse different kinds of images. Furthermore, the technology is becoming increasingly important in modern image transmission.

The basic components of digital image technology are depicted in Figure 2.1. In general, an image processing system consists of an image reading instrument, a computer and an output unit. Within this general system a high degree of variation can be found. The image reading instrument can be both analog and digital, varying from a video camera to nuclear magnetic resonance. The output can be produced as a yes/no decision, as an instruction to an industrial robot or as a digitally processed image. The computer performing the actual image processing, connecting input and output, can be anything from a personal machine to a specialized image processing machine. Four basic technological problems of digital image processing can be identified. First, the images must be digital or converted from analog to digital. Second, the output must be adapted to the specific application. Third, as the information content in an image by far exceeds the information content in symbols, image processing requires much faster computers with a larger memory than is offered by ordinary computers. Fourth, these three parts must be integrated into a well functioning system.

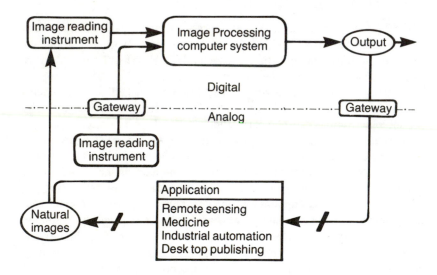

Figure 2.1   Schematic representation of digital image technology

Digital image technology: characterization of the innovation

How can digital image technology be characterized as an innovation? Christopher Freeman and Carlota Perez distinguish between four different types of innovation:[2]

1 Incremental innovations, which occur more or less continuously in any industry.
2 Radical innovations, which are discontinuous events unattainable through incremental adjustments of the pre-existing state of affairs.
3 New technological systems, which are far-reaching changes in technology affecting several branches of the economy.
4 New techno-economic paradigms, technological revolutions, which are so far-reaching in their effects that they have a major influence on the behaviour of the entire economy.

This taxonomy of innovation suggested by Freeman and Perez rests upon the characterization of innovation along two dimensions, the scope and scale of the technological change. In the scope of innovation they distinguish between minor and major changes and in the scale of innovation they distinguish between single innovations and interrelated clusters of innovations. If we combine these two dimensions of innovations we end up with a representation, Figure 2.2, of the Freeman and Perez taxonomy of innovation.

The classes of innovation are obviously neither independent nor mutually exclusive. An interdependence of minor and major changes can hardly be denied. Major changes are often induced through the accumulation of minor changes and minor adjustments following radical changes can often be necessary in order to increase the economic efficiency of the radical innovation. Furthermore, a hierarchical order of innovation can be detected: technological revolutions are made up by several new technological systems, which in their turn are made up of series of radical and incremental innovations. Nevertheless, the taxonomy can serve as a guide-line in the characterization of digital image technology.

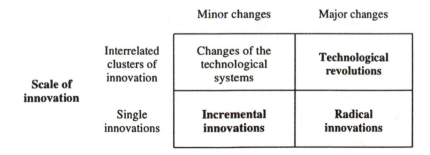

Scope of innovation

		Minor changes	Major changes
Scale of innovation	Interrelated clusters of innovation	Changes of the technological systems	**Technological revolutions**
	Single innovations	**Incremental innovations**	**Radical innovations**

Figure 2.2 Graphical representation of a taxonomy of innovation

Digital image processing is not confined to one isolated technology. It is comprised of a combination of technologies, computer technology, electronics, telecommunications, and others, moulded into a technological system of interconnected technologies. The present state of the development of image processing does not result from the work of a single heroic inventor or from a single grand invention. True, some innovations and the deeds of some great people stand out as being pioneering contributions: the work at MIT on perceptrons and on parallel processor computer architecture; the development at Bell Laboratories of light sensitive semiconductors; the work of Godfrey Newbold Hounsfield on computer aided tomography, for which he was awarded the Nobel Prize; and the development of magnetic resonance imaging technology, another Nobel Prize winning achievement. But, more importantly, behind these more spectacular contributions, there has been series of small interrelated innovations produced by individual actors in different countries and industries. As these actors extended the frontiers of digital image processing, they paired with other proponents of the technology, not randomly or according to the pre-existing structures, but according to the emerging logic of the new technological system. This new technological system, digital image technology, is also reaching out towards other technological systems, such as radiology, industrial automation, graphic production and geographic information systems. Together the emergence of digital image technology, the furtherance of electronics and computer technology and the changes in traditional technological systems coincide in 'the battle of the systems' between digital and analog technology.

In summing up, digital image technology is characterized as a new technological system comprised of series of radical and incremental innovations. This new technological system is, however, also a significant part of a technological revolution – the battle of the systems between digital and analog image technology.

EXAMINING SOME OF THE PRECONDITIONS FOR THE DEVELOPMENT OF DIGITAL IMAGE TECHNOLOGY IN SWEDEN

In the previous chapter it was argued that digital image technology bore the marks of modern technology in that it predominantly emerged as a result of the pursuit of scientific research at public institutions. What was the nature of the society capable of turning out this new technological system? Here we will take a cursory view of the history of the Swedish national system of innovation from which digital image technology emerged.

Swedes with an interest in industrial progress often take pride in putting forward the frontline position in technology of Swedish industry. Axel F. Enström once wrote;

> It is said, and it is true, that Swedes in general have a pronounced technical and mechanical bent. In other words, technical ability is one of the important natural resources upon which the nation can rely in its struggle for life. This gift for mechanics in the people is supposed to be the result of centuries of development, inasmuch as from ancient times the people have been accustomed to get their daily bread from tilling a poor soil. This bent is traditional, and traditional also is the endeavour to foster and train it.[3]

Enström based his admiration for the Swedish technical ability upon several observations and, taken in chronological order, he begins in the eighteenth century with the instigation of institutions – the Royal Academy of Science (1739) and the Ironmaster's Association (1747) – for the fostering of science, development and trade. The establishing of engineering schools and specialized laboratories at the beginning of the nineteenth century were taken as further evidence of the Swedish tradition of fostering and training technical ability. But what probably struck him as being most important was the seemingly close relationship between inventive activities and industrial development around the start of this century. Many of the current leading companies in Swedish industry were established at or before the turn of the century.[4] The establishment of these firms has to a large extent been associated with the nineteenth-century Swedish inventors and their heroic deeds.[5] These firms did not, however, thrive on a single innovation, but on continuous streams of radical and incremental innovation. Thus, in the course of industrial development the major source of innovation must have shifted from independent inventors (giving rise to new firms) to organized research and development (making these firms prosperous).

Is Sweden's technical tradition unique? If so, has it been able to sustain this alleged comparative advantage in technical ability? The pattern of industrial development in Sweden probably does not diverge from those of other similar countries. The instigation of academies of science and engineering schools parallels many other countries and most western countries exhibit an industrial development, with a close relationship between innovation and entrepreneurial activity, which is equal to the Swedish case. Also, the shift from independent inventors to organized research development and scientific research as the sources of innovation seems to be a general phenomenon. Simon Kuznets has stated that 'The epochal innovation that distinguishes the modern economic epoch is the extended application of science to problems of economic production.'[6] Hence, the industrial development in Sweden is not unique; other countries exhibit similar patterns.

Yet, compared to the size of the Swedish economy, the nation's industry has accrued a very strong position on the international scene. Maybe it is true that Sweden's most important natural resource is technical ability. The current relationship between investments in research and development and productivity growth does, however, indicate some problems in the Swedish system. In the 1980s Sweden was one of the leading countries with regard to expenditure on research and development. None the less, Sweden's measured growth in productivity is one of the lowest among the OECD countries. In Tables 2.1 and 2.2, Swedish expenditure on research and development and Swedish productivity is compared with some other countries. Note, however, that the tables cover different periods of time.

The only way in which the investments in research and development are reflected in foreign trade is by an increase in Sweden's net export of licences. In fact, Sweden exhibits consistent signs of a problem in its ability to appropriate the investments in research and development in domestic production and exports of advanced products.[7] Swedish industry's strength lies in a few, more traditional industries: metals/materials, forest products, transportation, power generation and distribution, and telecommunications.[8] Meanwhile its position in fast-growing high technologies, such as computer

Table 2.1 Gross domestic expenditure on R&D as a percentage of Gross Domestic Product

	1975			1981			1985	
1	United States	2.3	1	United States	2.4	1	United States	2.8
2	Germany	2.2		Germany	2.4		Japan	2.8
	United Kingdom	2.2		United Kingdom	2.4		*Sweden*	2.8
4	Japan	2.0	4	Japan	2.3	4	Germany	2.7
	Netherlands	2.0	5	*Sweden*	2.2	5	France	2.3
6	France	1.8	6	France	2.0		United Kingdom	2.3
7	*Sweden*	*1.7*		Netherlands	2.0	7	Netherlands	2.1
8	Norway	1.3	8	Norway	1.3	8	Norway	1.6
	Belgium	1.3	9	Canada	1.2	9	Canada	1.4
10	Canada	1.1	10	Denmark	1.1	10	Denmark	1.2
11	Denmark	1.0	11	Italy	0.9	11	Italy	1.1
12	Italy	0.8	–	Belgium	n.a.	–	Belgium	n.a.

Source: OECD Science and Technology Indicators, Report 3, *R&D, Production and Diffusion of Technology*, OECD, Paris, 1989.

Table 2.2 Productivity in Swedish industry compared with other countries, 1960–89. Increase in production per labour hour, yearly average.

1960–70		1970–80		1980–90	
1 Japan	10.8	1 Belgium	7.0	1 United Kingdom	5.4
2 Netherlands	7.1	2 Japan	6.6	2 Japan	5.3
3 *Sweden*	6.7	3 Netherlands	6.0	3 Belgium	4.9
France	6.7	4 Italy	5.9	4 Netherlands	4.0
5 Italy	6.5	5 Denmark	5.6	5 Italy	3.9
6 Belgium	6.2	6 France	4.5	6 France	3.7
7 Germany	5.9	7 Germany	4.1	7 Norway	3.6
8 Denmark	5.8	8 *Sweden*	*3.5*	8 *Sweden*	*3.2*
9 Norway	4.1	9 Canada	2.7	9 United States	2.6
Canada	4.1	10 Norway	2.6	10 Canada	2.5
11 United Kingdom	3.7	11 United Kingdom	2.5	11 Germany	2.3
12 United States	2.8	12 United States	2.4	12 Denmark	1.0

Source: *SOU 1991:82, Produktivitetsdelegationens betänkande* (Productivity Delegation Report), Stockholm: Allmänna förlaget, 1991.

technology, is declining.[9] This implies that the export channels for advanced electronic products are deteriorating.

Lately, Swedish industry has often been characterized as being immobile and incapable of entering high-technology areas. The absence of a nationally based electronics and computer industry is often perceived as especially problematic and efforts have been made to overcome this problem.[10] These efforts have so far not been successful in that they have neither been appropriated in terms of industrial production, nor have they had significant indirect effects on the dynamics of Swedish industry.[11]

The problems of appropriating the investments in research and development, and technical ability, do not, however, necessarily suggest anything regarding the quality of the research and development or regarding the technical ability as such.

What was the nature of the technical capabilities in Sweden in the fields from which digital image technology emerged? Sweden held a strong position in the development and construction of mechanical calculators, the predecessors of the first computers. In the pioneering years of the development of computer technology the strength in mechanical engineering was transformed in to emerging capabilities in computer technology. When the news of the first electronic calculators reached Sweden, a group was sent to the USA to study the development of computers. Soon after this, the interest in computing machines was formalized in an institution for the furtherance of Swedish computing capability, 'Matematikmaskinnämnden' (the board for calculating machines). Attempts to acquire an electronic calculator from the USA were futile; American export laws prohibited export of products of strategic importance. Consequently, machines had to be built in Sweden and so Matematikmaskinnämnden supported and supervised the construction of several electronic calculators in Sweden. The most important of the first computers was a machine called BESK, which was completed in 1953. For a short while BESK was the fastest electronic calculator in the world. It was used both in research and in the solving of practical industrial problems. BESK was followed by the construction of other machines at universities and in industry. Even though the first machines to a large extent were copies of their American ancestors, they also contained solutions and components developed through independent Swedish research.[12]

In the late 1950s the ability to construct calculating machines was transformed in to industrial production. Two large Swedish corporations, Saab (at first primarily for internal needs) and Facit AB, ventured to exploit commercially the emerging capabilities in computer technology. Matematikmaskinnämnden, which had played a significant role in the transfer of computer technology to Sweden, had fulfilled its task and so it was dissolved. The majority of the members of the committee continued their work by moving to Facit, some went to the telecommunication company L.M. Ericsson and others followed the committee as it was transformed into another public institution. Alongside Saab and Facit a third firm, Standard Radio and Telefon AB (SRT AB), also struggled to exploit the emerging technology. The firms' endeavours were not major victories but were not without their successes. However, the firms were burdened by insufficient economic performance.

Gradually Swedish efforts in computer technology became concentrated in one firm, Datasaab. In 1971 Saab and the Swedish State acquired SRT AB and renamed the company Stansaab. In 1974 Saab acquired Facit's computer electronics division and, finally, in 1978 Saab's computer division and Stansaab were merged as Datasaab. In 1981 Datasaab was acquired by Ericsson and became part of its effort to gain a position in integrated information systems. The effort proved to be a disaster and it threatened Ericsson's well-established position in telecommunications. In January 1988 Ericsson sold the computer division to the Finnish conglomerate Nokia: the Swedish effort to establish a national computer industry had come to an end.

The indirect effects of the efforts in computer technology were also limited. No internationally competitive support industries, such as electronics,

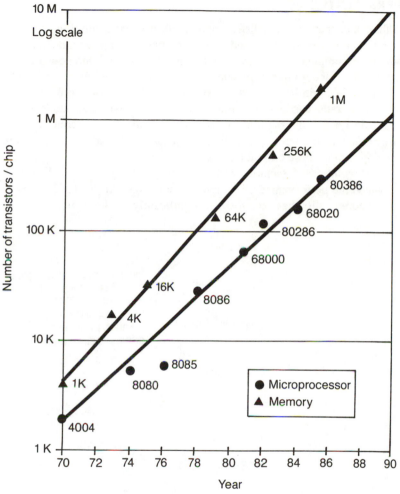

Figure 2.3 The evolution of memory and microprocessor capacity

Source: OECD, Information Computer Communications Policy: 20, *Major R&D Programmes for Information Technology*, Paris, 1989.

emerged. A parallel story can be found in the development of television technology in Sweden. Initially strong technological positions for Swedish industry were not transformed into lasting commercial successes. Of the industries mentioned, only in telecommunications has Sweden been able to hold and develop an internationally competitive position.

COMPUTER TECHNOLOGY: AN INTERNATIONAL PERSPECTIVE

Although the national Swedish computer industry was exhibiting problems and was slowly being dissolved, the international computer industry took automatic computation to new technological heights and into new areas of application. Electronic components, computers and other electronic products have become better, faster and cheaper. Apart from some defence motivated trade barriers, electronic components have been made freely available on the international market. In digital image technology the critical factors are memory and processor capacity. Figure 2.3, depicts the development of these critical factors.

The evolution of memory and processor capacity have in their turn enhanced the performance of computer technology. At the same time the cost of computation has been lowered significantly, as shown in Figure 2.4.

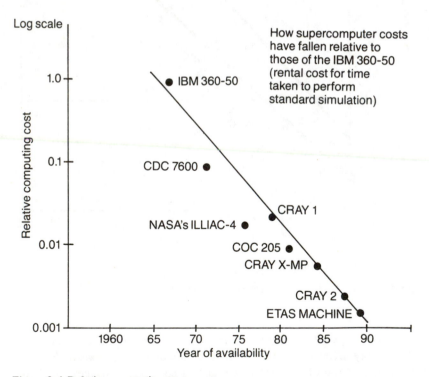

Figure 2.4 Relative computing cost

Source: OECD. Information Computer Communications Policy: 20, Major R&D Programmes for Information Technology, Paris, 1989.

Finally, the performance of computer technology is to some extent contingent on the computer architecture applied. The traditional von Neumann architecture with sequential data processing seems to be approaching its limit. By shifting to a computer architecture involving parallel process-ing,[13] new avenues of performance will be opened. The performance of sequential and parallel data processing architectures are compared in Figure 2.5.

We have now set the stage on which digital image technology emerged and evolved. The relationship between technology and industry is dis-cussed in Part II, before the development of image processing in Sweden is described more fully in Part III.

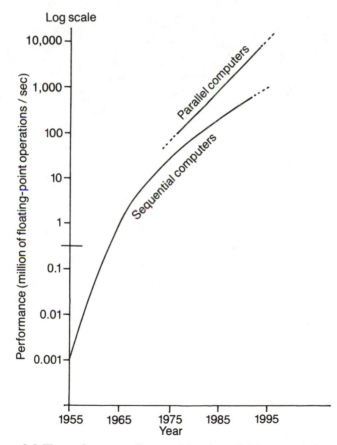

Figure 2.5 The performance of sequential and parallel data processing compared

Source: OECD. Information Computer Communications Policy: 20, Major R&D Programmes for Information Technology, Paris, 1989.

Part II
The act of insight

I have been primarily a theorist all my life and feel quite uncomfortable in having to preach the historian's faith. Yet I have arrived at the conclusion that theoretical equipment, if uncomplemented by a thorough grounding in the history of economic process, is worse than no theory at all.

Joseph A. Schumpeter, 1942

Part II is an inquiry into the nature of technological change and industrial dynamics. The aim is twofold: first, to lay the foundation upon which the study of the emergence of digital image technology in Sweden is based; second, and of equal importance, to provide the theoretical and method-ological underpinnings of the work. The theoretical equipment that is presented has not, however, been developed independently of what could be observed in the emergence of an image processing network in Sweden. The inquiry begins with an examination of the nature of technology, industry and knowledge and it continues with a discussion of the necessity of applying a contextual and historical perspective in studies of the relation-ship between technological and industrial evolution. The section is closed with a discussion of technological systems and networks of actors, and a framework for the understanding of the emergence of new industrial net-works is developed.

3 Perspectives on technology and industry

The predominant schools of thought in the social sciences are absorbed by the problem of how existing structures are administered. If we were to review sociology, economics, business administration or other academic fields we would most certainly find that the majority of the studies are concerned with some aspect of the administration of the current state of affairs. Novelties, such as technological innovation, enter into these studies, primarily in the shape of their impact on or consequences for pre-existing structures. Thus, social progress is viewed as a process of cumulative growth, where future structures are only extensions of the existing order. Yet, at least in hindsight, we are able to observe the existence of new structures: new technologies, new industries, new social systems or new ideologies representing discontinuities in the evolution of the society. The origin and emergence of these new structures are rarely studied. There is a general bias towards the study of the administration of older order and the implication of change upon pre-existing structures is not unwarranted. It is justified by its compelling importance in the progress of any system. This does not imply that an understanding of the emergence of new structures is unimportant. The interdependence of the emergence of a new structure and its subsequent integration into the pre-existing structure justifies increased interest in the emergence of new structures, both in its own right and as a complement to more traditional perspectives.

After a discussion of the general relationship between technology and economics, the perspectives on technology and industry will be explored, continuing on the three paths of inquiry set out in Chapter 1. The search for insight is begun by exploring the issues at hand, the forces behind the emergence of technologies, the forces provoking the emergence of new institutional structures and the nature of the link between science, technology and economics. Thus, the presentation will continue with a discussion of the nature of technological change. The focus of the discussion will then shift to the issue of industrial evolution. Finally the relationship between science and technology will be discussed in terms of the nature of knowledge.

TECHNOLOGY AND ECONOMICS

Technological change is an obvious and significant novelty, shaping the future direction of economic production and consumption. Mainstream economics has, however, shown very little interest in economic growth or its causes. Other problems were more pressing.[1] The problem of economic growth had been at the heart of the thinking of the classical economists, but, as time wore on, growth lost its grip on the attention and imagination of the growing body of mainstream economists.[2] To Adam Smith, the founding father of classical economics and of the political economy of growth, economic growth resulted from the interplay between extension of markets and division of labour. Left alone, people or the invisible hand of the market would take care of things: increasing the scale of the markets, enabling specialization, giving rise to even larger scales of production. Hence, in effect, he told people of his time that economic growth was unproblematic.[3] Malthus and Ricardo did not agree. To them growth was problematic and they focused their interests on the limits to growth, on the notion that population growth would exceed the growth in food production and on the diminishing returns in the use of land. Later, John Stuart Mill formulated a theory of economic growth, suggesting that it resulted from the increase in either the production elements – labour, land and capital – or their productiveness.[4] In spite of these early achievements the interest in economic growth did not expand. On the contrary, growth and development were very much viewed as 'universally available and achievable, hence inevitable'.[5] In the neoclassical theory of mainstream economics, the central elements of growth – institutions, population, and technology – were treated as autonomous data. The causes of growth and its implications were mainly neglected.[6]

On the outskirts of mainstream economics some individuals and schools of thought did, however, give close attention to some aspects of the problems of economic growth and change. The German historians, the American institutionalists and the Marxists provided a critique of the economic performance under a capitalistic regime, discussing the pains of growth. Yet others, Such as Veblen, Weber and Schumpeter, focused their efforts on explaining the forces behind industrial dynamics, the sources of economic growth.[7]

After World War II, politicians and consequently also economists became more concerned with the problems of growth. Economic growth was thought to be essential in order to ensure national independence and security.

Hence, the primary goal was growth: 'if ahead, stay ahead; if behind; catch up'.[8] The increasing interest in growth focused on three problems: (1) the sources of growth; (2) the effects of growth – national and social inequalities; and (3) the speed of growth – or why some countries seemed to be catching up while others were falling behind.[9] The heritage of the classical economists, especially that of Mill, was picked up by the early growth accountants of the 1950s. They found that only a small fraction of measured productivity growth could be attributed to increased productivity of individual production factors or total input growth. Approximately 90 per cent was attributed to the advance of (the unidentified and unmeasured) total factor productivity.[10] Robert Solow labelled this unknown element 'technical change' and showed that it corresponded to shifts in the aggregate production function. In this way he generalized the neoclassical growth model. Moses Abramovitz called it 'a measurement of our ignorance' and, since it could not be measured, it later became known as simply 'the residual'. All of the early growth accountants carefully explained that the large unmeasured residual included other components apart from technological change, such as education, economies of scale and better resource allocation.[11] Later studies have aimed at decomposing, attributing portions of total factor productivity to other measured components, and thus reducing the residual. None the less approximately 50 per cent has remained unexplained and is attributed to the advance of knowledge or technological progress, an element which is still very much enclosed in ignorance.[12]

Technology touches upon us all. We live in a mechanized world with complex interactions between humans and the human-made world. Technological artefacts and methods of production have increasingly been applied to solve problems of everyday life and of economic production. Changes in the human-made world through technological development or innovation are considered to be one of the most important dynamic forces behind the progress of our modern society.[13] A quick look around will probably be sufficient to convince us that technology has an important role in shaping society. It was the perception of the significance of technology in industrial progress that led Torstein Veblen to state: 'All industrial innovation and all aggressive economy in the conduct of industry not only presumes an insight into the technological details of the industrial process, but to any other than the technological experts, who know the facts intimately, any move of that kind will appear hazardous.'[14] Perhaps Veblen overstated the role of technological experts – the engineers. None the less the impact of technology can hardly be denied in a society where automobiles, electric light, television, nuclear power stations, computers and other technological artefacts have become a dominating feature even of everyday life. As Usher says:

Broadly conceived, technology is an important part of the central core in the evolutionary process. It is an essential aspect of the accumulation of knowledge and the development of skills. It does not exhaust the field of the development of the mind, but it is a characteristic segment of the whole. . . . In its own right, and as an aspect of the general process of innovation, technology has powerful claims upon our attention.[15]

The generation of technological change or innovation and the realization of these changes in the progress of society are some of the most intriguing issues in the study of economic change. These issues are not addressed in the neoclassical growth model. The early growth accountants identified technical change as an important factor determining economic growth, but they undoubtedly left us in ignorance regarding the nature of this factor.

The critical issue has not been resolved. The advance of knowledge or technological change is a primary cause of long-term economic development and our knowledge of the nature of technological change and its effect upon growth remains limited.[16] Growth is a complex issue; in order to understand its causes and processes, it is not enough to relate growth factors to changes in the output. We also, as Abramovitz suggests,

want to understand and explain the movements of these immediate determinants. And such explanations will involve investigations which, in almost every instance, lie outside the normal boundaries of economics. . . . The economics of growth is, therefore, the field of work in which the dependence of economics upon its sister social sciences appears in a supreme degree.[17]

Long before the coming of growth accounting others had already realized that technological change was a prime mover of progress. One of the first modern economists to focus on the dynamics of economics was Joseph A. Schumpeter. He saw the capitalistic system as the engine of change and argued that population growth or technological change had a positive effect upon the interest rate and profits. If technology remained unchanged there would be no profits encouraging entrepreneurial activities and in the circular flow of economic life the marginal product of capital would be driven down to zero. But this was not the circumstance that first caught Schumpeter's attention. Unlike his contemporaries who mainly visualized the problem as being how existing structures were administered, Schumpeter saw the creation and destruction of structures as the relevant problem.[18] As Marx had done before him, Schumpeter viewed the economy as an ever changing system. He introduced inventors and entrepreneurs, creating and realizing new combinations, threatening and eventually breaking pre-existing structures and thereby transforming the economy from one structure to another.[19] According to Schumpeter social progress was not merely a process of cumulative growth. It also embodied a fair number of revolutionary changes. He perceived the inventors and entrepreneurs as the engines of these revolutionary changes. The inventors and entrepreneurs were thought to be primarily but not solely motivated by and rewarded with extraordinary profits. The magnitude of these profits depends on the duration of the temporary monopoly created through the innovation. Perfect competition, on the other hand, excluded extraordinary profits and thus also the incentive to innovate. According to Schumpeter monopolistic competition is justified by its positive effect upon innovation. In Schumpeterian economics the process of creative destruction takes precedence over price competition. Technological competition is more compelling than price competition and the monopoly created by innovation is always temporary, constantly subject to the threat of creative destruction.

Another theorist preoccupied with the close connection between technology and economy was the American institutionalist John R. Commons. Unhappy with contemporary economic theory, with the possible exception of the works of Veblen and H. D. Macleod, he set out to develop an economic theory of collective and individual activities, thus taking adequate account of the institutional elements of the economy.[20] Commons took a different stance from Schumpeter. His interest did not focus on the elements of a capitalistic regime, profits and rents, but on the elements of an institutional regime, collective and individual action, and their effects upon the course of economic life. Commons perceived the economy and economic change as a dynamic interplay between complementary and limiting factors, which continually are changing places.

> What was the limiting factor becomes complementary when once it has come under control; then another factor is the limiting one. . . . This is the meaning of efficiency – the control of the changeable limiting factors at the right time, right place, right amount, and right form in order to enlarge the total output by the expected operation of complementary factors.[21]

This is achieved through volitional processes of routine and strategic transactions, where the resolving of limiting factors are characterized as strategic transactions and the operation of complementary factors as routine transactions.

The doctrine of complementary and limiting factors has three different but inseparable applications: scarcity, efficiency and going concerns. 'The technological economy is efficiency; the business economy is scarcity; the going concern economy is technology and business; the national economy is political economy. Each is a special case of strategic and routine transaction.'[22] Even though Commons did not particularly address the issues of technological change and economic change, he is very specific in his general framework regarding the relationship between technology and economy and regarding the forces behind change.

Schumpeter, Commons and others suggest that technology and economy are intertwined. More importantly, they state that economic entities – firms, industries and nations – do not have an equal opportunity to develop, apply and exploit advances in knowledge or technology. Causes of growth cannot, meaningfully, be reduced to the homogeneous production factors of land, capital and labour. Efforts to advance knowledge and technology – to pursue research and development, to invent – are controlled by social, economic and institutional structures. But these structures are partly controlled by previous advances in technology, some of which might long since be forgotten. The outcome of advances in knowledge and technology is in its turn also controlled by the prevailing social, economic and institutional structures.[23]

Studies of the problems of economic growth have focused our attention not solely upon technological change but also upon the close relationship between technology and business and upon how technological change is translated into economic performance. On the aggregated level economic performance is usually judged by growth of GNP, by distribution of wealth and by inflation and unemployment.[24] On a disaggregated level economic performance can be determined by growth of turnover or by return on investment. The impact of technological change on aggregated economic performance will be the result of the sum, both positive and negative effects, of the impact on the disaggregated level. Thus, the economic performance of technological innovation will be filtered through accompanying changes in the industrial structure, the creation of new structures and the destruction of obsolete structures. The economic impact of technological change can appear directly through cost reduction or the increase in sales resulting from an innovation or it can appear indirectly through cost reductions and increases in sales that it prompts in other related areas. The major impact can, furthermore, accrue from the subsequent adjustments prompted by the original innovation. In either case we would have a hard time tracing the benefits from innovation. Nevertheless, the economic impact of technological change will accrue through the changes in the industrial structure.

Technology and economics: a short summary

Technological change is one of the most compelling dynamic forces behind long-term economic development. Growth accountants did identify this crucial link between technological change and economic progress, but they have left us in ignorance as to the nature of the link. Others, however, have shown that the relationship is neither symmetrical nor straightforward. On the one hand we have economic performance, economic growth, distribution of wealth, inflation or unemployment. On the other hand we have the reciprocal relationship between technology and business: between technological change and institutional change or changes in the industry structure. The relationship between technological change and economic performance is summarized in the following four statements suggested by a group of neo-Schumpeterian economists:

1 Technological change is a primary cause of long-term economic development.
2 The dynamic mechanisms of economic development are radically different from those allocative mechanisms postulated by traditional theory.
3 The dynamic mechanisms have to do with both technical change and institutional change or the lack of it.
4 The socio-institutional framework always influences and may sometimes facilitate and sometimes retard processes of technical and structural change, coordination and dynamic adjustment.[25]

The primary interest here is more on the relationship between technology and the social, economic and institutional structure and less on measurable level of economic output. The focus is on technological change and changes in the industry structure. Since we will be preoccupied with this throughout the volume, it is necessary to take a closer look at the two major components, technology and institutions. We shall begin with the nature of technological change and then proceed to technology and industrial evolution.

THE NATURE OF TECHNOLOGICAL CHANGE

Technology is one of these infuriating words that can mean everything and nothing and it is almost impossible to decode its meaning. The aim here is to present not a conclusive definition of technology, but rather a workable one. In a recent paper, the Swedish historian of technology, Svante Lindqvist, discusses the meaning of technology. He presents different definitions of technology, from the use of machine and tools and applied science to all rational and efficient activities. He ends up with a definition of technology that is also workable in this context: technology is human methods of satisfying needs and wants through the use of physical objects, or all purposeful activities that change the material world.[26] A simple definition is not sufficient to be able to understand what technology is. It is also necessary to define the role of technology in society. It is possible to discriminate between at least three traditional functions of technology: productive, military and symbolic.[27] The first two roles are rather straightforward; technology is used for economic production and for military purposes. In the third role, technology is perceived as being used for symbolic reasons or to increase our social status, a role which perhaps is more debatable. Could there be such a thing as conspicuous technology? Even though most people would like to think that technology results from rational behaviour, it cannot be denied that military and symbolic considerations also will affect the direction and pace of technological development. What about technological innovation or change?

Technological development is most commonly depicted as radical technological innovations or series thereof, glorifying the heroic inventors and their spectacular ideas. Their names and achievements are for ever written in society's special 'Halls of Fame' for technology: the patent system, the Nobel Prize and the history writings. Long since forgotten are their predecessors, their associates, their less successful contemporaries and the innumerable heirs of their achievements, collectively adapting their innovation to productive work. Who cannot accurately account for the achievements of James Watt, Thomas Alva Edison, Alexander Graham Bell or Charles Babbage? But who remembers John Newcomen, Francis Upton, Elisha Gray, Per Georg Scheutz or other unsung heroes of technological change? However, is not every inventor and every innovation dispensable, will there not always be someone or something to act as replacement? Here the heroic theory is implicitly contrasted with the social theory of discovery, where the course of science and technology is regarded as a continuing process of cumulative growth, with discoveries tending to come in due time.[28] But is this not a false disjunction? In the process of technological and economic change is it not only the totality that counts? Schumpeter would absolutely agree with this conjecture. The first sentence in his *Theory of Economic Development* is: 'The social process is really one indivisible whole.'[29]

While technological achievement is explained by human ingenuity, societal progress is often described in terms of chains of technological breakthroughs, each one replacing its antecedents. Animal power was replaced by wind and water mills, which were made obsolete by steam engines, which were replaced by electricity. We move from unsophisticated to sophisticated technology; from cave paintings, hand writings, mechanical and electrical typewriters to electronic word processing. Older technology is successively being replaced by revolutionary innovations, disrupting the prevalent societal and industrial structure. New structures are created or pre-existing ones are altered, making them more able to cope with the technological change. Radical innovations not only embody a potential to replace obsolete technologies but also open new avenues of continuing technological and social change, where the new technology enters into a variety of related fields or industries. The computer replaced a mixture of methods of mathematical computation but, since then, through continuous development, it has been applied in areas, such as word-processing and automatic tellers, which were unimagined by the inventors. And we presume that the new technology is superior to the old, in that we think that it contributes positively to the rate of productivity growth.[30]

But do these chains of isolated technological changes reveal more than the ABC of a complex historical process? The French historian Fernand Braudel encourages us to believe otherwise. In reviewing the history of furniture he writes:

> But are the several histories of these items of furniture really the history of furnishing? However characteristic it may be, one piece of furniture does not reveal a whole picture; and the whole picture is what matters most. Museums, with their isolated objects, generally only teach the basic elements of a complex history. The essential is not contained within these pieces of furniture themselves but is in their arrangement, whether free or formal, in an atmosphere, an art of living both in the room containing them and outside it, in the house of which the room is a part. How, then, did people live, eat and sleep in these furnished interiors of the past – which were of course havens of luxury?[31]

What Braudel says about furniture holds true also for the study of technological change: do the histories of pieces of technology reveal the history of technology? However characteristic one isolated innovation or technology might be, it does not reveal the whole picture; 'and the whole picture is what matters most'.[32] The essentials lie beyond particular technological innovations, in their relation to the context in which they occur and of which they become a part. The focus on radical innovations and heroic inventors has furnished important insights into the process of technological change, the nature of innovative activity and why some individuals and firms are willing to accept the inescapable uncertainty related to innovative activity. This focus does, however, de-emphasize the subsequent adjustments and improvements in technology and economic structure. As these are often of higher or equal importance in the generation of performance, this perspective ignores one of the most important aspects of economic development. The impact of radical innovations is often increased by subsequent technological development. Initially, this development will probably be dominated by product innovation nurturing the emergence of a new industrial structure. As process innovation increases, integrating the production process, reinforcing the emergent structure and obstructing the possibilities of further product development, the degree of product innovation will level off.[33] Consequently, technological artefacts or innovations can never be understood in isolation. Technologies combine into technological systems of complementary components and pieces of knowledge. Technologies depend upon and interact with one another in intricate ways. The smallest unit of observation is therefore not single innovations but interrelated clusterings of innovations, technological systems.[34]

How, then, do new technological systems unfold and develop? Thinking about an individual innovation, such as the radio or the aeroplane, its development can seemingly be traced back along an imaginary line from its state of development, at a chosen point in time, to its origin; from the jogger's freestyle radio to the achievements of Guglielmo Marconi; from the 'Euro-fighter' to the Wright brothers' flight with Kitty Hawk. The imaginary line describes a development of increasing perfection from the first rough idea to the final state-of-the-art. The underlying logic of this is that technological development can be described as a sequence of activities, where every stage of the development sets the conditions for the next. It mirrors the construction of houses: we start by building a sound foundation, upon which we put walls, over which we place a roof, then we do the interior decoration and finally we lay out the garden and build a fence. No foundation means no interior decoration. Technological development can similarly be expressed interms of a sequence: scientific discovery/invention, innovation, diffusion/transfer.[35] In this, the economic outcome of scientific discovery arises from the diffusion/transfer of innovation changing the average production practice in the industry or in the nation (see also Figure 3.1).

Yet, comparing the present state of an innovation with its origin, the dissimilarities are often more striking than the similarities and the develop-

Scientific discovery/invention

↓

Innovation

↓

Diffusion/transfer

↓

Economic and industrial change

Figure 3.1 The traditional view of technological development

ment cannot be explained without additional, often parallel, processes of invention, innovation and transfers: development is not a cumulative sequence but a cumulative synthesis.[36] Turning to technological systems this becomes even more obvious: the development of technological systems is characterized by on-going invention, innovation and transfer. Each of these activities is of course partly controlled by the others, but not necessarily in sequential order. Moreover these activities are also controlled by different mechanisms and values. The mechanisms and values spurring invention differ from those prompting innovation, and differ from those facilitating diffusion and transfer. To simplify the discussion further let scientific discovery/invention be represented by creation of novelty, innovation by development, and diffusion/transfer by use. The emergence and evolution of a technological system is thus perceived as the interrelated concurrent processes of creation of novelty, development and use (see Figure 3.2).

Do the observed economic performance of the western world and the changes in the social order result only from the streams of continuing innovation, revolutionizing the technological order? An unconditional positive answer to this question would be quite wrong, leading us astray in the garden of technological determinism. Schumpeter made this observation, arguing that it would be quite wrong to say 'that capitalistic enterprise was one and technological progress a second, distinct factor in the observed development of output; they were essentially one and the same thing'.[37] The message conveyed by Braudel is that technological artefacts or innovation should be seen from both the technological and social contexts of which they are a part of or in which they occur. In the same way, pieces of furniture in Braudel's words have certain roles and positions in the room and in the house, reflecting the social life of the inhabitants. Likewise, pieces of technology are interrelated, not randomly but according to a specific logic, and the essential lies beyond the individual pieces or innovations, in the totality, both in the relationship between the individual pieces and in the context of the society fostering and being captivated by them. Braudel becomes even more specific regarding the role of technology in social progress, when he states that

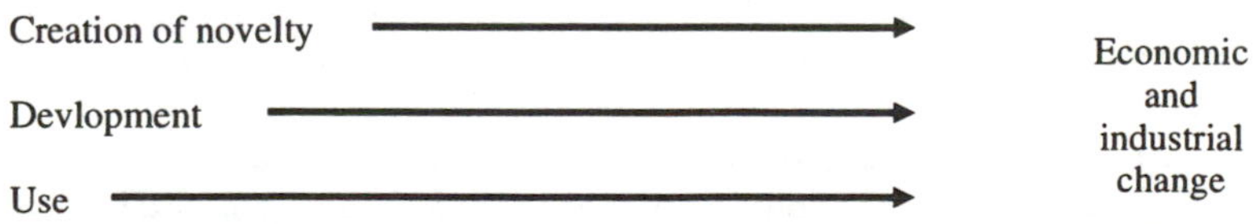

Creation of novelty ⟶

Devlopment ⟶   Economic and industrial change

Use ⟶

Figure 3.2 The emergence and evolution of new technological systems as parallel processes

Technology ultimately covers as wide a field as history and has, of necessity, history's slowness and ambiguities. Technology is explained by history and in turn explains history; but the correlation is in neither case fully satisfactory. In the realm of technology, co-extensive with the whole of history, there is no single onward movement, but many actions and reactions, many changes of gear. It is not a linear process.[38]

Technology most certainly possesses the capacity to shape society, but technology is not autonomous. It is the result of human endeavour: the researcher's search for a solution, the businessperson's hunt for profit or the politician's quest for power. And 'no innovation has any value except in relation to the social pressure which maintains and imposes it.'[39] Many examples show the same process.

The steam engine, for example, was invented a long time before it launched the industrial revolution – or should one say before being launched by it? The history of inventions, taken by itself, is therefore a misleading hall of mirrors. A splendid sentence by Henri Pirenne neatly sums up the question: America, when the Vikings reached it, was lost as soon as it was discovered, because Europe did not yet need it.[40]

The nature of technological change – a short summary

The most important finding in this section is the definition of technology as clusters of interrelated technologies structured into technological systems. Furthermore it was argued that the development of technological systems could not be explained by a sequential model. Instead it was suggested that creation of novelty, development and use should be regarded as interrelated concurrent processes continuously prompting the technological system to change.

In summing up the nature of technological change we must, however, inevitably note that technology and technological change are important parts of society and human progress. 'Technology is indeed a queen: it does change the world.'[41] But, at the same time, it is also socially constructed, laden with the attitudes and values of the society that promotes it.[42] The role of technology in social progress can only be fully understood in the context of the society that promotes and maintains it and is also promoted and maintained by it.[43]

We will now leave this track for a short while and instead discuss technology and industrial evolution and hence the nature of industry. We will return in the next chapter to the contextuality of technological change and industrial evolution and how this process is influenced by its history.

TECHNOLOGY AND INDUSTRIAL EVOLUTION

The works of Schumpeter have many sides and there is a slight shift in focus between the young and the old Schumpeter. The young Schumpeter elaborated on how new structures emerged from actors performing acts of innovation and entrepreneurship, thus creating extraordinary profits, attracting imitators and pressing the profit level downwards. The older Schumpeter, on the other hand, was primarily interested in the impact of market structure on the level of innovation. Working on two distinct but interrelated sets of problems he has induced successors with different lines of reasoning. The young Schumpeter was taken up by economists studying technological change. Here we will take a quick glance at how the older Schumpeter has affected the field of industrial economics. The basic issue is the impact of market structure on technological development. In one of the more influential textbooks in industrial economics F. M. Scherer says: 'Here we shall be concerned largely with a possible causal flow in the opposite direction: from market structure to technological innovation. Is progress faster or slower under monopolistic conditions, or does it make no difference?'[44] The same line of reasoning is found in the survey by M. I. Kamien and N. L. Schwartz of the literature covering market structure and innovation.[45] Here the heritage of Schumpeter is synthesized in two broad hypotheses. The first states that there is a positive relationship between innovation and monopoly power and the second that large firms are disproportionately more innovative than small firms.[46] Less attention is given to the critical issues of how economic structures are created and destroyed, of how new industries emerge and of the role of individual firms, inventors and entrepreneurs in the advancement of this process.

In mainstream industrial economics the primary interest is the structure, conduct and performance of industries. Traditionally, an industry is defined as a group of producers of goods perceived as close substitutes, which are available to a common group of buyers. Producers of goods that are relatively distant substitutes are not included in the industry.[47] This theoretical, product oriented, definition of industry thrives on homogeneity. A homogeneous group of sellers produces a homogeneous set of products, to be sold to a homogeneous group of buyers. The nature of competition between the incumbents of the industry, combined with the threat from potential entrants, determines the overall economic performance of the industry. Increased competition drives down the profit level and thus the attractiveness to potential entrants. The economic performance of individual firms is determined by the relative success of their competitive behaviour. These industries are transformed through the seeking of differential advantage by the incumbent firms. Less successful firms will earn a less than sustainable return on investment and eventually they will exit the industry. When the overall profit level of the industry exceeds the sustainable return on investment and cost of entry, new entrants will be attracted, squeezing the profit level. The industry will transform through natural selection of the firms best adapted to the conditions of the industry. Individual firms will entry and exit, but the industry with its core technology will persist.

An industry is thus identified as a group of naturally selected competitors, where the performance of all others becomes the natural criterion for evaluating individual performance. Successful strategies will be imitated instantaneously and without cost, resulting in increased homogeneity in competitive behaviour of incumbent firms. A competitive symbiosis evolves where entry deterrence is given higher priority than intra-industry rivalry. Hence, the capacity of self-resurrection slowly deteriorates. Competition will no longer function as the propelling force behind development and industries cannot, as Schumpeter proclaims, be revolutionized incessantly from within.[48] Sources of innovation, resurrection and revolution are increasingly to be found outside focal industries. Basic research at universities is of increasing importance in the generation of new technologies: computers, biotechnology and image processing are but a few examples of new technologies emanating from basic research. The inter-industry flow of technology is one of the major forces behind the resurrection of some industries: developments within computer technology have been instrumental in the recent revitalization within telecommunications. Suppliers and buyers are assuming more active roles in the innovative process. Development and change is a result not of intra-industry rivalry but of the interaction between complementary actors and the integration of complementary technologies.

Theories defining industry as a group of naturally selected producers of close substitutes are inherently static. They can explain neither the emergence of new industrial structures nor the major extensions of old structures that are brought on by technological change.[49] Natural selection is a concept borrowed from biology. The biological theory of evolution is comprised of two basic mechanisms: one generates variety and the other, natural selection, selects and retains only the useful variety.[50] Genes are the biological entities which are subject to evolution. Variation and natural selection improve the fitness, the reproductive capacity, of individual genes in the gene pool and thus the organism evolves over time. Note that it is the genes, and not the organism, that are selected. Natural selection operates without foresight, without plans and without purpose and yet it is capable of producing the most complex organisms.[51] Darwin ends his *Origin of the Species* by highlighting this quality of the biological theory of evolution:

There is grandeur in this view of life, with its several powers, having been originally breathed into a few forms or into one; and that, whilst this planet has gone cycling on according to the fixed law of gravity, from so simple a beginning endless forms most beautiful and most wonderful have been, and are being, evolved.[52]

Given such grandeur in the biological theory of evolution, how can it ever be stated that theories defining industry as a group of naturally selected producers of close substitutes are inherently static? We should perhaps not borrow metaphors as often as we do. They turn back on us as if they were explanations when they are meant to focus the attention on the unexplained.[53] Thus, while biological evolution provides important insights into the understanding of industrial evolution, industrial evolution cannot be explained by natural selection. First of all, social entities or their populations, companies, corporations or organizations can never be the basic unit of natural selection. They are too unstable to be the basic unit. They are too short-lived to be subject to natural selection. Furthermore, since they constantly merge or otherwise blend with each other, natural selection as it is known from the biological theory of evolution would be impossible.[54] The firms or their competitors can thus never be the basic unit of industrial evolution. The question is, do there exist basic units of evolution, with stable qualities comparable to the biological gene, within the social sphere? In one of the more convincing applications of evolutionary theory in economics, *An Evolutionary Theory of Economic Change*, the problem of the basic unit of evolution is resolved by the introduction of routines as the genes of economic evolution.[55]

A second and more important objection to the casual use of biological evolution in the study of industrial change strikes at the heart, the definition, of the industry. The position of an individual producer in an industry which is defined as a group of producers of close substitutes is totally different from the position of individual genes in the set of genes constituting a living organism. While firms are considered to be free agents, unattached to other firms, the genes exist in a highly complex system; 'they collaborate and interact in inextricably complex ways, both with each other, and with their external environment.'[56] Furthermore, it is often difficult to separate the social entities from the environment that constitutes the selection mechanism.[57]

Technology and industrial evolution: a short summary

Heterogeneity rather than homogeneity, interconnectedness rather than independence, and mutual adaptation rather than one-sided selection are the relevant attributes of a definition of industrial structure that are required if we are to study the emergence of new industrial structures. Thus, substitutability is less suitable as a stratifying concept and complementarity a more relevant one when it comes to analysis of the emergence of new industrial structures. In this study, as well as in many other studies of industrial dynamics, the industrial structure is perceived as an evolving system of interconnected parts: a network where the parts consist of actors interconnected through the activities they undertake and the resources they employ to perform these activities. The overall system is defined as a network of actors interconnected through exchange relationships.[58] Any attempt to explain the evolution of this system must be founded upon an understanding of the interaction over time between the evolution of the parts and the evolution of the whole system.

We are thus not refuting the grandeur of the biological theory of evolution, but basically focusing on other qualities of the metaphor: on the qualities of the webs of interlocking relationships underlying the process of evolution and on the path-dependent character of the evolution generated by problem-solving and adaptation and self-reinforcing mechanisms in complex contexts. What is suggested is a historical and contextual perspective on the emergence of new industrial structures, new industrial networks.

THE NATURE OF KNOWLEDGE

Advance of knowledge, most often expressed as growth of scientific knowledge, is typically assumed to be one of the major causes behind the economic prosperity of the Western nations.[59] Technology comprises not only artefacts but also knowledge components, and so technological innovation is often assumed to result from progress of knowledge. But what is knowledge? Is there one conclusive answer to this straightforward question? Probably not, but it might be agreed that knowledge is intangible and impossible to comprehend fully. Also agreed might be the role of knowledge in society and the significance of the pursuit of knowledge in relationship to technological and industrial evolution. Håkan Håkansson states that '[n]ew knowledge in terms of new product or process ideas often emerges at the interface between different knowledge areas. In exchange situations different kinds of knowledge come together (are combined and confronted) to create innovative situations.'[60] Knowledge is a compelling constituent in the course of technological change and industrial evolution, but its true nature is, at best, secluded in the shadows of philosophy. The present inquiry into knowledge will not be as pretentious as the heading suggests and only a few features pertaining to the problem of technological change and industrial evolution will be discussed.

It can be argued that assumptions regarding the nature of the state and the growth of knowledge have an immediate impact on the understanding of progress. In his classic article, 'The Use of Knowledge in Society', F. A. von Hayek states that, if we assume that we have perfect knowledge regarding the initial conditions, all remaining economic problems can be solved by pure logic. He continues by claiming that the peculiar character of economic order 'is determined by the fact that the knowledge of the circumstances of which we must make use never exists in concentrated or integrated form, but solely as the dispersed bits of incomplete and frequently contradictory knowledge which all the separate individuals possess.' He also claims that the solving of economic problems really is all about utilization of knowledge not given to anyone in its totality. Knowledge is also to some extent contextual, and contingent upon particular circumstances of time and place. In this respect individuals accrue advantages over all others in that they have access to unique information that can be put to beneficial use, but only if the decisions depending on it are left to specific individuals or are made with their active co-operation.[61] Decisions or innovations can be improved or can ascend through interaction between individuals with access to pieces of knowledge predisposed by their particular circumstances of time and place. Von Hayek states the proposition more specifically than Håkansson did above; solutions to economic problems are produced by the interaction of people, each of whom possesses only partial knowledge.[62]

The issue addressed by von Hayek was the construction of a rational economic order. But, like Schumpeter, he perceived the problem as the administration of an ever-changing order and he stressed that economic problems arise always and only in consequence of change.[63] Hence, dynamic economics must be construed upon assumptions of imperfect and partial knowledge. The question is how to characterize the particular circumstances of time and place of knowledge. Can we specify the effects that this will have upon the course of technological change and industrial evolution?

How has the idea of individualized, imperfect and partial knowledge, expressed by von Hayek, been articulated in more recent theories of technological change?[64] The Italian economist Giovanni Dosi characterizes knowledge in three dimensions: articulated versus tacit, universal versus specific, and public versus private knowledge.[65] He paints a picture of knowledge as a continuum from perfect – articulated, universal and public – to imperfect and partial – tacit, specific and private. These dimensions are far from mutually exclusive and it is not unlikely that the latter two follow from the first; the distinction between tacit and articulated knowledge. In discussing knowledge assets, Sidney Winter adds some other taxonomic dimensions: observability in use, degree of complexity and whether it is independent or an element of a system.[66] For the present purpose it is, however, sufficient to distinguish between tacit and articulated knowledge, bearing in mind that this articulation of imperfect and partial knowledge has further implications regarding the nature of knowledge.

Returning now to the initial question, what is knowledge? Let us include in the term knowledge other enigmatic concepts, occasionally used synonymously, such as competence, skills, know-how and capability. Knowledge consists of a tacit, implicit and non-codifiable component as well as an articulated, explicit and codifiable component. Some elements of knowledge can be well articulated and coherently coded in textbooks and manuals, thus enabling meaningful communication, knowledge transfer or teaching, of these particular elements. Yet some elements of knowledge cannot (at least not at the moment) be adequately expressed: 'we know more than we can tell'.[67] Some elements of knowledge are tacit and they cannot be properly communicated. The tacit elements of knowledge are effective barriers to the transfer of knowledge and technology: the individual practising the knowledge does not even have to recognize or be aware of it. Tacit knowledge is commonly considered as resulting from learning processes, from hands-on experience or trial-and-error experimenting. A collective of individuals, an organization, a business firm or simply a network actor can be perceived as an agglomeration of elements of knowledge and competencies, some tacit and some articulated.[68]

A historical example of the essence of tacit knowledge is provided in a study of the transfer of the Newcomen steam-engine to Sweden.[69] Thomas Newcomen, later described as a common ironmonger, and his assistant John Calley, by combining a number of well-established complementary competencies and without knowing or understanding the underlying theoretical principles, constructed a very successful prime mover. Needless to say Newcomen and Calley were not without predecessors in their quest for converting thermal energy into mechanical energy, but in the first decade of the eighteenth century they succeeded in developing a practical working steam-engine which proved to be of great benefit to the British mining industry.

The working principle of the Newcomen engine was fairly easy to understand from the available published prints of the early engines, even if these were more like advertisements than complete working instructions. But an elementary understanding of the basic working principle was quite different from the knowledge and hands-on experience needed in order to design and operate the engine. The Newcomen engine won immediate acceptance in the British mining industry. In the early eighteenth century practical experience of Newcomen engines was rare, however, and the engines were constructed and operated by Newcomen and his associates. But, as the stock of engines grew, so did the knowledge and experience resulting from designing and operating the engine. During the eighteenth century about 1700 Newcomen engines were erected in England.

In England an organization for the construction and operation of the Newcomen engine was established and, with a growing installed base, there followed a familiarity with the technology, favouring even more instalments. The situation in Sweden was utterly different. The engine could not just be shipped to Sweden; it had to be constructed there and be adapted to the specific local context. In Sweden knowledge of designing steam-engines was sparse and the necessary experience of practical operation was non-existent. A series of technical and social circumstances coincided, keeping the Newcomen engine from being widely spread in Sweden, and so repressing the development of the practical experience, the tacit knowledge, necessary in order to construct and operate the engine. While the positive feedback loops in England led the Newcomen engine on to a winning path, the negative feedback in Sweden hampered learning, restricted the diffusion of the engine and preserved the barriers towards the development of steam technology.[70]

The tacit elements of knowledge suggest that knowledge cannot be universal, available to all. Knowledge is to some extent specific and access to it is restricted not only because its diffusion is deliberately avoided, a recurring phenomenon in research and development, but also and perhaps more importantly because it occasionally is impossible to communicate. Knowledge is contextual: it is unequally distributed and partial. The tacitness, contextuality and partiality of knowledge have significant implications for the theoretical propositions regarding the development, use and diffusion of knowledge. Even the codifiable knowledge is to some extent context specific.

First of all, knowledge is not equally available to all actors or all individuals. The notion that knowledge, once it is produced, is available without cost to all others does not hold. The appropriation or utilization of knowledge 'on the shelf' is not free.[71] The technological capability of firms differs and consequently so does their ability to appropriate knowledge. The utilization of knowledge is not equally costly to all actors. Owing to previous experience some actors can utilize specific elements of knowledge more economically than others.[72] It is not even the case that the utilization of knowledge 'on the shelf' necessarily has to be less costly than the original production of the knowledge. This observation sets the distinction between original innovation and subsequent imitation in a new perspective, implying, contra-intuitively, that imitation is more problematic and costly than is commonly suggested. The distinction between innovation and imitation is thus an artificial one. The two processes are in many respects similar in nature and they are often separated only by the fact that one, by means of different social institutions, principally the patent system, is defined as being first and original and all others as being second and mere copies.

Continuing on this line of reasoning, the production of knowledge is contextual, burdened with the specific circumstances in which it occurs. The communication of knowledge from one context to another, from one individual, firm, industry or country to another, is not unproblematic. Transfer of knowledge requires due adaptation of both the knowledge subject to transfer and the knowledge possessed by the receiver. Some parts of the knowledge might be embodied in technology, but some parts will inevitably be disembodied, represented by the tacit knowledge of the experienced constructor or operator. These assumptions concerning the nature of knowledge not only are suggestive when it comes to the transfer of technology but also imply severe restrictions regarding the trading of technology. The notion of a perfect market for technology is inconceivable, given that some tacit knowledge is required to reap economic benefits from technological innovation which is derived from advances in knowledge. This logical consequence of the contextuality of knowledge would have a significant impact upon the transformation of scientific discovery to economic production.

The nature of knowledge: a short summary

We have touched upon the intricate relationship between knowledge and technology and between advances of knowledge and technological change. The issue will probably never be fully resolved and only some general features have been highlighted. The relationship between knowledge and technology is asymmetrical. Technology contains some elements of knowledge: some elements of knowledge are embodied in the artefacts of the technology. But not all of the knowledge which is required to develop or operate a technology will be embodied in the products: some elements of knowledge will be disembodied. A special form of disembodied knowledge is associated with the interrelatedness of technologies into technological systems. This type of knowledge can of course also be embodied, as it is in so-called network technologies, such as railways, telecommunications and electricity. But these are not the only technologies organized into systems. In other technological systems, such as digital image technology, the interrelatedness is more subtle and disembodied. We have every reason to assume that knowledge concerning the interrelatedness of technology does not exist in concentrated and integrated forms. The pursuit of activities in technological systems thus requires the interaction of actors each of whom possesses only partial knowledge regarding inter-relatedness. It should be clear that knowledge can be embodied in technological systems, unknown or unattainable by network actors. But knowledge, explicit and implicit, is also embedded in networks.

In general it may be suggested that the accumulation of knowledge and the development of technology will converge. The relationship between the advance of knowledge and technological change is, however, also asymmetrical. We cannot simply state that technological change follows from advances in knowledge: the Newcomen engine was developed without a clear understanding of the underlying theoretical principles. The opposite causality is not closer to the truth, though it is possible to observe several cases when advances in knowledge follow from technological change: the theoretical principles underlying steam-engines were developed long after the technology had been established. Science owes probably more to technology than does technology to science. But the relationship between the two is more reciprocal than directed. The scientific, technical and economic spheres do feed back on each other, but not necessarily in a sequential order and not to a great extent. Progress within each sphere is prompted and controlled by specific mechanisms, institutions and values peculiar to that sphere. It is perhaps most important that these spheres are linked at all.[73]

SUMMARY

Technology most certainly has the power to shape society, but it is not autonomous and it has no value except in relation to the social pressure which fosters it. Steam-engines or computing machines were invented long before they launched the industrial or information revolution – or was it the other way around, were they launched by their revolutions? To become familiar with technology and technological change it is therefore necessary to proceed beyond the spectacular innovations and the great, heroic people behind them. Society would probably be different if the telephone had never been invented, but would this have arrested progress? Would the removal of any innovation or any inventor halt progress? In the development of technology and progress of society no innovation and inventor is indispensable. There will always exist alternative solutions to any problem addressed and there will always be humans attempting to solve perceived problems. Human ingenuity and changes in the human-made world are compelling ingredients in the progress of society, not in their singularity but in their multiplicity, variety and ambiguity.[74]

It was first suggested that the dynamics of technological and social evolution could be captured by focusing on two structures of society, technology and institutions. This basic model has since been significantly modified. The basic components and the relationships between them have been retained, but they have been defined differently. Technology has been defined as technological systems and institutional structures as networks. In studying the emergence of new technologies and new industries, it is thus suggested that the emergence and evolution of technological systems and networks is the relevant issue (see Figure 3.3).

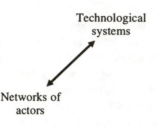

Figure 3.3 A basic model of the link between technological systems and networks of actors

In the next chapter we will add two other dimensions to technological systems and industrial networks and take a closer look at contextual and historical perspectives and at the concept of technological systems. The concept of industrial networks and a framework for understanding the emergence and evolution of new technological systems and new industrial networks are then presented in Chapter 5.

4 A contextual and historical perspective

In a study of organizational development in the Imperial Chemical Industries, Andrew Pettigrew argues that change can be understood only as a continuing process in the context in which it appears and he suggests a contextual and historical perspective on processes of change, whatever the content of the change might be.[1] Here the primary interest concerns not changes within individual organizations but the emergence of new technologies involving agglomerations of firms and organizations. This does not mean that the perspective suggested by Pettigrew is less valid. On the contrary, as noted in Chapter 3, the relationship between technological change and social progress is reciprocal. Technology possesses the capacity to shape society, but it is neither autonomous nor neutral: it is the result of human effort and it is laden with the attitudes and values of the society that promotes it. Here the primary interest is not society as a whole but a part of society – industry. It has furthermore been argued that technological innovation and business activities must be studied in the context of technological systems and networks of actors. As these structures are the results of the past, the contextual perspective necessitates a historical one.

The purpose of this chapter is to discuss and develop a contextual and historical perspective on progress and change. The chapter opens with a discussion of how context affects change, continues with a discussion of how history matters, and concludes with a discussion of how the suggested perspective is translated into actual analysis of change processes.

IN CONTEXT

No Man is an island, entire of itself;
every man is a piece of the continent,
a part of the main;
if a clod be washed away by the sea,
Europe is the less,
as well as if a promontory were,

as well as if a manor of thy friends
or of thine own were;
any man's death diminishes me,
because I am involved in mankind;
And therefore never send to know for whom
the bell tolls; It tolls for thee.
                              John Donne (1572–1631)

Donne wrote this poem when, during a serious illness, he heard the death
bell knelling for another, making him aware of the interdependence of men
and women in the life of humankind as a whole.[2] Ernest Hemingway cited
it in his epic story of human solidarity in the Spanish civil war. Humankind
is one volume of many authors. The idea expressed by Donne has a bearing
also on our own field of study. No technology is an island, nor is any
business an island.[3] They are all pieces of continents, parts of the main.
Adam Smith realized it when he stated that the division of labour was
limited by the extent of the market. Marx saw it when he derived the social
structures and conditions from the economic relations of production.
Neither the contextuality of technology nor the relationship between technology and society are novel findings of modern research. In contemporary
research on technological change and social progress there is a growing
consensus, even if this cannot always be detected in individual pieces of
research, regarding the relationships within and between the two basic
components. When it comes to the nature and direction of these relationships some general disagreements can, however, be detected, all the way
from pure technological determinism to pure social construction of technology. In the following some different notions of technological systems
and of how they have been related to social progress will be traced.

Veblen did identify the interdependency of technologies and his call for
engineers as managers of industrial progress was the result of his perception of industrial systems, which he defined as '[a]n inclusive organization
of many and diverse interlocking mechanical processes, interdependent
and balanced among themselves in such a way that the due working of any
part of it is conditioned on the due working of the rest'.[4] To Veblen only an
engineer could understand the complexity of industrial systems and thus
only an engineer could supervise this system efficiently. Today most of us
are probably inclined to believe that Veblen was overly optimistic regarding the possibility of managing the industrial system. Nevertheless,
men such as Frederick W. Taylor and Henry Ford thrived on integrating the
parts of the American system of manufacturing into an efficient system of
mass-production.[5] His faith in engineers aside, the major contribution of
Veblen was his identification of industrial systems as sets of interrelated
technologies contingent upon human action.

Commons, a great admirer of Veblen, also addressed the problems of the industrial society. The specific ideas put forward by Commons can easily be regarded as generalizations of Veblen's thoughts on industrial systems. The idea of complementary and limiting factors is well in line with Veblen's observation that mechanical processes were interlocked, interdependent and balanced in such a way that the due working of any part was conditional on the due working of the rest. Commons did not share Veblen's strong belief in engineers, but he stressed the volitional side of economics in his routine and strategic transactions. To Commons the going concern economy consisted of one objective, technological, side of complementary and limiting factors and one volitional, managerial, side of routine and strategic transactions.

Before we continue with some of Veblen's many followers let us briefly re-examine a different systems approach suggested by the economic historian, Abbott Payson Usher. Contrary to Commons, whose primary interest was the going concern economy, Usher set out to explain technological change and social progress. In his study of the history of mechanical inventions, Usher presents his unique theory of social evolution, the particular system of events. Turning against the early concepts of social evolution, expressed as sequences of stages that were presumed to describe the entire social structure, Usher claimed that adequate historical analysis required concentration on particular sequences of events. Instead of maintaining that the totality of the present was derived from the totality of the past, he formulated the proposition more specifically, that every event has its past. The analysis of social evolution required studies of processes of innovation and processes of diffusion through imitation. Usher articulates a gestalt theory of innovation, where he proposes an analysis of the processes of change with explicit reference to the place of individual effort in the general social process. Usher was not, as were Veblen and Commons, interested in the interrelatedness of the prevalent technological systems. His focus was on particular sequences of events and their place in larger systems of relationships.[6] A similar stance is taken by Siegfried Giedion. Recognizing the development of mechanization as an ever-unfolding historical process observable only at the end, he suggests that the outcome of a century of mechanization is a society where relations are far more complex and interlocked than in any earlier society. But, while noting the impact of mechanization, he also firmly points out that it is blind and without direction. Mechanization springs from the mind of humans and '[t]o control mechanization demands an unprecedented superiority over the instrument of production. It requires that everything be subordinated to human needs.'[7]

Another scholar on the list of pioneers studying the link between technological and social change is Lewis Mumford. A basic communist, a student of Veblen and sympathetic towards Usher, Mumford studied how the Western civilization had been affected by the development of the machine.[8] Mumford, stating that technics and civilization as a whole resulted from human choices, inclinations and aspirations, conscious as well as unconscious, was probably more inclined than Usher to perceive technology as a social construction.[9] Where Usher stressed technological innovation as the engine of social evolution, Mumford underscored social progress as the engine of technological change. A sociological perspective on the nature of invention is provided by S. C. Gilfillan. He perceived the invention process as a whole and demonstrated the length of the process. Mainly concerned with the social aspects of the process, Gilfillan pointed out that inventions are changes in a system which necessitates further invention and he showed that technological change was made up of innumerable minor improvements, with only infrequent major inventions.[10]

Usher, Giedion, Mumford and Gilfillan may be considered as classical forerunners to the contextual approach to the history of technology.[11] The contextual historians, Melvin Kranzberg, Lynn White jun. and Thomas P. Hughes to mention but three, have aimed at historical synthesis of the dynamic interplay between the functional characteristics of technologies or technological systems and the complex social, cultural, political and economic context in which they prevail. John M. Staudenmaier, in closing his book on technology's storytellers, describes contextual history as

> a vulnerable process in which the historian is deeply affected by the humanity of the subject matter. To reject as ahistorical the ideology of autonomous progress is to recognize that technological designs are intimately woven into the human tapestry and that all of the actors in the drama, including the storyteller, are affected by the tensions between design and ambience. By telling the stories of technological developments while respecting the full humanity of the tale, the contextual scholar rescues technology from the abstractions of progress talk and, in the process, takes part in the very ancient and very contemporary calling of the historian, reweaving the human fabric.[12]

The Swedish economist Erik Dahmén influenced by Schumpeter, Veblen and the Swedish institutionalist Johan Åkerman, clearly saw the systemic nature of industrial development. Dahmén's particular interest was in entrepreneurial activities and industrial transformation and he has developed a theory of industrial dynamics where the two major constituents are development blocks and entrepreneurs. Maybe he was influenced by Veblen who previously had stated that; 'any technological scheme is more or less of a balanced system, in which the interplay of parts has such a character of mutual support and dependence that any substantial addition or subtraction at any point will involve more or less of derangement all along the line.'[13] Dahmén develops his concepts by referring to development blocks as

> a set of factors in industrial development which are closely interconnected and interdependent. Some of them are reflected in price and cost signals in markets which are noted by firms and may give rise to new techniques and new products. Some of them come about by firms creating new markets for their products via entrepreneurial activities in other industries. This, too, may include the creation of new techniques and new products. In both cases, incomplete development blocks generate both difficulties and opportunities for firms.

Dahmén furthermore distinguishes between two extreme cases of transformation: positive transformation pressure characterized by opportunities, and negative where the necessity to adapt and adjust is immediate.

Development blocks are construed upon the complementarity of technological, economic and other related factors and upon the notion of structural tensions, that is, the absence of particular complementary factors. Now the definition of the concept falls into place. Development blocks refer to sequences of complementarities which, by way of series of structural tensions that is, disequilibria, may result in a balanced system.[14] The concept of development blocks is not merely suggestive when it comes to industrial transformation. It also offers an alternative to traditional economic aggregates and it should be obvious, from the discussion of technology and industrial evolution above, that the definition of industrial networks to a large extent has been influenced by the works of Dahmén. A final observation regarding development blocks, which is not immediately apparent from the definition but which arises from some of the examples provided by Dahmén, is that transformation processes drift towards conclusive solutions.

Lately, we have observed an increasing interest in the interrelatedness of technologies and in the nature of technological systems. Nathan Rosenberg informs us that the 'growing productivity of industrial economies is the complex outcome of large numbers of interlocking, mutually reinforcing technologies, the individual components of which are of very limited economic consequence by themselves.'[15] Paul A. David offers a very precise definition of technological systems when he states that they are characterized by technical interrelatedness and prospects of economic benefits from system integration.[16] The network benefits or network externalities originate from two different circumstances. First, as is stated in the straightforward definition above, the benefits arise directly from the integration of the interrelated technologies. Second, and this is perhaps not as obvious, network externalities, and thus potential benefits, are apparent when the overall economic performance of the system is dependent on the number of users and when the economic value for an individual user increases with the growing total of users.

Hughes provides a more articulated, and less operational, definition of technological systems, where he combines the internal and functional technical interrelatedness with the social, political and economic context in which it prevails. He suggests that the nature of technological systems goes beyond the interrelatedness of physical artefacts, such as generators, transformers, transmission lines, consumption measuring devices, and light bulbs and electrical apparatus in the electric light and power system.

> Technological systems also include organizations, such as manufacturing firms, utility companies, and investment banks, and they incorporate components usually labelled scientific, such as books, articles, and university teaching and research programs. Legislative artefacts, such as regulatory laws, can also be part of technological systems. Because they are socially constructed and adapted in order to function in systems, natural resources, such as coal mines, also qualify as system artefacts.[17]

Let us halt here to see what we are up against. We have been through several different inquiries into the nature of technological change and social progress. The unifying theme has been the contextual approach to the issue. We have seen a range of different definitions of technological systems. There were the straightforward, more mechanistic, definitions presented by Veblen or David, focusing primarily upon the interconnectedness of technologies, and there were the more complex definitions, by Mumford and Hughes, setting the technical interconnectedness into a larger social, political and economic context. For our purpose it seems operational to maintain the distinction between the more mechanistic technological system on the one hand and the social, political and economic context – the institutional structure – on the other. And, as suggested above, the latter will be perceived as networks.

Technologies depend upon and interact with one another in intricate ways. Only in schools do technologies appear in their pure and simple forms. They are interconnected into technological systems of complementary artefacts of different technologies and pieces of knowledge. Technologies are interconnected into systems, not randomly but according to an internal logic, not ordained but set by the historical development of the system. The logic of the system will at every moment embody the seeds for further development. Resolving imbalances in a technological system (which Commons called limiting factors, Dahmén structural tensions, Rosenberg bottle-necks, and Hughes reverse salients) will lead not only to the development of the system but also to new imbalances in other parts of the system. The dynamics of the sequential resolving of imbalances advance the technological systems and what was once a limiting factor will in the next moment be a complementary one. The resolution of imbalances requires human action; Commons called such efforts strategic transactions, Dahmén entrepreneurial activities, Schumpeter and many others innovations and entrepreneurial activities, and Hughes system-building. Of course not all imbalances can be resolved and if not compensated for in other parts of the system, they can threaten the whole system. Nor are all solutions to be found where the imbalances are perceived.

Technological systems are not, however, all about resolving imbalances through innovation. There is an everyday life also in technological systems, a going concern of complementary factors. Some have shown that day-to-day rationalization in going concerns contributed more to economic productivity than did radical innovation.[18] On the other hand it is difficult to refute the strong relationship between radical innovation and day-to-day rationalization.

Technological change and social progress does not, however, concern only technical factors. Institutional factors might be of equal or even greater importance. In Sweden as well as in other countries, firms, organizations and even individuals are struggling to develop electric vehicles. There are still some technological imbalances to be resolved, specifically with regard to battery technology and the relationship between effective power and volume and weight, but it is mainly an institutional problem. The prevailing automotive technology has been gaining momentum for a century and contemporary society is almost perfectly adapted to automobiles with combustion engines and to mass – automobile – transportation. Thus the prevailing institutions of automotive technology will favour conservative technological innovation and will penalize radical ones. A Swedish entrepreneur reports that it took him three months to develop his first electric car but it took him six months to have it registered and inspected according to Swedish law.[19]

In addition to institutional factors, geographical factors can play a significant role in shaping technology. In his account of the history of steamboat technology, Louis Hunter points out how a particular geographical factor, the shallow waters of the Mississippi river, shaped the technological design of steamboats. Consequently, the design was less viable in areas with deeper waters.[20] Hughes claims that different regional areas, exhibiting natural and human variations, will shape technology into different technological styles. He shows how the character of electric power systems were accidently shaped by local characteristics such as climate and seasonal variations in daylight, the location and character of rivers, lakes and seas, the availability of mineral deposits, soil and vegetation, elevations, transportation, industry, and demography.[21]

Local or national, institutional and geographical characteristics shape the particular design of technological systems. These qualities are even more explicit if we turn to art and architecture. The art historian Nikolaus Pevsner writes:

> In acknowledging the international unity of the new style, it ought not be forgotten that in Hoffmann's elegance, in Perret's clarity, in Wright's expansive broadness and comfortable solidity, or in Gropius's uncompromising directness, national qualities are represented at their best. But the art historian has to watch personal as well as national qualities. Only the interaction of these with an age produces the complete picture of the art of an epoch, as we see it.[22]

Well, art is not technology: the degree of freedom is much higher in art than in technology. Nevertheless, technology, especially emerging technology, will also be laden with both local and personal qualities. In many ways technology grows out of local needs and social circumstances. And whatever the origins of a technology its impact upon industrial production will be contingent upon the ability to shape it according to the local needs of the users. The successful transfer of technology from one local context to another, from one nation, region or industry to another, requires that the people and institutions employing it must be able to understand it, experiment with it and evaluate the economic repercussions of its use.[23]

An excellent example of the local qualities of technology and the subsequent problems of technological transfer is the futile attempts to transfer the Newcomen steam-engine, originating in eighteenth-century Britain, to Sweden and the United States. The development of the Newcomen engine in Britain arose from a number of factors: the problem of flooded mines, a favourable social organization, an ample supply of strongly energized fuel and the use of iron for construction. The Swedish historian of technology Svante Lindqvist has shown that a functioning Newcomen engine could be constructed in Sweden and that the failure in transferring the engine to Sweden resulted from a number of coinciding technical and social circumstances. The problem of flooded mines was not critical; the particular organization of ownership did not favour experimenting with new technology; compared to Britain the energy content of Swedish fuel was lower and the supply of fuel was a critical problem; and finally Sweden based its technology on wood rather than on iron, which made the construction less viable.[24] The attempts to transfer the engine to the United States also proved to be unsuccessful.[25] The Newcomen engine with its extremely low fuel efficiency seems to have been adapted to peculiarities of the local British context, flooded coal mines and an ample supply of inexpensive strongly energized fuel. This occurred more than 250 years ago and we might argue that the situation is different today and in many respects it is. The increasing globalization of modern industrial production might function as an institution facilitating technological transfer, leading to less accentuated differences between technologies emerging in different local contexts; on the other hand, the problem of transfer might also be amplified.

In context: a short summary

To sum up, no human, technology or business is an island, entire of itself. Each is a piece of the continent, a part of the main. Every innovation is embedded in a specific context, social as well as technological. The development of ploughs cannot be separated from the technique of ploughing, the quality of the soil, the social organization of the community, the holding of draught-animals, the nature and quality of available raw materials or the skills of the producers and users of ploughs. As Usher so vividly pointed out; 'The processes by which "man makes himself" include those procedures by which men transform their environment. Human evolution is doubly dynamic: man and the geographic environment react upon each other, and both terms are transformed.'[26]

Pre-existing technological systems result from the combined historical efforts of different actors working, independently or jointly, to solve locally defined problems. Each actor functions within historically defined boundaries. No actor can efficiently control the complexity of a full technological system. But, as the pay-off of collaborating with an actor controlling complementary technologies is often higher than abstaining from collaboration, the individual actors will form a community of interrelated actors, an industrial network. The combined efforts of the actors in the industrial network set the condition for future development of the technological system. Here again the process is doubly dynamic: networks and technological systems react upon each other and both terms are transformed.[27]

HISTORY MATTERS

The road not taken
Two roads diverged in a yellow wood,
And sorry I could not travel both
And be one traveler, long I stood
And looked down one as far as I could
To where it bent in the undergrowth;

Then took the other, as just as fair,
And having perhaps the better claim,
Because it was grassy and wanted wear;
Though as for that passing there
Had worn them really about the same,

And both that morning equally lay
In leaves no step had trodden black.
Oh, I kept the first for another day!
Yet knowing how way leads on to way,
I doubted if I should ever come back.

I shall be telling this with a sigh
Somewhere ages and ages hence:
Two roads diverged in a wood, and I –
I took the one less traveled by,
And that have made all the difference.
                    Robert Frost (1874–1963)

The technological and social embeddedness of innovation creates a decisive momentum, which drives the development of technological systems, not towards an optimal, a conclusive or a completely balanced state, but in accordance with the restrictions and opportunities set by the historic development. Veblen observed the power of the existing industrial systems and he attributed it to both technological and institutional factors.

> The state of industry in America and in the other advanced industrial countries will impose certain exacting conditions on any movement that aims to displace the Vested Interest. These conditions lie in the nature of things; that is to say, in the nature of the existing industrial system; and until they are met in some passable fashion, this industrial system cannot be taken over in any effectual or enduring matter. And it is plain that whatever is found to be true in these respects for America will also hold true in much the same degree for the other countries that are dominated by the mechanical industry and the system of absentee ownership.[28]

A path is laid by taking one rock at a time. Similarly, technology evolves by the solving of one problem at a time. In this way the past has a stronger grip over progress than all of the future opportunities combined.[29] Neither technology nor society is advancing towards any particular future state. They are both evolving from their present states. New technologies are not enclosed in the shadows of the future, but in the ambiguity of the past. We may trust ourselves to dream, to have visions, but dare we predict? This does not imply that the present is derived from the past and the future from the present: we are not slaves of the past, but we are its children.[30] Progress is propelled by circumstances embodied in history and, regardless of whether we are historians or not, historical analysis is necessary if we are to acquire a better understanding of progress and the forces prompting it.

One very obvious way in which history matters in the study of technological change and social progress is the time lag between original invention and its successful implementation. The electronic computer can be said to have been invented in the mid-1940s and since the 1960s the rumours of a computer revolution have been whispered everywhere. Yet, it is only recently that a widespread use of computer technology has been witnessed and still there is no immediate evidence of an economic impact. On the contrary, one is struck by the paradox of rapid technological innovation combined with disappointingly slow gains in economic productivity. The story of the computer is not without precedent. The economic historian Paul David reflects the development of computer technology in a not-too-distant mirror and compares it with the development of electricity.[31] Even if he hesitates to take the analogy too far, he presents a striking similarity in the development of these two general purpose technologies, especially regarding the time lag between the establishing of the technologies and their economic impact.

Many examples tell similar stories: a long period between technological change and its economic impact and a huge difference between frontier technology and technology in use. The future factory-concept has been the topic of manufacturing technology for decades, and yet surprisingly little has happened on the factory floors. Digital image technology is no different: the original ideas turned up around thirty years ago and it is still too early to say that the technology is successfully implemented in today's society. It began when some groups of researchers independently started to experiment using computers to analyse data contained in images. Since then the path to the image processing technology of today has been filled with temporary successes and failures and enclosed by futile attempts and unexplored routes. Current digital image technology is neither optimal nor conclusive. It plainly is and whatever is is right.[32]

As time wears on and individuals and organizations, with vested interests, put money and effort into specific technological or social solutions, development accumulates momentum: it becomes path-dependent and small historical events, such as investments in particular technological solutions or specific institutional circumstances, can lock the industrial evolution into different paths. The particular path travelled can make all the difference.

Prevalent technological systems are founded on the accumulated achievements of the past. The history of any specific system could have taken a number of different paths and the particular one followed does not necessarily have to lead towards an optimal solution. We do not have to go very far to find suboptimal technologies that have persisted despite their overt inefficiency. Consider the persistence of the Anglo-Saxon measures of distance; or the three different standards for television broadcasting, which seem likely to survive even the development of High-Definition-Television. From the railways in Sweden comes another example, with the technological shift from steam to electricity and the construction of the D-train, one of the most successful and long-lived Swedish designs of trains, manufactured from 1924 to 1957.[33] Swedish Rail decided that the back-and-forth movement characteristic of the dominant design of steam engines should be retained after the shift to electric motors. The persistence of this peculiarity was of course not without rationale: it was argued that only a back-and-forth motion could produce the torsion necessary to start the train set. The large company ASEA argued unsuccessfully for bogies and motors on every axis, a technological solution more appropriate for an electrical manufacturer.[34] The effect of the decision was that the rotating motion from the electric motor was transformed into a back-and-forth motion, which in turn was transformed into a rotating motion of the wheels. Another consequence was the preservation of the structure of the locomotive industry, in that there was no need for continued division of labour and specialization. The major Swedish manufacturers of steam locomotives, Nykvist and Holm AB, Motala Verkstäder, and AB Svenska Järnverks-verkstäderna, could continue to be significant suppliers, alongside ASEA to whom the future of train technology belonged.

David provides another example of the durability of an obviously sub-optimal technology – the persistence of the QWERTY-keyboard.[35] In the development of the first typewriters the configuration of the keyboard was open to choice. Ultimately it should be adapted to the mechanics of the typewriter and allow for efficient typing. The first typewriters to hit the American market had a keyboard, known today as QWERTY, an up-stroke mechanism, and a flat paper carriage. With the up-stroke mechanism there was a risk of typebar clashes. The flat paper carriage, having a non-visible printing point, meant that a typebar clash was not immediately obvious to the typist and so the clash would be reproduced. The keyboard was therefore configurated deliberately to hamper the speed of typing so as to minimize the risk of typebar clashes. The configuration also meant that the word TYPEWRITER, the brand name of the first typewriter, could rapidly be pecked out by sales representatives wanting to impress potential customers.

For efficient typing, the QWERTY-keyboard makes no sense. Since it was deliberately constructed to reduce the speed of typing, we might suspect that it would have been abandoned once it had been made obsolete through the development of new mechanics, where the risk of typebar clashes is reduced or totally removed. Yet it has persisted even in the age of personal computers. We have a technological imperfection at our fingertips. It has not persisted owing to a lack of more efficient configurations: it has survived despite the existence of much more efficient alternatives. One alternative placed the sequence DIHATENSOR in the home row: ten letters from which more than 70 per cent of the words in the English language can be composed. Later, in the 1930s, QWERTY was challenged by a serious contender, the DSK configuration, which reportedly allowed for 20–40 per cent faster typing. But despite several technological shifts since then it has persisted. The technological solution of up-stroke mechanism and flat paper carriage was not especially problematic. Well before the turn of the century alternative mechanical solutions, reducing or eliminating the risk of typebar clash, were developed. From 1890 type-writers with visible printing points, eliminating the reproduction effect of a single clash, were available. The configuration had not accumulated a strong installed base: by 1880 the entire stock of QWERTY-typewriters did not exceed 5000.

It is clear, from a rational point of view, that QWERTY should have been abandoned, but it has survived. What are the basic forces behind the persistence of the apparently inefficient configuration? Why was the con-figuration of keyboards already locked in before we entered the twentieth century? Probably a number of circumstances coincided to favour QWERTY as the universal design of keyboards. The fact that it was first and was also associated with the largest manufacturer certainly helped but was not sufficient. More decisive was the development of methods for fast typing, i.e. touch-typing, which required the memorizing of the configur-ation of the keyboard and thus created an idiosyncratic relationship between the keyboard and the typist. But why still QWERTY? There existed several different keyboards and schools of typing. A crucial event was perhaps a public competition between eight-finger and four-finger typing methods. Eight-finger typing was developed by Ms Longley, the founder of the Shorthand and Typewriter Institution in Cincinnati in 1882. She happened to teach with a QWERTY-keyboard although many of the competing configurations would have served equally well. The eight-finger method taught by Ms Longley was challenged by a four-finger method which was taught on a rival design. The eight-finger method won and, even if the competition really did not concern the keyboard, it proved the superiority of QWERTY in the eyes of those running typing schools and those publishing manuals. It thus acquired momentum and the intercon-nectedness of keyboard and typing method and the installed base have enabled it to persist even through a series of technological changes. The origin and survival of QWERTY resulted from a series of events, some rational but most purely coincidental. If it had not been for some of these events we might as well have been locked into a different path and maybe we would have ended up with a better configuration of our keyboards. But, as Stephen Gould says at the end of his opus on QWERTY,

> why fret over lost optimality? History always works this way. . . . For if history were not so maddeningly quirky, we would not be here to enjoy it. Streamlined optimality contains no seeds for change. We need our odd little world, where QWERTY rules and the quick brown fox jumps over the lazy dog.[36]

The case of the QWERTY-keyboard illustrates the contextuality of technology. There is technological interrelatedness not only between purely technical factors, such as keyboard configuration and typebar mechanics, but also between technical and human factors, namely keyboard and methods of typing. In the case of the D-train the technological interrelatedness between the back-and-forth motion and necessary torque was not so entrenched. This peculiarity of steam locomotives was finally abandoned and the Swedish locomotive industry was restructured. ASEA became the major supplier of railway technology.

Two other characteristics of technology in context are system scale economics, which favours the dominant solution, and quasi-irreversibility of technological change, which immunizes inferior technology from the attacks of superior technology. It also illustrates the consequential fact that dynamic processes take on an essentially historical character and it suggests that the study of economic history is necessary in the making of an economist.[37] Likewise, the study of business history is essential in the making of managers and researchers in business administration, and the study of the history of technology is essential in the making of engineers. If we are to reach a better understanding of the dynamics of industrial evolution, all of these related fields of history must be combined, and maybe others added, because history really matters in the making of tomorrow.

It is clear that historical events are important factors begetting processes of technological and industrial change. In our everyday lives too the role of history is indisputable. But how does history enter into the social sciences? It is notable that history rarely enters into the analysis, either in orthodox economics or in mainstream business administration. The role attributed to history in mainstream, non-historic, social sciences would be discouraging to any historian or anybody else with an interest in history. Nevertheless, history has not vanished completely from the research agendas and it is worth taking a short glimpse at how history has been taken into account in economic analysis.

In arguing for turning economics into a properly historical social science, Paul David distinguishes between four classes of how history has entered into economic analysis: two quite ordinary, classes which he labels 'mild to moderate history' and two perhaps more controversial classes which he labels 'strong history'.[38] As he moves through these classes he goes from an economic analysis where history plays a minor part to those where history is subsumed to beget the course of actions and events. The mildest, and completely uncontroversial, way in which history enters into economic analysis is through time lags between cause and effect. The direction is always the same; effects follow from causes, not instantaneously but with a slight delay in time.[39]

A more significant, but still moderate, role for history is found in models where the outcome is derived from particular dynamic sequences of intervening events. These models are commmonly based upon a notion of generalized accumulation, where the presence of 'A' is a precondition for attaining 'B': specific conditions or sets of conditions must be present for dynamic processes to pass from one state of development to another. A special class of models within this category is represented by random walk or state dependence with unique temporal sequences of moves. Unrestricted, where all moves are perfectly reversible, the dynamic process described by these models will eventually shake loose from its past; 'where the process is likely to end up eventually is independent of the place at which it started, or where it was at any specified intervening times.'[40]

Turning now to the second category discussed by David, strong history, we find models associated with path-dependent dynamics of economic systems, in which the role of history is substantially stronger. According to David, path-dependence connotes the fact that;

> the influences of past events and of the states they bring about must be communicated – like the deepening of the wheel-ruts by each successive vehicle – through some definite chain of intervening casual events, effects and resultant states – down to the present state, whence they can be passed on to future events.[41]

Path-dependence does not preach historical determinism, where the totality of the present is derived from the totality of the past. It simply suggests, as Usher also pointed out, that every event has its past, its present and its future, where irreversible events or activities effectively disconnect some regions of the state space from the rest. All roads do not lead to Rome and as way leads on to way, the particular path followed will make all the difference.

David discusses two explicit forms of path-dependence: lock-in by small historical events and path-dependent transitions. The first refers to dynamic processes, which can be locked into particular evolutionary paths through seemingly insignificant and entirely random events. The economics of QWERTY discussed above is an excellent example of how a semi-random, if not totally random, configuration of the typewriter keyboard locked in the development of typewriters and typing. The work of Brian Arthur shows that issues, such as competing technologies and industry location, can be analysed as processes locked in by small historical events.[42] And even if the event shaping the future is random and initially insignificant, it is possible to make statements regarding the probability of the possible outcomes, one of which is sure to emerge.[43]

Path-dependence of transition probabilities refers to a class of models where history really matters in the sense that knowledge of the present is not sufficient when it comes to predicting the future: some knowledge of the past is also necessary. The dynamics of a system is governed not only by where it is but also by where it is coming from. The past or rather the path through the past defines the range of possible actions. The present determines precisely what actions will be taken. In path-dependent dynamics, history is transmitted through a series of positive feedbacks, through which the system gains momentum: pushing it forward in a direction set by the past. Yet some forces – technological innovation, economic conditions or political ambitions – function in the present, inducing the system to drift. These forces do not affect the system directly, but through particular sequences of events. What, then, is the positive feedback: the carriers of history? This is a matter which explicitly as well as implicitly has been discussed above in relation to the contextuality of technology and the economics of QWERTY. Only five major sources of feedback will be presented here. Some have already been discussed but some, through their commonality, have been excluded from the discussion so far.[44]

1 Economies of scale in production: as the cost of production falls with increasing numbers of units produced, past performance in production is transmitted to the economics of production of the future.
2 Learning processes: learning always favours the existing. Regardless of the mode of learning – 'Learning by Doing', which is more aligned with the concept of economies of scale, or 'Learning by Using', which is more contingent upon technological interrelatedness – learning loads the dice on future development.[45]
3 Technological interrelatedness: the interrelatedness of technological systems creates an indivisibility, where the functioning of the parts is contingent upon the functioning of the whole, thus endorsing the development of prevalent systems, and deterring revolutionary changes to the parts.

4 Network externalities: refers to the notion that the user-value of a good or a service is dependent upon the total number of users. The user-value of the telephone is extremely low for the first adopters, but as the number of users increases so does the user-value. Network externalities punish the early adopters and reward the laggards.[46]
5 Networks: the industrial and institutional structure, here referred to as industrial network, is a carrier of history through rules and regulations, routine transactions, relationship-specific investments and through socialization of action.

These five sources of positive feedback are obviously not mutually exclusive. They influence and interact with each other in intricate and complex ways, creating a decisive momentum pushing the dynamics of systems into path-dependent evolution. These mechanisms reinforcing past achievements do not merely pertain to the evolution of prevalent technological systems and industrial networks. They are also informative regarding the problems associated with the emergence of new technological systems and networks and the obstacles that have to be overcome in order for novelties to become established. These feedback mechanisms counteract novelties to the same extent as they preserve the pre-existing structures.

History matters: a short summary

Dynamic processes – technological change, economic growth, social progress or whatever – are path-dependent, which necessitates historical perspectives on change. Current events cannot be fully understood without knowledge of how they have been shaped by past events, some (such as QWERTY) situated in the remote past.[47] In this sense every process is unique and it is in these unique sequences of events that the explanations for the outcome of dynamic processes should be sought. The particular path travelled, with its uniqueness and dependency on chance, will make all the difference. Or as Benedetto Croce puts it: 'The material of history is the singular in its singularity and contingency, that which is once and then is never again, the fleeting network of a human world which drifts like clouds before the wind and is often totally changed by unimportant events.'[48] Against the uniqueness and dependency upon random events of history and dynamic processes stands the ambitions to reach generalizable knowledge. While history most often is preoccupied with the uniqueness of events and sequences of events, social sciences are all about theoretical abstractions and generalizations. Maybe it is futile to seek to integrate the two: unique processes and timeless generalizations are indeed contradictory.[49] Nevertheless, timeless generalizations founded on a historical perspective are at least better than ahistorical generalizations.[50] Schumpeter goes even further, stating that 'theoretical equipment, if uncomplemented by a thorough grounding in the history of the economic process, is worse than no theory at all'.[51]

SOME NOTES ON METHOD

History matters and future outcomes are controlled by the course of events. A historical phenomenon, however, can never be understood apart from its moment in time.[52] Social processes are thus formed by the recurrent connection of the past with the present and so history is made; a history which exists and cannot be changed. 'The past is, by definition, a datum which nothing in the future will change. But the knowledge of the past is something progressive which is constantly transforming and perfecting itself.'[53] How should social processes be approached to transform and perfect the knowledge of past and present events?

Social processes are by nature complex: filled with constituent and chaotic elements and in their entirety often totally unintelligible. Recall, once again, Schumpeter's words: 'The social process is really one indivisible process. Out of its great stream the classifying hand of the investigator artificially extracts economic facts.'[54] Being an economist Schumpeter naturally searched for the economic facts, but economics are but one aspect of the social process: it is really one indivisible whole. To capture the essence of a social process the economic side must be complemented by other aspects. Only by approaching history from several angles can the knowledge of the past be transformed and perfected. The unravelling of social processes calls for an open mind and, as Marc Bloch puts it, 'in history, as elsewhere, the causes cannot be assumed. They are to be looked for'[55] It is the task of the inquirer into social processes to sift and separate those facts that may be called constituent and that are the true pointers of the development. 'Once this has been done the material does the rest.'[56] This should be the gist of any inquiry into social processes: to look for the causes behind the process and to report these; to produce and communicate knowledge; to learn and to teach. The major problem is to identify the underlying causes, that is, to learn from the past how history should be told. Once this is done the material does the rest.

It is the privilege of a scholar of any discipline or of any theoretical leaning to use a sensitive classifying hand to extract relevant facts. This inquiry into technological change and industrial evolution is conducted within the realms of marketing, broadly defined. As marketing rests firmly upon the duality of economic and social theory it is natural to seek also to extract social facts from the great stream of events characterizing the social process.

Even so, our ontological starting point is that there is a reality, which exists independently of our own consciousness, of which it is possible to get objective knowledge.[57] The question is whether the study of this reality, the reconstruction of the past, can be conducted independently of our own consciousness, of our own preconceptions and implicit or explicit theoretical propositions. Can a story be told as it really was, as Leopold von Ranke put it – 'wie es eigentlich gewesen'?[58] The famous phrase of T. S. Ashton, 'The facts do not wear their hearts on their sleeves', encourages us to think otherwise. The choice of theory or theoretical shifts will delineate the subset of facts that are deemed relevant and hence worth bothering to record or remember.[59] Reality is complex and according to the business historian Håkan Lindgren it can be compared to 'cobwebs of nodes and lines', categories and causal relationships, 'being structured both horizontally and vertically and integrated with other complex cobwebs in an infinite tunnel of time.'[60] Reality is, and by itself neither contains categories nor reveals causal relationships. The nodes and lines, the categories and casual relationships are theoretical constructs, abstractions founded on empirical observations or the theoretical inclination of the investigator or, as most often is the case, a combination of the two.

Consequently, even though we might assume that the past exists independently of our consciousness and might firmly believe that we can obtain objective knowledge of it, we cannot deny that our knowledge of the past will be based upon our preconceptions and implicit or explicit theoretical propositions. 'For undoubtedly there can be no history without a point of view; like the natural sciences, history must be selective unless it is to be choked by a flood of poor and unrelated material.'[61] We cannot free ourselves of past experience and as we enter into a new study, we bring with us specific ambitions and preconceptions. According to Karl Popper, the way out of this difficulty is to introduce a 'preconceived selective point of view into one's history; that is, to write that history which interests us'.[62] The initial purpose of this study was to explain the emergence of a new industrial network. I entered into the study with an ambition to combine two growing schools of thought, the network approach and dynamic economic theory, hence the interest in the dynamics of technological innovation and industrial change. It cannot be denied that this non-rational choice of theories has had an impact upon my understanding of the development of digital image technology in Sweden. The 'choice' of theory locked me into a particular path of theoretical reasoning.[63]

The choice of theory determines what facts or subset of facts are worth recording and remembering; the field from which constituent components will be sifted and separated. The present study is no exception. The perspective that has been presented in this chapter suggests one possible delineation of the relevant facts pertaining to the study of technological innovation and industrial evolution. In this case it implies that relatively higher importance has been attributed to context and time-related facts regarding the interconnectedness of technologies and the relationships between firms over time. Other, perhaps more traditional, perspectives would inevitably extract different subsets of facts from the same reality, probably emphasizing the role of individual inventors or particular innovations in the course of industrial change. The underlying frame of reference does not only affect what we will see, it also indirectly determines the results. While I am destined to put forward conclusions regarding technological systems and industrial networks, others are bound to give priority to the support of the notion that progress is brought about by individual inventors and their heroic deeds.

Inquiries into social processes are thus determined by the underlying, explicit or implicit, theoretical propositions. But what kind of knowledge of social processes do we seek? In this respect there exists a giant breach between history and economics. In history the purpose is to deal with individual cases, most often to describe a unique process. In economics, on the other hand, the aim is to establish general laws pertaining to classes of social processes. One of the aims of this study is to bridge the gap between history and economics and thus to handle the contradiction between the study of unique processes, in this case the emergence of image processing in Sweden, and the ambition to generate more general knowledge about these processes, in this case about technological innovation and industrial evolution. History and economics are brought into harmony through compromise, where the aim is not to search for the one and only true history or to establish a general law of evolution. The purpose is rather to explore social processes by employing economic and social models. In the following I will continue to argue for theory-laden studies of historical processes and to discuss the characteristics of the particular method of historical analysis employed in this study. Finally, some methods of generalization will be discussed.

Lindgren informs us that 'the hard core of the historical method is the linking-up of the thing to be explained to more abstract concepts in a dynamic analysis.'[64] The latter part of this statement is far from being controversial: history is all about processual analysis of long-term change. The first part should be neither surprising nor controversial, if we disagree with the general notion that the totality of the present is derived from the totality of the past and instead formulate the role of history more specifically in that every event has its past. We must have a method of moving from particular events, or rather sequences of events, to higher levels of aggregation and abstraction. Historical analysis implies the move from unique observations, through successive abstraction, to the phenomenon to be explained, unifying the particular sequences of events in their particularity with the general trends of an ever-changing reality. Historical interpretations should be sought rather than general laws of social evolution. The task of historical interpretation is to disentangle causal threads of development and to describe the accidental manner in which these are interwoven.[65] As Carlo M. Cipolla suggests, the aim of a historical study 'is not to twist facts to prove a theory, but rather to adapt the theory to provide a better account of the facts'. In the process of scientific inquiries into unique historical events, it must therefore 'be perpetual feedback between the formulation of problems and the process of gathering evidence'.[66]

John R. Commons describes the method of analysis as the phases of analysis, genesis and synthesis or insight, where analysis refers to the process of classification, genesis refers to the analysis of the changes that are continually going on in all factors and finally synthesis, or the concept preferred by Commons, insight, refers to the uniting of the changing parts into a changing whole.[67] To put the process of thinking proposed by Commons into the present context, analysis can be interpreted as the classification, based upon the present state of knowledge, of the unique observations; genesis as the analysis of the particular sequences of events; and finally insight as the unification of particular sequences of events into a changing whole.

The scheme through which knowledge of historical processes is generated is a complex activity of analysis, genesis and insight, deliberately constructed by the investigator in order to understand, predict or control the complex social processes of reality. The process is never finished. New insights set the stage for re-classification of observations, calling for re-analysis of the changing parts and producing opportunities for more insight. And there is always plenty of room for new insight.

> The older insights have been wonderful and important for their time and place – never to be forgotten or set aside. The new insights are needed and in turn they need the aid of the old, because 'the world's economic dilemma' is more puzzling than ever before, and yet similar dilemmas have occurred in the past.[68]

The proposition that learning is a process of constant reiteration should not be read as a suggestion that the growth of knowledge is purely accumulative. New insights might contradict as well as corroborate old insights. I do not simply know more now about technological innovation and industrial evolution than I did before I started to study the emergence of digital image processing: my acquired knowledge is also more specified and better articulated.

Neither is the process necessarily moving only in one direction. New insights can, as the social psychologist Karl E. Weick has pointed out, predate the categorization of observed events.[69] The process of acquiring new knowledge could work the other way around; from insight and genesis to analysis. An example of this could be the development of the Newcomen engine discussed above, where insights in the form of a new engine were produced without analysis and genesis, that is, without knowledge of the underlying theoretical principles. These were developed much later, after the innovation of the second generation steam-engines.

The method of inquiry as a complex activity of analysis, genesis and insight implies that theorizing – the process of learning – is more implicit in this case than in most other studies. It is a process of uniting empirical observation with theoretical insights; combining inductive and deductive reasoning; integrating unique observations, classification of hard data or articulated knowledge with theoretical insights, higher levels of understanding or expressions of tacit knowledge. The process of theorizing around dynamic processes, characterized as they are by multiple change and multiple causation, calls for true pluralism. In the successive abstraction of unique observation, in the pursuit of insight through analysis and genesis, anything goes. In the sequential reiteration of analysis, genesis and insight, pluralism is essential: poems, prayers or promises, theoretical reasoning, anecdotal evidence or quantitative methods of analysis, anything goes in the pursuit of insight.

'The only principle that does not inhibit progress is: anything goes.'[70] But it is more than that. Disabling learning would be the greatest mistake: no stone should be left unturned in the pursuit of knowledge. No factor or observation can be discarded without first having been evaluated. Disciplinary boundaries must be broken. The point that a factor is sociological or an observation geographical cannot mean that they should be excluded from an analysis of technological and economic change. No method can be discarded without first having been tested.[71] The only action that would be totally wrong would be to refrain from trying additional methods or alternative modes of reasoning, that is to refrain from pluralism. Note here that what is advocated is not an extreme form of pluralism, but a pluralism within the realms of existing observations and within the actual line of reasoning. To attain the normal standards of persuasiveness and coherence it is necessary to narrow the perspective. Thus, while learning should be open and free, teaching must be focused and argumentative. How one learns or from what is irrelevant; it is essential that one learns. And the story to be told is not how one has learned, but what.

The standard of persuasiveness comes from the belief that there exists no absolute truth. The aim is thus to build one, not the, image of reality: to argue for a perspective rather than to prove it. The image to be built must, however, be a complete image; there is just one reality and it is this whole reality we aim to reveal. The image must be coherent. It must be internally coherent; the story told and the theoretical reasoning should each hang together. It must also be externally coherent; the story told and the theoretical reasoning should be united.

This study of the emergence of image processing in Sweden is far from an accurate representation of the often tedious efforts and the seemingly endless endeavour of the underlying work. Only a minor part of the analytical effort put into the study is presented. The story of the emergence of image processing in Sweden could have been, and has been, told in many different ways. In the first attempt to portray the process, each and every research and development project was presented as a separate process, as a particular sequence of events. The story, based upon several different case studies, revealed some interesting properties.[72] First of all, it revealed a surprising stability of the individual efforts of technological development. Even though many of the projects went through major institutional changes, primarily in the transfer of the projects from scientific institutions to business firms, these changes were only to a lesser extent reflected in changes in the course of technological development. Second, and more important, it revealed an interrelatedness between the different stories. There seemed to be a pattern where the different projects, which were initiated in different contexts, were moving towards each other, forming an apparent network structure around the emerging technology, only to be attracted to other technologies and other actors and so dissolving the emerging network structure. Had I been interested in a different question, for instance economic performance and the organization of research and development in digital image processing, this structure of the story would have been perfectly adequate. But, since my interest was focused towards the whole picture of industry dynamics and the relationship between technological change and industrial innovation, the structure of the story was deemed inadequate.

The observation of different phases in the development of image processing was the point of departure in the second attempt to depict the story.[73] Different sequences of events were divided into three periods, and the development within the different periods were lumped together. The development of digital image technology in Sweden was therefore divided into three distinct phases. Each and every phase followed logically from the preceding ones and was a precondition for the succeeding ones. This was a first attempt to unite the unique observations of changes of the parts with the changes of the whole. This exercise confirmed the observation that the story could be told as three distinct periods, but the story as such was insufficiently integrated. And major rewritings were still needed. Some attempts at integration were made, focusing on specific problems in the development of new technologies and industrial change.[74]

A third attempt at a total revision of the story was discontinued half-way through owing to a perceived lack of insight into the underlying theoretical principles. Combining new theoretical insights with the existing empirical observations resulted in (as seen in Chapter 5) the abstraction of the particular systems of events into three facets of technological development and industrial evolution: genesis, coalescence and dissemination, where different underlying processes seemed to dominate the course of events at different periods. To confirm the general pattern of evolution, quantitative methods of network analysis were employed. Only this last analytical effort is reported in the present study. From the structure of the book it might appear as if the theoretical reasoning preceded the empirical study. This is, however, an illusion. The theoretical framework was developed simultaneously as empirical data were collected: causes were not assumed, they were sought.

Up to now a method of historical analysis has been suggested and what may be called internal validation of the theorizing based upon single case studies – unique processes – has been discussed. A question still not touched upon is how general the findings of studies of unique processes are. First, it should be observed that we are dealing with unique processes, so the process itself cannot be generalized. Yet, the aim of applying methods of successive abstraction is to produce testable theoretical propositions. The purpose is to find the general pattern behind the observed changes in the reality. The observed pattern could thus ideally be generalized through subsequent scientific tests, confirming or contradicting the present results. We can also argue for a more general applicability of the findings by comparing them with other studies of unique processes. We should, however, be cautious in our use of other studies and employ at least some rudimentary source criticisms before we use them as an external validation of our studies.

Some concluding notes on method

The pursuit of knowledge in the social sciences can in conjunction with the pursuit of technological change be treated as processes of particular systems of events subject to lock-in by small historical events, that is, as path-dependent evolutionary processes. What we end up with are not conclusive, eternal, everlasting truths. The accumulated knowledge does not even necessarily have to converge towards the truth. We are only adding to the huge bulk of research reports, providing yet another statement, posing different arguments in a continuing scientific dialogue. With luck our studies will be read and understood and, where history shows that we were on to something, others will be there to reproduce our findings and our successors can also compensate for our mistakes. The particular method of analysis and theorizing advocated here suggests that the results are embodied in the path pursued. In consequence, I am more inclined to argue for the plausibility of the findings rather than to present conclusive results. Some of the major findings of this study are embedded in the structure of the presentation: in the telling of the story.

TECHNOLOGICAL SYSTEMS AND INDUSTRIAL NETWORKS IN THEIR PARTICULAR CONTEXT OF TIME AND PLACE

All through this chapter it has been argued that events must be seen in their particular context of time and place. Adding these arguments to the basic model presented in the previous chapter provides an extended abstraction of the interdependence between technological systems and industrial networks (see Figure 4.1.)[75]

However, a remaining problem is that, by adding new dimensions, clarity is not automatically brought to the initial dimensions. This is especially enigmatic in the present study since the basic components, technological systems and industrial networks, are generic concepts covering the same ground. The concepts are not mutually exclusive and in many cases they are interchangeable. In the following we will very much fall back on a more mechanistic definition of technological systems, like the one presented by Paul David, that they are characterized by technical interrelatedness and prospects of economic benefits from system integration. Networks, on the other hand, will be perceived more as a social system of interconnected relationships.

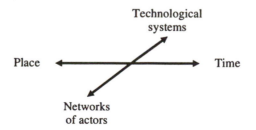

Figure 4.1 Technological systems and industrial networks in their particular contexts of time and place

SUMMARY: A HISTORICAL AND CONTEXTUAL
PERSPECTIVE ON TECHNOLOGY AND INDUSTRY

In summarizing the ideas laid out in Chapters 3 and 4, the major statements made regarding technological innovation and industrial evolution are that the phenomenon is socially constructed and path-dependent and that it is embedded in a context of technological systems and social networks.[76] Technology and industry are socially constructed in that neither of these strives towards optimal solutions. They are not balanced or in equilibrium, they are not unbalanced or in disequilibrium; they simply are and they have been unfolded by social actors addressing perceived problems. Hence, it would not be fruitful to make value judgements regarding the process of change. The social construction is, however, limited. The process cannot shake loose from its history. It is path-dependent. What is holding it back – and also driving it forward – is the inertia of technological systems and social networks.

The story of technological change and industrial evolution in the emergence of digital image technology in Sweden will be presented in Chapters 6, 7 and 8. But first it is necessary to elaborate further on the nature of networks and technological systems and to develop a framework for understanding the emergence of a new technology and a new network.

5 Industrial networks

Networks of actors and technological systems

In the previous chapters it was argued that it was necessary to study change in the context of time and place. From a general model of the relationship between technology and institutional structure, a more specific model of the reciprocal relationship between technological systems and networks of interrelated firms was derived. The nature of technological systems has already been discussed, so the focus in this chapter will be on the nature of networks. The purpose more specifically is to define the nature of the link between technological innovation and the evolution of networks. We will begin by looking at some antecedents of the network theory and then quickly move to an inquiry into technological change, followed by a discussion of the relationship between technological systems and networks. The chapter concludes with the presentation of a framework for understanding the emergence of new technological systems and new networks.

INDUSTRIAL NETWORKS: SOME ANTECEDENTS

Network theories are becoming increasingly recognized as analytical tools applicable to the analysis of the nature of industrial production and consumption. What do network theories in general suggest? If theories of the firm state factors that determine or control the behaviour of the firm, then network theories suggest that a specific firm's behaviour is controlled by its relationships with other firms and not by internal factors or by aggregates of unspecified units, such as competitors and markets for supply and demand.[1] The behaviour of the whole network would then be controlled by its specific pattern of interrelated firms.[2] But this pattern is also controlled by the technological system, which in its turn is controlled by changes in the network. The concept of industrial networks will be used to cover both technological systems and networks of interrelated firms. Thus it is the interplay between technological systems and networks of interrelated firms that begets the evolution of industrial networks.

The aim here is to provide the antecedents of the specific theory of industrial networks developed by some groups of European marketing researchers.[3] Firmly rooted in industrial organization, inter-organizational theory and system analysis, this research tradition rests upon the layers of the function of organized behaviour systems, the behavioural theory of the firm and the interdependence of firm behaviour and environment. Here a path to industrial networks will be laid by relating the accumulation of theoretical knowledge to the changing conditions of industrial production.

The rise of modern capitalism and the organization of industry

The giant corporation, mass-production technology and the dominant schools of thought in industrial economics emerged almost simultaneously. The shift from craft technology to mass-production both necessitated and facilitated corporate growth. Many of the rising giants were organized so as to encompass the greater part of the underlying technology. The Edison Electric Light Company not only manufactured incandescent-lamps and electric dynamos but also constructed, operated and maintained electric service stations.[4] The Ford Motor Company exhibits a similar organization: centred around the manufacturing of automobiles, Ford also controlled tool manufacturing, steel-works, gas stations and automobile outlets.[5] The pattern was to strive for maximum internal control. Thus, when the Ford Motor Company discovered a growing production of car radios that could be fitted into Ford automobiles, so competing with internally manufactured radios, the interior of the car was changed in such a way that only Ford's own radios could be installed.[6] Specialization and division of labour was primarily perceived as being effectuated within the growing corporations. It gave rise to increased productivity through the capitalization on the enhancement of the skills of the work force and the division of labour between workers and machines. Altogether it gave rise to economies of scale prompting internal corporate growth.

The emerging industrial structures with a limited number of large corporations were far from the idealistic dichotomy of monopolistic and perfect competition. The complete theoretical distinction between monopoly and perfect or pure competition, impaired by assumptions of homogeneous inputs and output and perfect information, was negated by the facts of intermixture in real life. Edward Chamberlin addressed the discrepancy between theory and reality in his pioneering work, *Theory of Monopolistic Competition*, presenting a synthesis of monopoly and perfect competition.[7] By introducing the concept of product differentiation, Chamberlin brought heterogeneity to the theory of competition.[8] He observed that, when products are differentiated, buyers are given a basis for preference, and will therefore be paired with sellers, not in random fashion (as under pure competition), but according to these preferences. Under pure competition, the market of each seller is perfectly merged with those of his rivals; now it is to be recognized that each is in some measure isolated, so that the whole is not a single large market of many sellers, but a network of related markets, one for each seller.[9]

Chamberlin only used the concept of network in an everyday sense. His main interest, and that of his contemporaries and successors, was in the nature of industrial competition. The observed heterogeneity was handled by the grouping of firms into industries according to the substitutability of their products. The notion of industries or trades was of course not new and the major contribution was rather the formulation of theoretical propositions regarding the relationship between the characteristics of industries and industrial competition. This product-oriented definition of industries and the relationship between the characteristics of industries and competition has permeated the preponderance of studies of industrial economics and its impact on Western thinking is indisputable: national statistics and anti-trust regulations are irrefutable evidence of its predominance.[10]

Industrial systems and organized behaviour

Others responded differently towards the observed increase in heterogeneity of inputs and outputs: primarily by focusing on the complementarities rather than on the substitutes and on industrial systems rather than on industries. This represented not only a shift in focus but also a shift in interest. The main issue was not intra-industry competition, but the functioning of total market or industrial systems, where the functioning of the parts was considered to be contingent upon the due functioning of the whole. R. F. Harrod and J. A. Hobson described the forces of production and consumption as 'forming common funds of industrial energy pulsing through the whole framework of industry, as the blood course through the various organs and cells of the body, giving organic unity to the entire system'.[11] This analogy between the course of economic action and the blood system was also put forward by Schumpeter in his discussion of the circular flow of economic life. He used the analogy in setting up the general perspective but abandoned it, referring to its inaptness to reveal processes of discontinuous change, when he came to the dynamics of economic life.[12]

Wroe Alderson, one of the founding fathers of modern marketing theory, went one step further.[13] Assuming perfect heterogeneity, Alderson's functionalistic approach to marketing was a total commitment to a systems approach of organized behaviour in heterogeneous markets. In his analysis of heterogeneous markets Alderson employed the concepts of transaction and transvection, stating that

> The function of exchange is accomplished at successive levels by means of transactions, but the process of bringing any given item to the ultimate consumer is accomplished through a series of sorts and transformations called a transvection.[14]

Through the concept of transvection Alderson accentuated the interdependencies of transactions and hence the complementarities of the market system. By focusing on transactions and transvections Alderson emphasized the importance of horizontal and vertical interdependencies to the functioning of organized behaviour systems. Alderson was, like Schumpeter, absorbed by the dynamics of economic life. Like Schumpeter, he stressed the importance of technological change, stating that

> The treatment of technological change occupies a key position in a theory that attempts to show the dynamic character of marketing behaviour. . . . the fundamental basis of market dynamics is located in the fact that markets are both heterogeneous and discrepant. . . . A (heterogeneous) market which is discrepant in the short run will display a long-run tendency toward equilibrium but will never actually achieve this steady state.[15]

In the emphasis of disequilibrium Alderson's work is similar to others studying dynamic processes. What was perhaps new was the recognition of heterogeneity as a major force, driving dynamic processes.[16]

Depending on the issues at hand, approaches towards the observed heterogeneity followed two different routes: either, as Chamberlin and his adjuncts did, addressing issues of industrial competition by grouping the heterogeneous commodities into more homogeneous groups, or, by focusing on the complementarities of industrial systems, addressing issues of the nature of industrial activity in the context of interconnected market or industrial systems. The latter was done by Alderson, who inquired into the function of organized behaviour systems by introducing the vertical interconnectedness of sorts and transformations in transvections. The difference between the two routes pursued is more than the difference of micro and macro perspectives on industrial production: the different general methods of aggregation used in the two approaches are totally irreconcilable.[17] To combine the two schools of thought, addressing both the nature of competition and the function of industrial systems, a synthesis of intra- and inter-industry competition and co-operation is required.

Taking the virtues of economies of scale to the extreme would lead us to believe that one corporation or a few of them eventually would dominate industrial reality. Specialization and division of labour and the extent to which economies of scale can be realized are not unlimited. Even if such were suggested by Adam Smith's famous conjecture that the division of labour is limited by the extent of the market, in the present times of globalization and integration of markets there would be opportunities for even more specialization. Economies of scale are subject to diminishing returns: unit costs will not continue to decline indefinitely with increases in production volume or size of the corporation. Technological as well as market and managerial factors check the realization of economies of scale and industrial production appears to be a trade-off between production volume and adaptability to changing conditions: between economics of production and economics of organization and marketing.

The organization of economic activity has become increasingly problematic. Advantages of firm size and mass-production can be, and have been, set off by a continuous stream of technological innovation, crises of control of the heightened flow through production and consumer preferences for individuality and choice. The supposedly ever increasing flow of goods and services through the systems of mass-production and mass-consumption invoked friction and problems of control of production, inventory, distribution or consumption. Some of these problems are social, such as the organization and rationalization of bureaucracies and the routinization of decisions and transactions; and some are technological, such as the development of means of communication and means of handling information, sometimes called a control revolution. The resolving of these problems highlights the highly tricky nature of organization and administration of large firms in complex industrial systems.[18] The advantages of mass-production were offset by the complexity of the whole system. Investments in production capacity had to be matched with corresponding investments in the markets for inputs and outputs. Furthermore, neither the suppliers of inputs nor the buyers of output remained passive. They actively sought to improve the outcome of their investments. The result of this is a situation where the economic performance of an investment made by one corporation is to some extent dependent on other elements of the industrial system over which the corporation in question has little or no control.

As the industrial systems of mass-production have matured, the components have become increasingly standardized, opening avenues for specialization and division of labour beyond the scope of the manufacturer of finished goods. In many industries we can observe the exploitation of economies of scale in the production of components. This development is perhaps most obvious in the computer industry, where the exploitation of economies of scale have primarily been located within the semiconductor industry but where the computer industry represents the bulk of the value added. Other industries, such as the manufacturing of automobiles, exhibit similar patterns.[19] Hence, by division of labour between different firms within the industrial system, specialization could be taken to new heights. Economies of scale unexploitable by a single firm could be realized by a series of consecutive firms. This should have positive effects on the overall economic performance, but it will also make the performance of an individual firm subject to the performance of adjacent firms. The present tendencies, combined with new production technologies and changing consumer preferences, have increased the possibilities for flexible specialization.[20] Where the development of interchangeable parts once was instrumental in the emergence of mass-production and mass-consumption, it now seems to foster a new phase in industrial development with the exploitation of economies of scale with flexible manufacturing and with individuality in consumption.

Consumers preferring choice is nothing new. One of the major crises facing the Ford Motor Company centred on the fact that the consumer preferred the choice and style offered by General Motors before the low priced, standard automobile offered by Ford. The resurrection of the Swedish automobile industry in the 1980s was to a large extent also due to consumer preferences for alternatives. In the 1970s the Swedish automobile manufacturers, Saab and Volvo, were doomed: they were considered to be much smaller than the assumed optimal scale. But changing consumer preferences in terms of choice of the size of the car enabled Saab and Volvo to survive and prosper in well-defined market niches. In flexible manufacturing, the recently ascending outgrowth of the factory of the future, the final user is bestowed with a greater discretion over production decisions. Ultimately, the decisions of what and when to produce would be made by the user, while the producers would decide only on how to produce. Realizing flexible specialization would thus require efficient flows of information and goods from production to consumption.

The industrial systems of mass-production have grown larger and more complex, constantly appending and uncoupling components, changing the interrelationships of the systems. When further growth of the rising giants of production seemed hampered by the limitations of the market, they extended their reach by setting up multinational operations and extended their scope by becoming multi-product firms.[21] This added to the already problematic situation of economic organization. Internally, the visible hand of managerial hierarchy was falling apart: the rising giants were reaching or going beyond the limits of organization. The advantages of large size were set off by worker dissatisfaction and by the inability to act upon anything but very large changes. The quest for worker motivation and

flexibility, presumed virtues of small organizations, encouraged corporations to try new forms of internal organization. Simultaneously the giants'
access to resources, markets for inputs and outputs, have become increasingly
critical and too important to be left to the whims of the market.

A new reality is in the making: a wide variety of firms from very small
to extremely large, far from the perfect competitive conditions of smallness
and similarity, where only loosely organized firms strive for their existence
in a complex environment disclosing market arrangements which, in consecutive order, connect systems of production and systems of consumption.
There is a new reality where multi-product firms cross industrial borders
and multinationals cross national borders, craving new theoretical insights
into the problems at hand.

Maybe the industrial reality did not change and maybe neither did the
world view of the theorists. But at least theorists focusing on the economic
organization within and between firms were becoming increasingly recognized. In general they addressed the failure of the economic organizations
of pure hierarchy or pure market. They perceived firms and organizations
as social entities rather than as production functions. They focused on the
behaviour of firms and organizations in changing environments, setting
internal organization in the perspective of external organization.

The behaviour of the firm

As we proceed down a path of alternative views on economic organization
we slowly pull away from the rationalistic view. A major step in this
direction was taken by the now classic work of Richard M. Cyert and James
G. March on a revised theory of firm decision making.[22] To them firms
were social entities and, as an alternative to the pre-dominant economic
theory, they formulated a behavioural theory of the firm. The theory
specified an alternative framework 'for dealing with the modern "representative firm" – the large, multi-product firm operating under uncertainty in
an imperfect market'.[23]

The basic constituent of the revised theory was an alternative perspective on organizational goals, expectations and choice. The organizational
goal was survival rather than profit maximization and it was the result of a
social bargaining process based upon existing coalitions of organizational
participants. The aspiration level was perceived to be set by the combination of past goals, past performance and the past performance of others.
Organizational expectations refers to the process through which information is made available. They described the formulation of expectations as
search processes, where the direction of the search was affected by the
nature of the problem stimulating search. The intensity and success of the

search was, on the other hand, affected by the extent to which goals were achieved and the amount of available resources, organizational slack. Here it should be noted that the firms were striving for satisfactory rather than optimal results. Finally, organizational choice was perceived as taking place in response to a problem, invoking and identifying alternatives consistent with prevailing goals and using standard operating rules in making the final choice. From here Cyert and March continued to discuss decision making of firms as quasi resolution of conflict, uncertainty avoidance, problemistic search and organizational learning.[24]

It should be obvious from this discussion that the behaviour of firms portrayed by Cyert and March, characterized by sub-optimization, local rationality and limited search, is far from the rationalistic assumptions regarding firm behaviour, reacting optimally towards the stimulus of price, suggested by economic theory. Most of the modern thinking regarding decision making within firms is firmly based on this path-breaking work of Cyert and March

Firms' dependence on the environment

The next rock to be laid in making a path towards industrial networks is to relate more specifically the decision making within firms to their environment. The behaviour of complex organizations was addressed by James D. Thompson, whose interest was in the effects of the basic sources of uncertainty, technologies and environments, on how organizations designed and structured themselves.[25] Focusing on the interface between internal organization and external environment, he suggested that the organizations, through buffering, smoothing, adaptation and rationing, would seek to seal off their core technologies from environmental influences. Technological requirements produced interdependencies within the organizations and, as organizations were always embedded in a larger system, he also argued that organizations must be interdependent with entities in the environment, not subordinated to authoritative control. The internal interdependencies within the technical core were to be handled through coordination while the interdependence with the environment should be handled through boundary-spanning activities of adjustments to uncontrollable constraints and contingencies.[26] Note here the significance that Thompson attributed to technology. Not only would it shape the internal organization of organizations but also the larger system within which the organization was embedded.

Thompson concluded his inquiry into complex organizations by suggesting that 'there is no one best way, no single evolutionary continuum through which organizations pass; hence, no single set of activities which constitute administration.' Yet he maintained that under norms of rationality the design of organization would be contingent upon the requirements of technologies and environments. He followed up by stating that 'Appropriateness of design, structure and assessments (of complex organizations) can be judged only in the light of the conditions, variables and uncertainties present for the organization.'[27]

Jeffrey Pfeffer and Gerald R. Salancik went one step further in the direction pointed out by Thompson, purporting that no organizations are completely self-contained or in complete control of the conditions of their existence. Organizations are, to a greater or lesser extent, always subject to external control. Organizations depend on their environment by virtue of the fact that they must inevitably acquire resources by interacting with their social environment.[28] In accordance with the reasoning of Thompson, Pfeffer and Salancik perceived the environment as the basic source of uncertainty. The concentration of power, the scarcity of critical resources and the pattern of interconnectedness between organizations determine the degree of conflict and interdependence in the relationship between organizations, two factors which in their turn determine the degree of uncertainty facing an individual organization.[29]

Problems arise not only because organizations are dependent on their environment but also because this environment is not dependable. Neither can it be fully comprehended or predicted by the organization. Does an objectively defined environment exist? This question signals a compelling problem: does organized action result from actual or perceived properties of the environment? The social psychologist Karl E. Weick assumes a more extreme standpoint in that he suggests that the environment is created, enacted, through organized action.[30] Hence, relating internal organization to external environment is problematic. Yet, the survival of organizations is dependent not only on the efficiency of internal adjustments but also on the ability to cope with and adjust to ever-changing environments.[31]

Systems for production and consumption of goods and services are being extended over national and industrial borders. Industrial activities have become increasingly interconnected. Firms engaged in industrial production are gradually becoming dependent upon each other in their pursuit of interconnected industrial activities. In the study of social or industrial change researchers are increasingly becoming inclined to address issues of the interrelatedness of firms and organizations in industrial markets. And inter-organizational issues are increasingly taking precedence over intra-organizational ones.

Networks: a response to the changing conditions of industrial production

Observing the changing conditions of industrial production, a group of researchers, primarily Swedish, found the industrial structures of firms and organizations resembling cobwebs of lines and nodes. Organized action, that is, the performance of interconnected industrial activities through the transaction and transformation of economic resources, was found to be embedded in a specific structure – a network. Empirical research showed that the major part of the exchange in industrial markets took place within the realms of relationships between firms; relationships that furthermore proved to be stable over longer periods. Where these exchange relationships were established through evolutionary processes, the relationships evolved slowly through the interaction between the firms, but once established they were rarely broken. The character of the relationships was found to be affected by the internal organization of the two parties and by product and production technology. Within the relationship, logistical and technical problems seemed to dominate over price considerations: exchange in the industrial market seemed to be regulated by problems rather than by price.[32]

Perhaps most importantly, it was concluded that the individual relationship was affected by the parties' other relationships. The exchange relationships were interconnected into networks, where individual relationships were affected by the properties of the whole network. Industrial markets were observed to be coordinated not only by the visible hands of the managers or the invisible hands of price mechanisms but also through the adjustments and adaptations within long-term relationships. Networks represented a coordinative mechanism, a governance structure separated from the traditional dichotomy of markets and hierarchies.[33]

Firmly rooted in the traditions of industrial economics, system analysis and inter-organizational theory, the group conceptualized a network perspective on the behaviour of firms in, and the function of, industrial markets. Inductive reasoning based on empirical research of industrial markets suggested that firms were linked together into networks, since they produced or used complementary or competitive products. Articulation of a network approach to industrial markets resulted from a combination of empirical findings and theoretical insights provided by Cyert and March (regarding decision making within firms), by Thompson and Pfeffer and Salancik (setting the behaviour of firms into the context of environment) and by Alderson (regarding the function of organized behaviour systems).[34]

Industrial networks: a general view

Resting on the assumption of perfect heterogeneity, industrial networks can be defined as consisting of actors linked together by their performance of complementary or competitive industrial activities, employing or consuming economic resources to process other resources.[35] Here are the constituent components of the prevailing network model, that is, actors, activities and resources, all three defined as being perfectly heterogeneous. Actors differ in respect to purpose, scope and scale, which means that business firms, social organizations and public institutions at different levels of aggregation may be considered as actors. A general condition, however, is that the actor should have the capacity to retain at least some degree of autonomy. Activities are comprised of acts of transformation and transaction interconnected into activity cycles and transaction chains. Resources are heterogeneous and are both tangible, such as capital and land, and intangible, such as knowledge, competence and skills. Heterogeneous resources are employed to transform, or to transact, other heterogeneous resources, hence one dimension of resources is that they are complementary (see Figure 5.1).

Actors control resources and perform activities. But no actor controls all of the necessary resources or performs all of the complementary activities of activity cycles and transaction chains. Technological change and industrial evolution have driven out specialization and division of labour between actors, leaving the individual actors dependent upon other actors in their performance of activities and production and use of resources. The interconnectedness of activities and resources creates interdependencies between actors, which are too critical to be left to the whims of the market. Hence, actors handle these interdependencies by establishing long-term relationships, where they give up some of their independence and freedom to act in return for decreased uncertainty. The behaviour of an actor is controlled by other actors with whom the actor has exchange relationships. The economic performance of individual actors is thus contingent on the performance of the whole network. Actors are embedded in industrial networks functioning not only as a constraint on individual action but also as an instrument and medium for interactions and counteractions between actors and other entities in their world driving further technological change and industrial evolution.[36]

At every point in time an industrial network exhibits a specific structure of relationships based on specific combinations of interconnected activities and resources, where the future of the network, new relationships and new activities and resources, is enclosed in past relationships and in past combinations of activities and resources. In the real world an industrial network

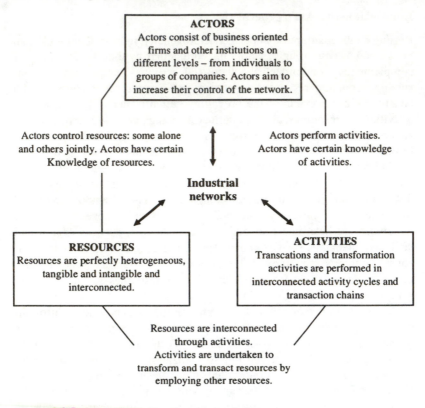

Figure 5.1 Industrial networks: the perceived view

Source: Håkansson, H. (ed.), *Industrial Technological Development: A Network Approach*, London: Croom Helm, 1987.

could, through continuing chains of relationships, be extended infinitely, until it embraced the whole world. This definition of network is, however, far from operational. Even if conclusive rules for setting network boundaries are inconceivable, some tools of delimitation are still needed. The pragmatic solution is to let the delimitation of networks be dependent on the specific questions raised. The boundaries are therefore set where mutual dependencies transcend into one-way dependencies. Boundary-spanning activities will nevertheless be those that are most forceful in the evolution of networks and so any delimitation must always be considered as temporal.

What, then, are the issues raised by the proponents of industrial networks? Network studies have been pursued along two lines of inquiries. First of all there are inquiries into the nature and evolution of organized action embedded in industrial networks. The absolute majority of the studies belong to this class of inquiry.[37] A second line of studies pertains to the nature and evolution of whole industrial networks. In this class of inquiry only a limited number of studies can be found: total network studies have been rare in the pursuit of network research.[38] Few, if any, have studied the emergence of new networks. The common denominator of most network studies is the focus on development and change: corporate growth, internationalization and technological development. Since this is a study of technological innovation and industrial evolution, the network approach to technological change should briefly be examined ·

TECHNOLOGICAL CHANGE IN INDUSTRIAL NETWORKS: THREE PROPOSITIONS

Actions or rather sequences of actions, organized, chaotic or unconscious, are undertaken by actors embedded in the social and technological contexts of industrial networks.[39] Technological innovation is one sequence of actions pursued in industrial networks. Technological change in industrial networks is affected by the existing structure of the network, the actors involved and their inter-organizational relationships, and the specific combinations of activities and resources. But it is also one of the propelling forces determining the future structure of the network. Hence, technology and technological change are fundamental aspects, reflected in several network studies, of the evolution of industrial networks. The results of more than ten years of study of technological change in industrial networks can be summarized in three general propositions: (1) technological development is an interactive process; (2) technological innovation results from local search processes elicited by locally perceived problems; and (3) the evolution of technology is a process of accumulation.

Technological change as an interactive process

The first proposition is that technological development in industrial networks is an interactive process. A significant part of the development takes place in the form of technical exchange between different actors; individuals, companies and research organizations. Håkansson argues accordingly that the

> interest should be focused as much on the interaction between different actors as on what happens within the actors. An innovation, therefore, should not be seen as the product of only one actor but as the result of an interplay between two or more actors; in other words as a product of a 'network' of actors.[40]

No actor is in complete control of the system of production and consumption in which, to a varying degree, the actor participates, performing activities and controlling resources. The actor can neither incorporate the factors underlying the supply side of innovation nor completely control the factors underlying the demand side. Suppliers, users and competitors can make significant contributions to the innovation process, both by inducing innovation and by contributing, with their specific competence, to the problem-solving. The innovation process can be improved through the interaction between different actors: combining complementary competencies, coordinating existing resources and mobilizing new resources, thus increasing the probability of success and reducing the risk and cost of failure.[41]

The rate of technical exchange and the subsequent theoretical interest in innovation as an interactive process seem to be increasing.[42] The observed increase in technological co-operation between firms can be attributed to two properties of industrial development. First, the highly developed vertical division of labour is the stylized fact of modern industrial societies, suggesting that a substantial part of the innovative activities take place in units separated from the potential manufacturers and users of the final innovations.[43] Second, increasing volumes of production lead to the massive increase in the costs of research and development experienced by most actors.[44]

The accentuation of the interactive facets of the innovation process does not suggest that the deeds of individual inventors, or internal research and development departments, are completely insignificant in the pursuit of technological development in modern industrial societies. It only suggests that whatever takes place within a firm must be set into the context of the co-operation between firms in an industrial network.

Technological change as local search processes stimulated by local problems

The next proposition regarding technological development in industrial networks is that it is characterized by local search processes stimulated by locally experienced problems or opportunities. Actors are constantly exposed to streams of events emanating from the technologically changing environments. And technological development unfolds as actors act, react, interact and counteract, responding to the streams of events facing them.[45] Which problem or opportunity to act upon and in what direction the solution or exploitation is to be sought is determined as much by the outcome of political processes as by economic and technological rationality. This proposition regarding technological development stands in contrast to the heroic theory of development. It focuses on the everyday life of innovation. Note that this does not necessarily preclude major technological breakthroughs. There is also an everyday life behind major innovations.

The direction of the search processes and the rate of innovation will be governed by the underlying stream of technological problems and opportunities, which in its turn is determined by the prevailing state of technology in the network, the technological base of past developments.[46] The implication of this contextual proposition on the nature of technological change is that technology will be differentiated between firms and networks. Technology is specific to the problems and opportunities spurring the local search processes; both the stream of problems and opportunities and the direction of the search processes are governed by the specific contexts of industrial networks. The network specificity of technology creates particular problems when it comes to the diffusion or transfer of technology from one network to another, requiring costly adaptations to or adjustments by the recipient network. Two implications follow from this: first, that neither transfer, diffusion, nor imitation is without cost – imitation can be as costly as the original innovation; and second, that the cost of transfer, diffusion, or imitation is different for different actors.

The problems or opportunities cannot always be sufficiently resolved or exploited at the point where they arise. Quite often the solutions are to be found outside the control of the actor experiencing the problems,[47] which brings us back to the first proposition: innovation is an interactive process. Mutual adaptation and adjustments, rather than the deeds of heroic inventors, engineers and scientists, are the hallmark of technological development in industrial networks, regardless of whether it pertains to original innovation or diffusion or transfer of innovation within and between networks.

Technological change as a process of accumulation

Knowing how way leads on to way and how the solving of problems arouses new problems, so triggering new search processes, bring us to the next proposition: technological change in industrial networks is a process of accumulation.[48] It is a cumulative process in the traditional sense in that it is a consequence of incremental technological change and gradual learning and it is as much a question of retaining previous experience, combining it with the prevailing circumstances, as it is of developing novel solutions.[49] But it is not a process of general accumulation; new knowledge or innovation, even after it is once produced, is not available free to others.[50] Technological development unfolds in sequences of problem-solving, where problems lead on to problems and where the solutions to these drive the technological frontier along a particular path. This does not proceed according to a master plan, or through the invisible hand of the market, but through the accomplishments of many actors, all of whom might be acting in their self-interest.[51]

The particular path of technological development is constrained by the interconnectedness of activities and resources in the industrial networks. Technological change in industrial networks is irreversible or quasi-irreversible. Innovation is created by adaptations and adjustments, necessitating adaptation and adjustment of interconnected activities and resources, thus locking the development into specific fields of development and locking it out from others. The network creates limitations and opportunities, a momentum, pushing the future technological development in the direction set by the past.[52] The network and the technology evolve through specific paths of accumulation.

Technology is a significant part of industrial networks.[53] Technological development is a compelling force driving the evolution of industrial networks, but this statement covers only half of the story. The evolution of the industrial network is also a compelling force driving technological change.

Heterogeneity and the evolution of industrial networks

In the introduction it was stated that in the network approach the behaviour of an actor is governed by its relationships to other actors. Why is this? Basically, it is because the actor faces the heterogeneity of the industrial network through its relationships and it is only by actors acting upon this heterogeneity that the network evolves. Heterogeneity thus constitutes the major force driving development in industrial networks as well as in the organized behaviour systems of Wroe Alderson. Dressed in economic clothing, heterogeneity of resources – one dimension of the heterogeneity in networks – can be defined as follows: a resource is heterogeneous if its value is dependent on which other resources it is combined with. By contrast, homogeneous resources have constant values independent of what other resources they are combined with.[54] The economic definition of heterogeneity is rather similar to that of network externalities, discussed in Chapter 2. The difference is that, while network externalities deal with the allocation of resources under imperfect market conditions, heterogeneity of resources is regarded as a factor begetting the evolution of networks.[55]

How does heterogeneity drive the evolution of industrial networks? Heterogeneity implies variation, which actors face through their relationships to other actors. Acting upon this, adjusting and adapting to each other, will induce changes in the network; some heterogeneity will be reproduced or self-reinforced, but to other actors this will signify further heterogeneity or variation. Transformed into a general model of evolution, this would mean that heterogeneity represents the mechanism generating variety and that the selection mechanism is reproduction and self-reinforcement. The problem, however, is to separate the generation of variety from selection. Selection might very well precede variety.

The heterogeneity of industrial networks is related not only to resources but also to actors and activities. This holy trinity of networks is, however, slightly different from the model suggested earlier of technological systems and institutional structures, where technological change and industrial evolution unfold in the dynamic interplay between the two. Given this particular interest in the evolution of industrial networks, the contemporary network model must be modified.

INDUSTRIAL NETWORKS REDEFINED

Industrial networks have been described differently in different studies. One fruitful way of handling the complexity of industrial networks has been to divide them into levels, a surface structure and a deeper structure. Jan Johanson and Lars-Gunnar Mattsson, two of the founding fathers of network theory, perceive what they label an industrial system as consisting of two levels, two basic sets of interconnections. One is an institutional set, still labelled industrial networks and defined as interconnected exchange relationships. The institutional set is perceived as a governance structure, through which the exchanges in the system of production and consumption are coordinated. The other level is construed upon a technological set, labelled production system, exhibiting an industrial logic of interconnected activities and resources. In this way Johanson and Mattsson accentuate the interconnectedness and interdependency of industrial networks and they move from stressing the individual elements of actors, activities and resources to emphasizing the interconnectedness and interdependencies of activity cycles, transaction chains and networks of relationships. The interconnectedness of the production system is handled by actors through internal organization and through relationships to other actors, producing the interdependencies of the governance structure of industrial networks. Combined production systems and industrial networks constitute the higher order concept, industrial systems.[56] Harrod and Hobson provide a comprehensive picture of an industrial system 'in which many clusters of businesses are grouped into trades, while these trades are arranged in order by series to carry on the work of converting the raw materials and forces of Nature into commodities and services for the use of man'.[57] The problem of using industrial systems as the principal concept is that an industrial network attains a connotation different from that of the contemporary network model.

Industrial networks: technological systems and networks of actors

How can industrial networks be delineated as the combination of institutional and technological structures? First of all, the industrial network is retained as the principal concept. Second, the institutional set is perceived as a network of actors held together by their exchange relationships and the technological set is viewed as a technological system. Industrial networks are still sets of interrelated actors performing interconnected activities, by transforming and transacting heterogeneous and interdependent resources.[58] An industrial network is, however, depicted as the union of a network of actors and a technological system (see Figure 5.2). To avoid confusion in the future, the word network will be used to denote a network of actors and industrial network will be used to denote the totality, the union of a technological system and a network.

Since the main interest is in the evolution of industrial networks as an interplay between social and technological structures, the more mechanistic definition of a technological system, suggested in Chapter 4, is maintained. A technological system is characterized by technical connectedness and prospects of economic benefits from system integration.[59] Remember, however, that the nature of technological systems goes far beyond the interconnectedness of physical artefacts, such as generators, transformers, transmission lines, consumption measuring devices, and light bulbs and electrical apparatus in the electric light and power system. Embodied in the technological system is an industrial logic of the nature of the production and consumption activities of the system; knowledge of product technology, of production methods and of natural resources.

Technological systems are globally defined and they are reflected in and

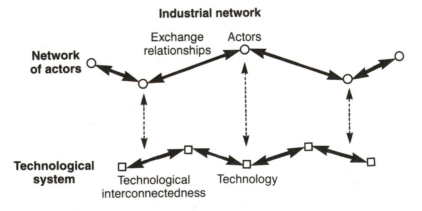

Figure 5.2 Industrial networks: technological systems and networks of actors

by networks of actors, which in turn are locally defined. Thus, the actual network is controlled not only by the technological system but also by the pattern of exchange relationships in the past and in the present. Owing to the historical pattern of interaction within local networks, the technological system will be reflected differently in different local networks. Local in this context does not suggest that networks are primarily demarcated by geographical boundaries. Local networks can extend over several different countries and several local networks can co-exist within the same country. That networks are locally defined simply implies that they can be separated from other networks which are reflected by the same technological system. The networks will over time become increasingly institutionalized as bureaucratic structures of government agencies, laws and regulations and common rules of behaviour accumulate. The structure of the network together with the institutionalized pattern of behaviour will affect the possibilities of changes in the technological system.[60]

Technological systems can be used to set the boundaries for an industrial network. Actors, especially large multi-product firms, are often engaged in several different industrial networks. The concept of a technological system enables us to delimit industrial networks in order to focus on particular networks of actors. But the concept is also useful when it comes to understanding the evolution of industrial networks. To be more than a tool for demarcating the network it is necessary that the technological system is identified by the actors. In the emergence of a new network, identification of something new and different manifests the evolution of the network. But identification alone is not sufficient to beget the evolution. It is also necessary that some actors – preferably several – are willing to sacrifice resources to the development of the new activities. The network must be legitimated. Finally, as no network can survive in isolation it must be adapted to the surrounding networks. Hence, the emergence and evolution of networks can be understood as three concurrent processes of identification – legitimation – adaptation.

Actors perform acts of innovation to resolve perceived problems in the technological system or adversities in their exchange relationships. If reproduced the innovation will be preserved in the technological system, functioning as a driving force for further changes in other parts of the particular network as well as in other local networks. The development and subsequent implementation of radical technological innovation and the emergence and evolution of new industrial networks thus embodies two sets of interrelated issues: the emergence of a new technological system, adapting and integrating the parts of the system to one another, and the emergence of a new network of actors, coordinating specialization and division of labour between actors, routinizing transactions and distributing the economic surplus, setting the scene for further integration within the technological system.

Starting out with what he labelled Wieser's principle of continuity, Schumpeter wrote that 'the economic system will not change capriciously on its own initiative but will be at all times connected with the preceding state of affairs'.[61] Yet, as he entered the path of industrial dynamics, he asserted that the new structures would emerge beside the old. He wrote: 'new combinations are, as a rule embodied, as it were, in new firms which generally do not arise out of the old ones but start producing beside them.'[62] Hence, his emphasis was on the capitalistic system capable of allocating resources for new ventures. In his later works he more willingly admitted that new structures could emerge from within pre-existing structures.

The economic structure in the Western world of today is in many respects different from the structure experienced by Schumpeter. The technological systems have grown larger and become more integrated; industrial networks have been extended globally and specialization and division of labour have become more apparent and distinct. Almost every economic field has become dominated by a few large multi-product firms. As a consequence economic activity has increasingly become embedded in socio-technical structures. A more potent social and technological momentum has been accumulated, causing the emergence of new industrial structures to be more aligned with the pre-existing structure than Schumpeter had reason to anticipate. Changes emerge from pre-existing structures and, if viable, they will eventually be re-integrated with the structures from which they originated. To realize changes, the semi-autonomous actors of industrial networks are dependent upon the support of others. But others will also induce changes which require reactions. And if change is problematic, the production of change is equally enigmatic, the costs of research and development and market introduction have risen tremendously and firms are increasingly seeking partnership in the development of new businesses. Hence, the emergence of a new industrial network is neither purely cumulative nor purely revolutionary. It is rather the result of a combination of accumulation and revolutionary change, where previously independent technological systems and networks are being linked into one unity, one whole, a new industrial network.

New technological systems originate from innovative activities within established industrial networks, which produce radical innovations representing discontinuities, which disrupt the established economic structure. The quest for innovative solutions to old and new problems craves the higher degree of freedom predominantly found within research and development departments of universities, national defence organizations and business firms and within newly established firms. As new technological systems, through different acts of innovation, diverge from the paths of the established industrial networks, the innovators, the newly established firms and the different research and development departments undertake to accumulate resources to transform the innovations into self-sustaining economic enterprises.[63] Simultaneously, new infrastructures, new industrial networks connecting the interrelated parts of the emerging technological systems must evolve. The performance of individual actors is therefore to some extent contingent upon the performance of the whole. A new industrial network cannot function in isolation. It must eventually be integrated with the structure from which it emanated. The emergence of a new industrial network is thus a continuous evolutionary process transforming industrial production and consumption from one structure to another, conveying new technological systems and new networks of actors. The final question is: how can the emergence and evolution of industrial networks be described, understood and analysed?

A FRAMEWORK FOR AN UNDERSTANDING OF THE EMERGENCE OF A NEW INDUSTRIAL NETWORK

Evolutionary processes in industrial networks have been the subject of several recent studies.[64] Being slightly different in scope, these studies share the common view that industrial networks are living, ever-changing, organisms. From these studies it can be concluded that the evolution of industrial networks is composed of two complementary but contradictory processes, the generating of variety and the organization of everyday life. Both processes are embedded in the pre-existing industrial network and are therefore bounded by historical evolution. The organization of everyday life refers to the process through which the activities and components of everyday life are coordinated, integrated or adapted to one another. The organization of everyday life is constantly disrupted by the generating of variety: the inducing of innovation or the establishment of new network relationships, motivated by perceived problems. The organization of everyday life primarily increases the degree of integration within the network while the generating of variety induces heterogenization and disintegration. A specific evolutionary pattern therefore results from these two parallel processes. As the processes are likely to dominate in different periods of time we can expect the evolution of an industrial network to move from integrative to disintegrative back to integrative, carrying a transforming structure.

Two different metaphors are conceivable in the study of the emergence of a new industrial network. First of all we could perceive it as a biological life-cycle, where the condition and interconnectedness of the complex system is set from the beginning;[65] And where the industrial network, properly fostered and nurtured, will move through the stages of birth, adolescence, growth, maturity, declining years and eventually death, bringing prosperity to society. On an aggregated level this metaphor suggests that periods of evolutionary growth will be nullified by revolutionary change.[66] The policy implications are obvious: the state should provide support during birth and adolescence, should tax it during growth, maturity and declining years and should facilitate and balance the death. The individual actor should strive to decrease the time span and cost of birth and adolescence, and to extend the time and increase the profits of growth and maturity, thereafter managing decline, exhausting final profits and timing the dismantling of the dying system.

The biological life-cycle metaphor is contrasted by a more action-oriented one, where the condition and interconnectedness of the complex system are not assumed to be set from the beginning. In fact it is assumed that this is what the evolution of industrial networks really is all about: the continuing formation, establishment and adaptation of the interconnectedness of the technological system and of the interdependencies of the network of actors; not in consecutive order but simultaneously, constantly expanding and contracting the industrial network, changing, integrating or disintegrating the interdependencies of the network and the interconnectedness of the technological system. The emergence of a new industrial network is thus characterized not by a sequence of life but by life itself: with growing, maturing, declining and dying elements constantly co-existing within the system. Here the policy implications do not come as easily and the inquiry into this issue must be postponed. The emergence of an image processing network in Sweden has been perceived as series of related and unrelated actions driving the industrial network in different directions. A problem with the action-oriented metaphor is that it does not seem to allow for novelty to emerge: 'Nothing was born; Nothing will die; All things will change.' Still, new industrial networks inevitably do seem to arise, but their evolution should be interpreted as life itself rather than as sequences of life.

New industrial networks – carrying new technological systems and new networks of actors – really do emerge. But they will grow out of the old order and are thus not new in an absolute sense.[67] New merely signifies a re-organization of the old order, but normally this would also include at least some novel elements; a new activity, a previously untapped source of resources or new actors. An industrial network does not ascend instantaneously in a once-and-for-all shape. Its evolution is only one facet of a more general social and technological development and as such it will unfold through parallel and continuous processes of formation, establishment and adaptation. However, since we are focusing on this particular facet, it is likely that, even if the processes are parallel, different processes will be found to dominate in different periods; furthermore, it is plausible that formation precedes establishment and that establishment precedes adaptation. The macro-evolution of an industrial network is the result of other processes: the evolution of a technological system and a network of actors. These in turn are driven by the micro-processes of actors developing new activities, exploiting new resources or forming new relationships.

Emergence and evolution of new technological systems

The shift in focus from individual innovations to technological systems necessitates a move away from the dominant model of technological development, which states that technical change is brought about through the sequence of scientific discovery/invention – innovation – diffusion/imitation. Instead it should be acknowledged that the evolution of technological systems has no real beginning and no ultimate end. The systems are a part of a constant metamorphosis of society. Their evolution is propelled by the creation of novelty, technological development and changing patterns of usage, but these processes do not unfold in sequential order. They are omnipresent concurrent processes feeding back on each other. Creation of novelty represents both scientific discovery and technological innovation and it is a continuous process, but its character will most certainly change cyclically over time; periods characterized by a few radical new discoveries will be followed by times of many less radical inventions which in their turn set the scene for yet other radical discoveries. The creation of novelty is propelled by the problems arising both in the pursuit of scientific research and in the development of technology. Technological development is another process with its own logic, it represents the establishment of the technological system and the integration of its constituent components into one whole connected system. Also this process is cyclical in its nature; times of increasing variety are followed by times of standardization and integration. Finally, there is the process labelled use, which represents the evolution of the user side of the new technological system. The user development will take the technology to new applications and to more users. Hence, the technological facet of the evolution of industrial networks can be treated as the continuous processes of creation of novelty, development and use, where creation of novelty and use represent the generation of two different forms of variety and where technological development represents selection and integration.[68]

Emergence and evolution of new networks of actors

Technology is not autonomous; technological change cannot be separated from the human ingenuity constantly pushing it forward. Thus the emergence and evolution of new technological systems cannot be separated from the evolution of the new networks of actors governing and developing the technological systems. This facet of the emergence and evolution of industrial networks is treated as the social processes of identification, legitimation and adaptation. As was the case with the creation of novelty, development and use, these processes do not necessarily unfold in a sequential order; rather they are omnipresent, continuously altering the structure of the industrial network. The undertaking of inventive activities is a salient feature of humankind. The transformation from a single invention to the emergence of a new industrial network is effected by the identification of a group of actors developing a cluster of interconnected inventions. The identification of a network as something new and different from the prevalent networks represents the origination of the new network. The fact that the activities of the actors constitute something novel does not, however, imply that resources automatically will be devoted to their development. To establish the new network, the development activities must be legitimated. Finally, when a new network has been identified and legitimated, it must be adapted to the prevalent networks.

SUMMARY: THE EMERGENCE OF NEW INDUSTRIAL NETWORKS

Only by combining the emergence of technological systems with that of networks of actors can the emergence of industrial networks be disentangled. By letting the continuous processes intersect, a model of the evolutionary process can be reproduced. A graphical representation of the framework for the understanding of the emergence and evolution of industrial networks is presented in Figure 5.3.

The study of the development of digital image processing in Sweden suggests that the emergence of a new industrial network can be described as three distinct phases: genesis, coalescence and dissemination. And even if the underlying processes are omnipresent they tend to dominate in different periods. Genesis represents the creation of variety and the growth of a new pattern of interaction. Coalescence represents the integration of variety into an emerging community of actors. Finally, dissemination represents the adaptation to the pre-existing structures and the dissolving of the industrial network.

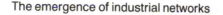

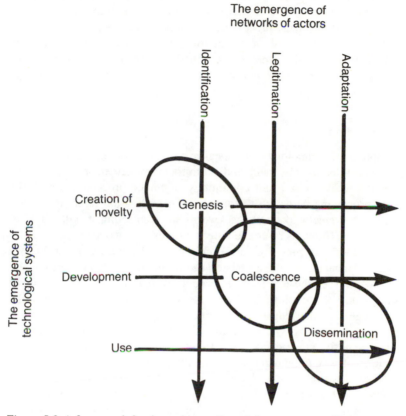

Figure 5.3 A framework for the understanding of the emergence of industrial networks

Genesis

Genesis is marked by the independent initiation of several different research and development projects and the origination of the new technological system. These projects were initiated within different technological systems and in different industrial networks and the actors of the emerging network were scattered geographically, functionally and technologically. As the projects deviated from their origins, the proponents of image processing had to initiate search processes for support and complementary resources outside their original networks.

Coalescence

As the emerging network was identified, the proponents of image processing began to interact with one another. The emerging network coalesced into a close knit community of complementary and competing image processing firms, developing image processing into a multi-purpose technology. As the network coalesced, the parts of the new technological system were adapted to one another, the technological system of digital image processing was integrated and the network produced several different image processing systems.

Dissemination

In adapting the technology to the specific needs of different users, inducing processes of learning by using and exploiting complementary investments made outside the close knit community of image processing firms, the image processing network disseminated. Dissemination refers to the extension of the network, both backwards by connecting it with supplier networks and forwards by connecting it with user networks.

The underlying processes are omnipresent. They do not unfold in a sequential manner, but will each become dominant in different periods. We have not yet seen the end of the emergence of digital image processing in Sweden and the evolutionary processes will continue to govern the development of the industrial network for digital image technology. A remaining question is: what determines the shift from one phase to another?

The genesis, coalescence and dissemination of the emergence and evolution of a new industrial network is based upon the empirical observation of the development of digital image processing in Sweden. It does not imply that this is an optimal route, or that all emergent networks will follow similar paths. The evolutionary pattern observed is not necessarily valid for the emergence of other new industrial networks. It is likely that new industrial networks emerge from everything and that they also disappear into everything. But there cannot be a general law of social evolution. It is hard to imagine that the outcome of such complex underlying processes can be generalized. Patterns of evolution are heavily marked by the specific time and context in which they occur. Genesis, coalescence and dissemination are descriptive tools generated by the study of digital image technology in Sweden, but the significant findings lie beyond the story told in the storytelling itself. Even if it is not meaningful to generalize the trajectory of an evolution, it is the role of scientific inquiry to search for the mechanisms generating the observed evolution. But the causes should not be assumed, they must be sought.

Part III

Novelty in thought and action: The emergence of digital image processing in sweden

> It is said, and it is true, that Swedes in general have a pronounced technical and mechanical bent. In other words, technical ability is one of the important natural resources upon which the nation can rely in its struggle for life.
>
> Axel F. Enström, 1927

The traditional Swedish view is that its prosperous industry rests upon an extraordinary technical ability. Industrial affluence in Sweden was founded at the turn of the century and the notion of technological prominence emanates from this time. Is the nation still relying upon its technical ability in its struggle for life or has this altogether been a myth? Digital image technology is an example of a field where Swedish actors acquired strong international positions from a technical point of view. From an economic point of view the results have been less satisfactory. The issue to be addressed in the story of Swedish digital image technology is how the technical ability was developed and how it has been exploited.

Before the presentation of the emergence of the digital image processing network in Sweden, the underlying principles governing the selection of information should briefly be re-examined. What information is included and what is excluded? The issues at hand are the emergence of industrial networks and the transformation of scientific research into industrial production. The focus has therefore been on the evolution of the cooperation between firms and other organizations and on changes in technology. Less attention has been given to individual inventors and entrepreneurs. This is not because they have been absent during the emergence of digital image processing, nor that their roles have been insignificant. The rise of image processing is filled with heroic individuals performing heroic deeds: Sixten Abrahamsson developing a drum-scanner; Torleiv Orhaug making pioneering contributions in the development of image processing and remote sensing; Nils Åslund persistently developing image-reading instrument systems; Per-Erik Danielsson and Björn Kruse developing parallel computer architecture and spinning off the first image processing company; Gösta Granlund constructing one of the more exciting image processing computers; Ingemar Ingemarsson and Robert Forchheimer taking the Swedish tradition in image transmission to new heights; Rolf Johansson making pioneering contributions in industrial automation; Lars Dahlström developing the first Swedish system dedicated for robotic vision; Björn Stenkvist and Ewert Bengtsson developing image processing systems for cytology. To a large extent these and other pioneers have taken Sweden to its technologically leading position in digital image processing. But these individuals are only the tip of the iceberg, behind them larger and smaller groups of fellow workers and researchers are likely to be found. Furthermore, it is argued that human ingenuity is more interesting as a phenomenon than are the individuals representing it. The focus is thus on networks of exchange relationships and technological systems and not on individual inventors and entrepreneurs.

The perspective taken is that the capacity to foster the development and exploitation of technical and industrial ability is contingent upon the capacity to foster the evolution of industrial networks.

6   Genesis

Digital image technology is an extension of computer technology and of course the existence and availability of computers were necessary conditions for the emergence of the new technology. The development of computing machines made it possible to mechanize solutions to old problems. It also made it possible to solve new sets of problems, whose emergence coincided with the development of the computer. Telecommunication and television technology, broadly defined, were two other important auxiliary sources in the emergence of image processing. Machine vision might seem futuristic and out of reach. However, combining two of the post-war high technologies, television and computer technology, by connecting a television camera to a computer and thus enabling machine vision, probably did not seem to be a far fetched idea.

In 1948, only a few years after the construction of the first computers, John von Neumann is holding a presentation on the general and logical theory of automata at the Hixon Symposium, where he discusses the possibility of mechanized image interpretation. He not only mentions it, but also indicates the direction in which to search to solve the problem.[1] Von Neumann audaciously suggests that

> Nobody would attempt to describe and define within any practical amount of space the general concept of analogy which dominates our interpretation of vision. There is no basis for saying whether such an enterprise would require thousands or millions or altogether impractical numbers of volumes. . . . It is therefore not at all unlikely that it is futile to look for a precise logical concept, that is, for a precise verbal description, of 'visual analogy'. It is possible that the connection pattern of the visual brain itself is the simplest logical expression or definition of this principle.[2]

Von Neumann's statement was not the starting point in the development of digital image technology, but it shows that prospects of mechanized vision were not merely a distant dream.

Initially, the primary problem was the reading of images into the computer: to process images one must first get them into the computer. The unavailability of digital images motivated an American research institute to digitalize a photograph of a 'Playboy Bunny'. This digital image of a female face was made freely available to everybody and, since almost every researcher into digital image processing had access to the image, it became the test card of processing methods. As solutions to the image reading problem were developed, other problems became critical: the huge amount of data embodied in images created specific processing problems. An ordinary colour photograph contains the same amount of data as 25 books of approximately 400 pages. Conventional computers could very well be used to process image information, but it was extremely time consuming and in almost every respect inferior to all other, predominantly manual, methods of image analysis. If image processing were to become technologically and commercially viable, special image processing computers capable of processing and storing huge amounts of data would have to be developed. In the late 1960s and early 1970s parallel data processing was developed, which still remains the dominant solution to the demand of high-speed processing capacity.

Another critical problem was the interrelatedness of input, processing and output, which suggested that the different problems could not be addressed separately. As the technology developed and became more standardized the process could be broken down into parts. Thus the possibilities for specialization and division of labour increased. This and the problems mentioned above appeared and were resolved within the realms of emergent networks and the developed solutions modified future technological development and the evolution of the networks.

FIVE CENTRES OF ORIGIN

Five centres of origin of the technological concept of digital image processing can be identified:

1 Optical character recognition related to the development of techniques to read data into computers.
2 Image transmission, and the development of picture phones.
3 Mechanization of previously manual analysis of images in research laboratories.
4 Radiology and the development of methods and instruments for the registration of soft tissue.
5 Remote sensing related to the development of air and satellite reconnaissance of early warning systems.

The common denominator of these remotely connected fields of interest was the increase in the degree of mechanization in the analysis or processing of natural images. As the capabilities within these technologies had developed differently in different countries, digital image processing emerged in different clothing in different countries. Sweden did not exhibit equal strength in the five centres of origin of digital image processing and all of the problems propelling the acts of innovation were not equally immediate.

Optical character recognition

In the development of the computer, human–machine interaction soon became problematic. This was particularly the case with the input procedure. The dominant solution was to code data into punch cards which were read into the computers. Several research and development activities were initiated in order to develop more functional ways of feeding data into computers. One of these ways was to develop a device that could read written or printed characters and transform them into computable units. This gave rise to a technological field labelled optical character recognition and the spread of this technology followed the spread of the early computer industry. The basic problem of converting an image of a symbol into digital information proved to be extremely difficult to solve efficiently, given the state of computer technology. When the computer terminal, keyboard and monitor became the standard solution to human–machine communication, one of the pressures compelling the development of optical character recognition disappeared. Consequently, the computer industry slowly lost interest in this field. The further development of optical character recognition was pursued outside the computer industry and the major impact of the technology has so far been in the development of fax-machines.

Picture phones and image transmission

Another significant field of interest in the emergence of image processing, and in the development of fax-machines, was image transmission. The major difference between image processing and image transmission is that the latter seldom involves elements of processing or analysis. In the adolescence of television technology, image transmission surfaced in actual tests and in the science fiction literature as interpersonal communication. Before television became a mass-communication technology, it was tested for interpersonal communication. The more futuristic ideas were materialized much later in AT&T's Picturephone, first presented at the New York World's Fair in April 1964.[3] Besides AT&T several other telephone

companies were making progress with picture phones. The Swedish company L. M. Ericsson regarded the picture phone as one of the most promising
research and development projects from 1968 to 1971 and they performed
the first transatlantic transmission of sound and image between two picture
phones in 1970.[4] L. M. Ericsson tested picture phone systems internally and
in their collaboration with Swedish Telecom. A system was also installed
at one of the largest Swedish commercial banks. The picture phone, however, captured more imaginations than it did business. None the less,
companies have persistently held to the concept of transmitting images
over the telephone and picture phones are still presented as the future mode
of telecommunication. The concept of picture phones has been expanded
into image transmission but the basic idea of a widespread picture phone
system survives and is being evaluated by telecommunication operators all
over the Western world.

The development of picture phones is an excellent example of the
interrelatedness of technology. Why could the scientific and technological
achievements of image transmission not be transformed into useful products of economic significance in the 1970s? After all, the capability of
transmitting sound and images simultaneously had been established, and
functioning prototypes were developed and tested. There is, however, a
huge gap between achieving something under favourable conditions and
the production of profitable products and services. The picture phone
functioned well in isolation, but it could not be implemented in the existing
system of telecommunication. The economic benefits of any communication system rely upon the availability of a substantial amount of nodes.
Image transmission requires a much higher transmission capacity than
ordinary transmission of sound and the limitations of the existing communication channels of the time allowed only small-scale use of picture
phones. Large-scale use of picture phones required a substantial increase in
transmission capacity and at the time this could be achieved only by
employing expensive satellite-technology. By itself this was a sufficient
cause for the delay in implementing picture phones. An additional, supply-
side, barrier to the development of picture phones was the unavailability of
low cost components, cameras and monitors, on which the picture phone
system was based. On the demand side, tests of picture phones eventually
showed that the primary need for the system was to communicate documents, not the ability to see the interlocutor. Compared to other modes of
communication, picture phones were a most inefficient technology for
transmission of documents. The development of the picture phone was
therefore locked into a situation where no evolutionary paths of development were open. Further development and implementation of picture phones
required a giant leap in technology and the demand for picture phones did

not motivate the commitment of resources necessary to make this leap. Picture phones remained a remote vision of a distant future, but they accentuated the need for improvements in the system of telecommunication, especially regarding the cost and capacity of transmission.

Research laboratories

Automatic analysis of images was also developed in numerous research laboratories, which based their research on the analysis of images. Some of these laboratories had already begun to make extensive use of computing machines by feeding manually interpreted image data into the first generation of computers, thus performing a rudimentary form of computerized image processing. To enhance the ability to process images an instrument capable of interpreting image data and reading them into the computer was needed. Two examples of fields of research spurring the development of image reading systems are spectrography and X-ray crystallography. In spectrography two-dimensional information is measured and processed. A manually operated mechanical instrument was the standard procedure for reading spectral recordings.[5] The obtained image data were read into the computer via punch cards. In the beginning of the 1960s a group of Swedish physicists, within Physics IV at the Royal Institute of Technology, set out to develop a machine for reading spectral recordings into a computer. By employing an electro-optical technique they were able to construct a spectral reader capable of performing the specified operations. The spectral reader was used in combination with one of the first Swedish computers.[6] This pioneering work in image reading later led to the development of a scanner, IRIS, for the reading of two-dimensional star plates.

In crystallography, x-ray diffraction of substances is used to describe and analyse the three-dimensional molecular structure of a substance. In x-ray diffraction a substance is irradiated with electromagnetic radiation. The three-dimensional structure of this substance is revealed in the diffraction pattern of this radiation. The diffraction pattern is registered on photographic film and by measuring the position and intensity of the diffracted radiation it is possible to reconstruct the molecular structure of the substance. Initially, the positions of the diffractions were measured with an ordinary ruler and the intensity was estimated by comparing the diffraction with a library of reference points. The problems associated with the measurements meant that only minor structures could be analysed. A Swedish crystallographer saw the possibility of mechanizing the measuring of diffraction patterns and of overcoming the tedious work of measuring and thus of enhancing the scope of the method. In the early 1960s he initiated the development of an automatic drum densitometer, a film scanner. The availability of this scanner made it 'possible to make fast routine determinations of interplanar spacings and diffraction intensities from X-ray powder photographs'.[7] The scanner resembled the above mentioned spectral reader in that it was based upon electro-optical technology. The film scanner and IRIS were manufactured by two different divisions of the emerging Swedish computer corporation, Datasaab, who perceived the instruments as interesting applications of computer technology. The film scanner was introduced in 1965 and IRIS in 1972; neither became a commercial success.

Other laboratories conducting research, which to some extent was based on the analysis of natural images, had not yet begun to make use of computers to process the information embodied in images. Laboratories of this kind could be found within different applications of science ranging from quality control of steel to cytology. The images to be analysed were often very complex and difficult to stratify, hence the difficulties in mechanizing the analysis. Across applications the variation of images is almost unlimited, but within a particular application or laboratory the variation is more limited. The dominant method of image analysis involved humans, basing their analysis on past experience or on the comparison of specific images with reference images. The developments within computer and television technology in combination with the homogeneity of the images within specific applications prompt an interest in the computeriz-ation of image analysis. A company that early on envisioned the possibility of computerized image analysis was the British company Metals Research Ltd.

Metals Research developed and marketed research metals and scientific instruments, primarily for the research laboratories of the steel industry. In the early 1960s a small group within the company began to develop an image analysis computer and in 1963 Metals Research presented a com-puter system for analysis of microscope images. The system consisted of a television camera and two monitors connected to a relay-computer.[8] The introduction of the second generation of image-analysing computers, Quantimet B, in 1964 signified a commercial breakthrough. In 1965 the research laboratory at the Swedish steel producer Fagersta AB acquired Quantimet B and before 1970 twelve systems were installed at other research laboratories within the steel industry.[9] Quantimet B was primarily used to analyse non-metallic inclusions in steel. The Swedish steel industry initiated a co-operative project regarding the usage of computerized image analysis in the steel industry. The commercial success of Quantimet B motivated Metals Research to change their name to Imanco Ltd, an acro-nym for Image Analysing Computers, and business was concentrated on computerized image analysis. The success continued and they acquired the more well-known producer of scientific instruments, Cambridge Instruments Ltd, a company whose name they adopted. The success of Metals Research, Imanco and Cambridge Instruments also propelled other producers of scientific instruments, such as Zeiss, Leitz, and Bausch and Lomb to initiate development of image processing systems.[10]

Radiology

Radiology represents a fourth source from which electronic image processing emerged. X-ray technology is certainly one of the most important innovations in medicine, in that it enables physicians to examine interior parts of the human body. X-ray is a form of electromagnetic radiation capable of penetrating solids. The penetration capability is higher in soft tissue than in hard and this difference can be registered on photographic film. This basic method of X-ray was quite sufficient for the examination of broken bones or punctured lungs, but had its limitations when it came to the examination of soft parts. This gave rise to extensive experimentation aimed at increasing the usage of X-ray as a diagnostic instrument. The easiest way was to alter the penetration regarding the soft tissue in question by injecting or otherwise inserting contrast liquid. The use of contrast liquid sometimes proved to be dangerous, as in the case of the examination of the spinal cord, and sometimes impossible, as in the case of the examination of an unborn child. Furthermore, even if we should not exaggerate the awareness, at that time, of the risk associated with exposure to radiation, X-rays could be detrimental to human health. These problems induced further experimentation regarding alternative methods of both penetrating the human body and registering this penetration.

The use of X-ray as a diagnostic instrument was increased by the replacing of the photographic film with a light sensitive electronic device combined with a capability for amplifying the signals. We can call this device an image amplifier. Through this development it became possible to convert the X-ray beam to analog electronic signals, which could be presented on a television screen. In many respects the technology of image amplifying resembled television technology. By employing electronics it became possible to decrease the energy in the X-ray beam and thus to reduce the exposure to radiation. The shift to electronic technology increased the possibilities for discriminating between different levels of penetration and it also made it possible to examine moving parts. The energy required by the electromagnetic radiation was also reduced by the development of new, more light-sensitive photographic film.

Electromagnetic radiation was, however, not the only radiation capable of penetrating solid materials or human bodies. Ultra-high frequency sound exhibited similar qualities and all around the Western world experiments were conducted using ultra-high frequency sound to penetrate human tissue. In the early 1950s Dr D. Howry and R. Bliss, an electronics engineer, constructed a system for scanning soft tissue involving the moving of a beam of ultra-high frequency sound through an arc. By timing the echoes electronically they were able to reconstruct representations of slices of insonated objects. Howry and Bliss claimed that their equipment was capable of revealing details of soft tissue of a kind unavailable from X-ray examinations.[11]

The basic technique employed by Howry and Bliss was, however, not unavailable in the further development of X-ray technology. By using a similar technique, moving the electromagnetic beam through an arc and registering it electronically, slices of human tissue could be reconstructed. This technique, often called tomography, was improved by A. M. Cormack and G. N. Hounsfield in their development of computer aided tomography, for which they were awarded the Nobel Prize. In computer aided tomography series of exposures are combined in a computer into a reconstruction of slices of human bodies or objects.

Remote sensing

Satellite reconnaissance and remote sensing represents the fifth – and perhaps most important – centre of origin of digital image technology. The early development of remote sensing was primarily aligned with the military need for analysis of reconnaissance images. Owing to strong military interest remote sensing represents the single centre that perhaps has attracted most resources. The Cold War and the race for supremacy in space and nuclear technology between East and West and the development of equipment and methods of unravelling the other side's progress were the most compelling driving forces behind the development of remote sensing and digital image processing in the USA and the Soviet Union.

Many modern technologies had their real breakthrough during World War II. One of these technologies was the use of air reconnaissance, which came to provide essential information for military intelligence. In the USA the development of satellite reconnaissance was initiated in 1946 through the presentation of the RAND-project: a study of the possibilities of satellite technology for scientific and military purposes.[12] In 1956, the US Airforce's high flying aircraft U-2 began surveillance over the Soviet Union. In 1957 the Soviet Union stunned the world by announcing the successful launching of the first satellite. The USA was deeply shaken, it had lost its supremacy in space technology. Consequently space and satellite technology was accorded highest priority and two years later, in 1959, the USA succeeded in placing a satellite in orbit around the world. The shooting down of U-2, in 1960, brought an abrupt end to air reconnaissance. As the development of satellite reconnaissance by then was gaining headway, the U-2 incident did not constitute a major setback for the military intelligence.

Testing of satellite reconnaissance showed that the result exceeded prior expectations[13]. But it also showed that some critical problems remained to be solved. One of these problems was associated with the high altitude from which the reconnaissance was effected. To be able to detect anything of interest the satellites had to be equipped with special cameras with extremely high resolution. Another critical problem was how to recover the images from the satellite. Initially this problem was solved by detaching the film cassette from the satellite and recapturing it with an aeroplane. This procedure of high altitude fishing was never considered to be an ideal solution and research was prompted in the field of television technology and in the transformation of photographic plates to series of electronic pulses. The development of satellite reconnaissance constituted a major driving force behind the development of image reading and generating instruments and of image transmission. As the volume of images generated from satellite reconnaissance increased, the analysis of these became problematic and the need to routinize the interpretation of satellite images became pressing. In the USA experiments were conducted where pigeons were used to analyse photographs, but even if some of these experiments were successful the developments within computer technology conveyed prospects of mechanized image processing. In the long run a development of computerized image processing appeared to be more productive than pigeons.[14] Even if the prospects were good, outcomes were often disappointing. Through the years the amount of resources employed in the development of remote sensing was allowed to vary with the variation in research and development results.

The most significant pioneering endeavour in the emergence of image processing in Sweden was undertaken by the National Defence Research Institute (FOA). In 1965 a newly appointed researcher, Torleiv Orhaug, with a background in radio astronomy and ionosphere physics, suggested a research activity related to remote sensing. There was no immediate military need for remote sensing, as in some other countries, but the field was regarded as promising for both civilian and military purposes.[15] After some tentative efforts involving holography FOA initiated a research project in computerized image processing related to remote sensing and, since no pressing military problem existed, they began by addressing more general problems of machine vision and by working on problems of a more civilian nature.[16]

At this time FOA was one of the more important research institutes in Sweden, not only for military purposes but also in general, and they had no problems in attracting a sufficient number of researchers with relevant competence in computer science and mathematics. To enable the feeding of image data into the computer FOA acquired one of the drum scanners mentioned above.[17] To learn more about the specific problem they co-operated with a group of geographers from Stockholm University. FOA also collaborated with one of the major Swedish suppliers of defence electronics on thermovision using IR-technology. FOA was also represented in the Remote Sensing Committee initiated in 1969. This committee was closely related to the Swedish Space Technology Group and its primary purpose was to motivate Swedish industry to participate in the development of remote sensing. When the Swedish Space Technology Group was transformed into the Swedish Space Corporation, remote sensing complemented the space activities of the company.

Apart from developing image processing FOA also made pioneering efforts in diffusing knowledge about image processing and remote sensing through seminars and different publications. To keep informed about the international developments within image processing they conducted several visits around the world. FOA not only developed remote sensing but also demonstrated to the Swedish research community that computerized image processing was possible.[18]

At this time the use of computers was centralized and the processing of images was extremely complicated, especially since FOA was not allowed to connect the drum scanner to a computer at the major computer centre in Stockholm. FOA had first to digitalize the image using the drum scanner in conjunction with an analog/digital computer. The image was then stored on magnetic tape and handed over to the computer centre together with the processing instruction. Some time later FOA received the results from the computer centre. In this way the simplest image analysis could take several weeks to complete. Although this was sufficient for the theoretical work at FOA, to be of practical use image processing technology had to be developed. The input and output units and the processing unit had to be integrated and the processing capacity had to be increased immensely.

In the late 1960s and the early 1970s the now established computer industry presented two technological breakthroughs: the mini-computer and the microprocessor. The mini-computer offered higher processing capacity but still far from enough for image processing operations. More importantly, the introduction of the mini-computer was accompanied by an organizational innovation. The concept of centralized computer processing was abandoned and research organizations obtained direct access to computer systems. Direct access to computers and thus control of the computer operations was a necessary condition for profound experimentation in computer science and related fields such as image processing. The introduction of microprocessors meant that industrial applications of computer technology became more feasible. Another important landmark in the development of image processing technology was the launching of the first dedicated remote sensing satellite, ERTS 1 (later called Landsat 1). ERTS 1 produced digitally stored images and made digital images widely available.

As sufficient solutions to the problem of feeding image data into the computer were presented, the problem of insufficient data processing capacity became critical. The computer industry had been instrumental in the earliest development of image processing, especially regarding optical character recognition and other input media such as the image reading system and the drum-scanner mentioned above. But as the computer terminal became the standard solution to the human–machine communication problem the computer industry lost interest in image processing. The data processing capacity offered by the mini-computer was more than sufficient for almost every possible application of computer technology and the computer industry saw absolutely no need for faster computers. If faster computers were needed they had to be developed outside the computer industry. The internal barriers to developing image processing technology, which faced the computer industry, perhaps provided one of the most pressing reasons behind the genesis of image processing networks.

A SECOND WAVE OF NEW VENTURES

In 1972, knowledge regarding the possibilities and prospects of image processing, together with the introduction of mini-computers and microprocessors, inspired the establishment of several research ventures in Sweden. They came independently from different directions: computer science, computer graphics, telecommunication, optics, electrical measurement, geography, geology, cytology and radiology; and they all initiated research, of differing aims and scope, in image processing. They combined their specific experience and different technologies, but they shared the same purpose, to develop the technology and methods of digital image processing. Instrumental in the encouragement of research in image processing in Sweden was the establishment of a new university, the University of Linköping. In Linköping three of the more radical research groups, the PICAP-group, the Image Coding Group and the GOP-group, were established. Together they formed an impressive community of image processing researchers.[19]

Most of the research was financed through public funding. The major sources of funding were FOA, the Swedish space program and the Swedish

National Board for Technical Development (STU). The public institutions assumed a passive role in the early progress of image processing. Apart from the forming of the Remote Sensing Committee in 1969, the public institutions reacted more to the proposals of individual researchers and groups of researchers than acting on their own initiative to promote a specific development. Research and development was, however, also undertaken within private firms unable to receive public funding. The introduction of the microprocessor increased the possibilities of applying computer technology to problems of industrial production. And in the development of industrial automation two of the largest Swedish companies, Saab and ASEA, initiated development of image processing technology. Spurred by a proposal from an independent inventor Saab in Jönköping, who previously had manufactured the image reading system mentioned above, initiated a project concerning the development of machine vision optimizing the outcome of sawing. As Saab had no previous experience of working within forest industry they acquired a company possessing this experience.[20] ASEA had recently initiated the development of industrial robots and as a parallel activity they initiated a project regarding the adaptability of industrial robots. Robotic vision was one ingredient in the project. To get a fresh start in image processing ASEA acquired an experimental system developed by the Department for Electrical Measurement at the Royal Institute of Technology.[21]

RECAPITULATING THE GENESIS OF THE SWEDISH IMAGE PROCESSING NETWORK

The independent initiation of a cluster of related research projects, combining new technologies with previous experience, slowly departing from their source of origin describes the genesis of the Swedish image processing network. The fact that image processing emerged from multiple centres of origin should not come as a surprise. After all, the social and technological momentum accumulated in different countries and in different industries is often significantly similar and it would be more surprising if we were to find only a single centre of origin of a new technology.[22] The genesis can be associated with neither a single point in time nor isolated activities of technological change. The identification of a new network and the creation of novelty in technology are processes over time involving complex sets of transfer of technology, innovation, diffusion of innovation and adaptation of innovation to local settings. And, as can be observed from the developments within FOA, the transfer of a problem may be as important to the creation of novelty as the transfer of the new technology itself. From the surge of creation of novelty, and not from the deeds of one particular heroic inventor, the new technological system emerged. Digital image technology arose from the flames of television and computer technology and a new network was identified. It was identified as new and separate from its origins. Instrumental in the identification of digital image technology was FOA, who not only constructed new machines but also primarily worked with the whole set of interconnected technologies and diffused this knowledge to others.

The development of image processing in Sweden is clearly related to changes in the social structure. The causality, however, does not necessarily run from technological to social change. The story reveals processes pointing in the opposite direction: social change begets technological. The employment of new researchers, the establishment of a new university and the decentralization of data processing were instrumental in the initiation of research related to digital image technology. At the same time, the impact of innovation on social structure cannot be denied. The genesis of the image processing network in Sweden was partly a result of the dynamic interplay between the emerging new technology and the emerging new network. It was partly the result of the barriers to developing image processing which were facing the computer industry. The identification of image processing actors and activities as being a new network was a necessary, but not sufficient, condition in the genesis of the industrial network. The fact that the new network also was identified as being different from the pre-existing ones was instrumental in the genesis of the new industrial network.

One important facet of genesis is the existence of a local structure capable of supporting the emergent new structure. In Sweden the defence industry and the emerging computer industry were important sources of local support. Both were instrumental in the establishing of an infrastructure for computer manufacturing and the computer industry was also important during the first years in that they manufactured the first image processing instruments. The Space Technology Group was equally instrumental in the support of emerging new structures and in general it can be claimed that these years were characterized by immense technological and social experimentation. It is possible that an experimental structure is more effective in supporting emerging industrial networks than directed public policy efforts would have been.

The swedish image processing network in 1975

The emergence of image processing technology follows a recently developed pattern in that basic research, often conducted at universities, is becoming increasingly important in the generation of new technologies.

The genesis of the image processing network is characterized by the initiation of a cluster of research undertakings related to the development of image processing technology. The major actors in the emergence of the new network had by the end of 1972 entered on to the path of the development of digital image technology. These actors were later to form the core of the image processing network. Figure 6.1 depicts the emerging Swedish image processing network in 1975.

Figure 6.1 shows a number of actors, some of whom have been grouped. These groups are called blocks and actors within a block are connected more to each other than to actors outside the block. It is obvious from the graphical representation that the image processing network generated under the genesis phase consists of five remotely connected blocks of actors and of some unblocked actors. (For a discussion of social network analysis and of how the graphical representation has been generated, see Appendix 1.) A closer look at the different blocks reveals that they are to some extent technology specific and that, in general, they consist of both research and development organizations and business firms. There is a high degree of heterogeneity between the blocks. Jointly, the five blocks and the unblocked actors portray capabilities in the complementary components of digital image technology: image reading systems, image processing systems, image transmission and different applications of digital image technology.

The most central actor in the network is FOA, acting both as a 'Merchant of Light' scanning the international research in image processing and as a 'Preacher' spreading the gospel of digital image technology to other researchers in Sweden. (For a discussion of how actor centrality is measured, see Appendix 1.) Apart from FOA, the emerging Swedish computer industry also holds strong positions in the network. In general the emerging image processing network is dominated by traditional firms and research organizations.

It is interesting to note that even if the emergent network transcends over geographical borders it is basically a local network of Swedish actors pursuing research and development in image processing. The applications of digital image technology developed in Sweden are all related to areas where Sweden has either a long tradition (picture phone, industrial automation and metallurgy) or a geographical comparative advantage (in this case space research, where Northern Sweden is bestowed with specific advantages, especially with regard to the reception of satellite information).

APPENDIX 1: NETWORK ANALYSIS

Networks, industrial as well as social, are complex and messy. Almost any empirical study of networks puts extremely high demands on the analytical

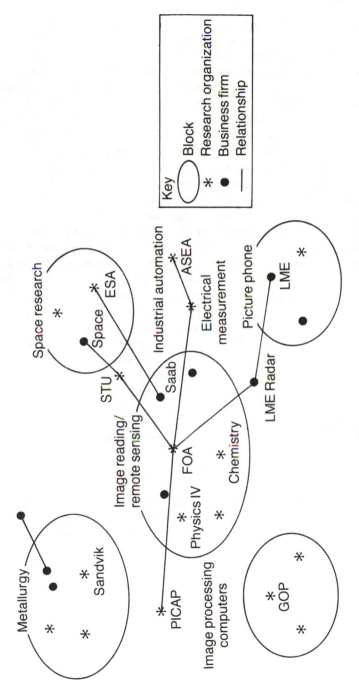

Figure 6.1 The image processing network in 1975. (Note that the graphical representation is not intended to depict the centrality of individual actors.)

skill and effort of the observer. Graph theory and its progenies of social network methods offer sets of different methods through which the structure of networks can be unravelled.[23] Social network methods can be used both to illuminate features of the total network structure and to comprehend particular components of the whole. Most commonly, network analysis is employed on three different levels of analysis. First, it is used to characterize the structure of the total network. Second, it is used to identify and characterize subgroups within the total network. Here two different approaches can be distinguished: one in which subgroups of actors more closely related to each other than to outside actors are identified and one in which a subgroup is defined as sets of actors holding similar network positions. Finally, network analysis is applied to characterize the specific network positions and roles of individual actors.

Relational data are collected through personal interviews with the leading individuals within actors pursuing research and development in image processing in Sweden. The relationships are primarily research and development collaborations, but the transfer of technology and the origin of some of the leading researchers are also considered to constitute relationships. Later, in the evolution of the Swedish image processing networks, spin-offs, commercial relationships and ownership have also entered as relationships. The relationships have been binary coded, but the output of the analysis has occasionally been complemented with additional information regarding the nature of activities performed and of the relationships. Data have been collected for three points in time, 1975, 1983 and 1989. Network analysis has been performed for all three years. The analyses for 1983 and 1989 will be presented later (Chapters 7, 8).

The years have not been selected arbitrarily. The year 1975 is chosen because it demarcates the year when all of the major actors in Swedish image processing had been established: it demarcates the ending of the genesis phase. The year 1983 is selected because it covers the major spin-offs from the university research and it demarcates the ending of the coalescence phase. The year 1989 is the last year in the study. The number of actors and relationships entered into the network analysis for the three years are shown in Table 6.1.

Table 6.1 Number of actors and relationships entered into the network analysis

Year	No. of actors	No. of relationships
1975	40	46
1983	57	93
1989	82	109

Does social network analysis reveal changes in the network pattern consistent with the suggested framework? Yes, it does. A basic analysis of the structure of the image processing network in 1975, 1983 and 1989 confirms the above assumed pattern of evolution. In Table 6.2 some traditional network measures are presented. We can see that the image processing network becomes increasingly integrated over the three phases of genesis, coalescence and dissemination. In 1989 the network density has decreased, suggesting the dissemination of the network. This interpretation is consistent also with the changes in the mean and variance of point centrality.

Social network analysis is not unproblematic. Graph centrality measures are highly dependent on the number of actors. Degree, the measure used for point centrality does not portray the full magnitude of actor centrality. So, even if both the graph and the point centrality measures are pointing in the same direction, the interpretation of the analysis can at best be suggestive. To take the structural analysis of the network further, we can perform different types of group analysis. Here EBLOC analysis has been used.

Table 6.2 Point and graph centrality of the Swedish image processing network, 1975, 1983 and 1989

Year	1975	1983	1989
No. of actors	40	57	82
Point centrality [a]			
Mean	2.25	3.193	2.65
Variance	2.188	7.384	4.57
Graph Centrality			
Density [b]	0.058	0.057	0.034
Integration [c]	90	182	212

Notes:
a. The measure used for point centrality is degree, that is, the number of direct connections to other actors that a specific actor has.
b. Density is a measure of the connectedness of the network, where the number of actual connections is divided by the total number of possible connections.
c. Integration is a measure of the distance between all actors in the network.

The graphical representations of the image processing network in 1975, 1983 and 1989 are based on EBLOC analysis of relationships between actors active in research and development of digital image processing.[24] In EBLOC analysis actors are blocked according to their relationships to other actors. Actors within a block are more closely connected to each other than to actors outside the block. Note that the spatial position of individual actors in the figures is not meant to depict the centrality of their specific network positions.

To get a clear picture of the network we must also analyse the positions of the individual actors. The most common measure of the position of individual actors in networks is different centrality measures. The Katz index, which is only one of many measures of centrality in network analysis, is chosen mainly for two reasons. First, it is one of the few complex centrality measures that is independent of the total number of actors in the network, which means that it can be used comparing the centrality of actors in different networks. Second, it is based upon the notion that both direct and indirect relationships affect an actor's position. The Katz index is computed from the adjacency matrix, where:

$$S_i = bA_{i+} + b^2(A^2)_{i+} + b^3(A^3)_{i+} + ... \qquad (i = 1, 2, 3, ... , n)$$

Here A is the adjacency matrix, (A^k_{i+}) denotes the i-th row sum of the k-th power of A and b is an attenuation factor.[25] Other centrality measures, degree, bavelas and beauchamp, have also been computed. They reveal a similar pattern, but also some minor difference. The Katz index for the image processing network in 1975 is presented in Table 6.3.

The Katz index of the eight most central actors in the image processing network in 1975 is given in Table 6.4.

Similar analyses were conducted for 1983 and 1989, the results of which are presented later in Tables 7.3 and 8.4.

Table 6.3 Katz index for the image processing network in 1975

Year	Min.	Max.	Mean	Median	Var.	Spread	b
1975	0.139	1.284	0.386	0.341	0.061	0.898	0.1111

Table 6.4 Katz index for the eight most central actors in 1975

Ranking	Actor	Katz index	Ranking 1989
1	FOA	1.284	26
2	Saab in Jönköping	1.025	12
3	Saab in Linköping	0.832	15
4	Physics IV	0.797	27
5	Saab in Gothenburg	0.594	19
6	Chemistry Gothenburg	0.588	_[a]
7	ESA	0.488	25
8	Sandvik	0.473	_[a]

Notes:
a. Deviated from the image processing network.

7   Coalescence

Digital image technology emerged almost simultaneously at different locations through actors engaging in highly specialized problem-solving. Only a few actors, if any, perceived themselves as proponents of a new technology. Instead, they entered evolutionary paths through research and development motivated by the solving of everyday problems. Some solutions shepherded the future problem-solving along paths directed towards the transmutation of computer and electronic image technology into digital image processing. These can be identified *ex post facto* as origins of Swedish digital image processing technology and as such they have entered this study. The evolutionary path of digital image processing in Sweden is comprised of several individual paths. Yet, we must remain open to the fact that similar problems in slightly different contexts might have induced other actors, using different or similar techniques, to produce solutions leading to different paths. If these actors had addressed their problems differently, the emergence of digital image processing in Sweden may well have followed a different path. And we cannot determine if the paths pursued produced a superior outcome than the paths never taken or less often taken would have done. This suggests that the emergence and evolution of new industrial networks to some extent are accidental. The process is, however, not purely accidental. Fortune favours the prepared mind and under favourable conditions fortune and the prepared mind can act together to produce change.[1] Thus, to induce innovations, prepared minds must encounter and perceive problems and opportunities in contexts favouring novel solutions.

DEVELOPING THE TECHNOLOGICAL SYSTEM OF DIGITAL IMAGE PROCESSING

Just as the pioneers of computer technology a few years before them had made reference to the human brain, the pioneers of image processing technology were captured by the analogy of human vision.[2] Human vision is, quite naturally, a narrower concept than the human brain and, contrary to computer technology, future applications of image processing were more obvious. The function and capacity of human vision constituted an important basis for comparison and the prophecy of the researchers was that machine vision in the future would be as general and as functional as human vision. To fulfil this vision it was necessary to combine previously only loosely interconnected series of artefacts and pieces of knowledge into complete systems of image processing. That is, into a system connecting image reading, image analysis and output. One problem was the development of systems with sufficient capacities to process the large amount of data contained in images. The major problem was, however, to adapt the different auxiliary components of image processing to each other, moulding them into a functioning system. Even to perform the simplest image analysis, the availability of a complete system was essential. Not only was it necessary to have access to the sets of functions of which the systems were made, but the functions had also to be performed in specific sequences, where every single function was dependent on all of the preceding and succeeding functions.

Technological systems of image processing were developed by actors, in Sweden and elsewhere, who were motivated by the possibilities of computerizing the analysis of image data. In general, however, digital image processing was not a sufficiently significant application to advance the development of electronics and computer technology. Consequently, none of the actors dedicated to the development of mechanized vision could control or even prompt the flow of technology ancillary to digital image processing. Thus, they were compelled to adapt to the underlying technologies; combining them into a novel system; adapting and integrating the complementary parts of the system, artefacts and knowledge, to each other. This is not to downgrade the development of digital image processing achieved through research and development – the application of novel findings and artefacts to new situations might be as problematic as the production of the original finding or artefact in the first place – it is only to place the development of digital image technology in its particular context.

Different problems and different resource bases

Digital image technology did not emerge from a single centre of origin. Neither was its emergence conditioned by the solving of a single set of problems. Actors of different origin, bounded by different historical paths, addressing everyday problems, created a variety of novelties related to the possibilities of machine processing of image information. The paths pursued by different actors defined not only the sets of problems to be solved but also the methods and techniques to be used in solving perceived problems.

The actors of the emergent image processing network had, through their historical paths, developed different resource bases on which the future development was to be founded. Different knowledge bases had evolved; some had acquired knowledge in radio astronomy, optics or spectroscopy and others in military intelligence, industrial automation or cytology. Furthermore, the actors employed technological practice of differing levels of sophistication. As these actors began to develop image processing, their initial work was, quite naturally, weighted by their past experiences.

The actors differed in terms of knowledge and technology in use. The availability of and access to interrelated resources, such as complementary technologies and user experience, also varied. The established companies could at least potentially make use of the resource base of the whole company, and they could also test the new technology in more realistic settings. The university researchers on the other hand had more limited access to resources and unless they themselves were the prime users of the novel piece of technology they had only limited access to information about user needs. Even among the university institutes some differences can be detected, especially with respect to their access to user experience; some projects were primarily motivated by the researchers' own need for image processing capabilities, while others were aimed only at the technology.

Finally, the actors' access to financial resources differed. Some of the research and development was pursued within the realms of established corporations, such as ASEA and Saab–Scania, or within rich research institutes, such as FOA; other research activities were pursued within universities, in both well established and recently formed institutes. The former group had access to larger amounts of financial resources, but on the other hand the researchers within these organizations were less free to choose problems. The researchers within established university institutes were also limited in their choice of problems.[3] Some research groups were established in connection with changes in the social and institutional structure, the employment of young researchers in established organizations and the establishment of a new university. These actors were granted a higher degree of freedom in choosing problems and methods of problem-solving. Thus, they were able to create history in the sense that they could bring their historical paths and prepared minds to contexts favouring new problems or new solutions.

Converging and diverging historical paths in the establishing of the new technology

The focus of the individual research groups differed. Some groups focused on the development of image processing computer systems, some on the development of computer software for image processing, some on specific applications of image processing, some on the image reading systems and some on image transmission. Thus, both corresponding and complementary research and development activities were undertaken. Research and development was initially primarily motivated by the solving of highly specific problems. The technological solutions to many of the specific problems, however, proved not to be sufficiently viable in economic terms or scientifically intriguing. The computer terminal proved to be a more viable solution to feeding data into computers than did optical character recognition. Other solutions, such as the picture phone, did not correspond to pressing problems. Consequently, digital image processing was either abandoned or extended to encompass sets of more general image processing problems. The computer and telecommunication industry abandoned image processing. But others continued and the aim of most of the growing research groups became directed towards the achievement of general computerized vision. As the aim of the different groups converged, so did their historical paths.

The significance of local context in technological development

Not all paths led to the evolution of image processing technology. The paths of both the computer and telecommunication industries deviated from image processing. Another path that wandered astray was the development of the drum-scanner. Professor Sixten Abrahamsson of the University of Gothenburg pioneered the image scanner technology by developing a drum-scanner.[4] The scanner was used in two contexts; by FOA as their main image reading instrument and at the Arrhenius-laboratories to read data from X-ray crystallography into a computer.[5] The drum-scanner was an important piece of equipment at both of these institutes, but neither of them continued to develop image scanner technology. At FOA the focus was on the development of methods of image processing and they were not particularly keen on developing the instruments as such. At the Arrhenius-laboratories the problem was to analyse molecular structures using X-ray crystallography and not image analysis in general. They continued to adapt the drum-scanner to their own needs and eventually they developed a different instrument better adapted to their specific problem. Professor Abrahamsson himself continued to develop scientific instruments but his death put an end to further achievements. The development of image scanners, a field in which Swedish researchers were pioneers, decayed.

The drum-scanner, applied in two different local contexts, gave rise to two different paths of development. The users of the technology adapted it to their specific needs according to the problems they were addressing. The nature of the local context in which the new technological system, or components thereof, are applied will have a significant impact upon the future development. Another example of this is provided by a spin-off from the robotic vision development at ASEA. In 1980 when ASEA decided to halt the development of robotic vision, pending the availability of more powerful microprocessors, the leading researchers behind the development decided to leave. As a group they continued the development of computer vision at Kockumation AB. But now the image problem was stated differently. Kockumation was active in the forest industry and the perceived image problem was related to the analysis of natural objects: measuring and quality control of lumber. The shift from human-made to natural objects required even higher resolution and processing capacity. As a consequence the group brought the ASEA-system to new heights, with better resolution and much higher processing capacity, making it a more general image processing system.[6]

What if?

If the evolutionary paths of the computer and telecommunication industries had converged on or coincided with the path of image processing, the evolution of the three would have followed another route. However, we cannot determine if alternative paths would have produced a more desirable outcome than the path pursued. We can only suggest that if some paths, which did not converge, had converged, the outcome would have been different. If the development and usage of the drum-scanner in Sweden had inspired the development of scanner technology, rather than image processing and X-ray crystallography, Sweden might, for better or for worse, have acquired technological leadership in image scanners rather than in image processing.

Adaptation of the components of the new technology to a functional system

To fulfil the future concept of a machine with as general and functional a vision as humans, the research groups extended their activities to embrace the total technological system of image processing. The quest for technological solutions to sets of general image processing problems was on.

The first image processing systems developed were predominantly binary, that is, they only distinguished between black and white. All images to be analysed had to be registered as a combination of black and white. A basic problem was the definition of the colour in the border area between black and white. Exactly when should white be turned into black? The solution to the problem was contingent upon circumstances related to the specific application and every set of rules would have only limited validity if applied to any other application. The binary character of early image processing reinforced the problem-specificity of the technical solutions. To actuate more general solutions it was necessary to go beyond the possibilities of binary images and to develop image processing for grey-scale and colour pictures. The shift from binary to grey-scale and colour images accentuated the need for specialized image processing computers.

Digital image processing had emerged as a combination of previously unconnected pieces of knowledge and artefacts; electronics and optics were combined into opto-electronics and computers and video-cameras were connected to enable processing of image information. The development of the parts, constituting image processing technology, was primarily motivated by circumstances unrelated to image processing. The technological system was therefore characterized by a low degree of standardization and a major problem facing the researchers was related to the adaptation of parts of the technologies to suit each other and so form complete technological systems. The basic problem was the development of the technological system itself.

THE COALESCENCE OF THE SWEDISH IMAGE PROCESSING NETWORK

The situation in Sweden in the early 1970s was such that a variety of specialized research and development projects, related to what later was to be known as digital image technology, had emerged. Collectively the emerging research and development activities in Sweden represented the essential parts of the technological system of image processing: image reading, computer systems and software for image processing, image transmission and application-specific experience. The individual research groups, however, could neither control nor prompt the development of the underlying technologies, nor were they able to dwell on the scientific and technological frontier in all of the essential parts of image processing.

The technological system of a country is forged by the accomplishments of the individual actors. Simultaneously, the outcome of each research and development endeavour is to a large extent dependent on the overall development of the technological system. The outcomes of different development activities are thus interdependent and each actor can increase the probability of success or decrease the risk or consequences of failure by co-operating with other actors within the same technological system. Co-operation between actors undertaking complementary research and development induces increased integration within the system. As actors within the technological system begin co-operating to get access to complementary research and development and to adapt the parts of the technology to each other, the emergent network will coalesce.

The significance of a critical mass

For genesis to transcend into coalescence a critical mass of similar and complementary research and development must exist. Critical mass in this context refers not only to sheer numbers but also to the degree of variation and complementarity of the going concern and research and development. Sheer numbers are important in that an increased number of actors engaging in specific research and development is accompanied by an increased probability of every actor encountering a peer with whom to cooperate. Numbers are also essential when it comes to the legitimacy of specific development activities. Variation and complementarity are critical in the sense that they denote the systemic nature of technology and thus promote co-operation.

During genesis a number of actors in Sweden had initiated a variety of research and development activities related to image processing: a critical mass of similar and complementary change activities was present. The presence of a critical mass thus means that all of the essential subsystems of digital image technology are present and that within all of these subsystems more than one alternative solution exists. In other related fields, such as image scanner technology, a critical mass did not accumulate. The presence of a critical mass suggests an availability of potential partners and that actors could benefit from co-operating with other actors. As some of the actors of digital image processing initiated co-operation, the emerging network began to coalesce. The actors deviated from their origins, attracted by a common set of solutions (digital image processing) to a variety of problems, and coalesced into a recognizable network of actors resembling the technological system of digital image processing.

As the image processing network coalesced, the actors grew closer to other actors engaged in the development of digital image processing and moved further away from their origins. The coalescence process implies contraction and contains a tendency towards isolationism. This process is to some extent reflected in the fact that more image processing systems were sold in Sweden between 1960 and 1970 than between 1970 and 1980.[7]

For the network to coalesce and the actors to deviate from their origins, the actors must attract new resources: the pursued research and development activities must be legitimated to ensure continuing evolution of the network. Coalescence thus implies the formation of a new industrial network and it hinges upon the duality of the legitimating of the development activities and the development of the technological system.

Legitimating image processing activities

In Sweden, image processing research and development did not fit into the traditional structure of research funding. The research and development was primarily multi-disciplinary and did not correspond directly to any of the existing research funding institutions, which mainly were intra-disciplinary. Instead, it was STU – whose societal role had traditionally been to encourage technological development and to support innovators outside the industrial community – who assumed a somewhat modified position by funding both basic research and technological development of digital image technology. Others who assumed the role of funding the emergent new technology were the newly established institutions, such as the new university in Linköping and the Swedish Space Corporation. Within these institutions the fact that the technology was new was by itself legitimating research and development in the field. Another new institution with the specific purpose of legitimating image processing was the Swedish Association for Automatic Image Processing, instigated in 1976 by five leading individuals representing five different research groups.[8] Apart from legitimating digital image processing, the association was an important mediator of social contact between researchers, in industry and at universities. An often discussed subject within the association was what was to be included within or excluded from the concept of digital image processing. Quite naturally, given the nature of the association, the concept was defined from a technological and not from a problem-oriented per-spective and lower levels of technological sophistication were most often belittled or excluded from the definition. The standard set by the Swedish Association for Automatic Image Processing and by the coalescing net-work of digital image processing was that more technology was better.

STU issues a special initiative for the commercialization of digital image processing

As digital image processing technology was legitimated and the industrial network coalesced, an increasing amount of resources was devoted to continued development. And where public policy had previously assumed a passive role it now actively supported the rise of what was assumed to have the capacity to become a new Swedish frontline technology. In 1979 STU inaugurated a five-year special initiative concerning the development of image processing technology in Sweden. Special initiatives formed a newly launched policy instrument to institute concentrated efforts in specific technological fields. The purpose of this special initiative was to generate competitive development and production of digital image processing in Sweden, by combining the available resources for research and development with the capabilities of Swedish industry, and thereby to produce and market high-technology products. Ideally, the initiative was to bridge the gap between scientific research and industrial production. The special initiative arrangement was chosen in order to reach a sufficient volume of market-oriented development projects, relative to competing nations, which means other industrialized Western countries. The special initiative was a natural continuance of STU's previous engagement in image processing. Less than 5 per cent of the total sum was allocated to projects with no pre-history of STU-grants.[9] Nevertheless, the special program for image processing was more in line with the traditional role of STU than the antecedent support for basic research had been.

STU did not, however, cut back on their support for basic research in image processing. They continued to promote university research and to fund most of the university institutions engaged in the production of knowledge related to digital image processing. Thus, the mission of the university researchers did not solely become confined to product development. They also conducted basic research and developed educational programs, first in the doctoral program and later for graduate students, and they also provide courses for the industry on the theories and methods of image processing.[10]

In total, the program was comprised of SEK 18.5 m, a fairly large sum of money from a Swedish perspective. But compared, say, to General Motors' support for research and development in industrial automation and machine vision during the same period it was less than 20 per cent. The SEK 18.5 M was distributed among six different actors pursuing nine defined projects, representing state-of-the-art of image processing technology in Sweden.[11] All projects, except two minor ones, concerned the development of specialized computer systems for image processing. The basic idea behind STU's initiative was that STU and different industrial partners should share the cost of development in each project. This ambition could not be realized in every case; the major part of the available funds was still allotted to university research for which no industrial partner existed, at least not initially. Only a few projects were directly related to concrete industrial applications and only two projects, the OSIRIS and the automatic inspection of PC-boards, seemed to satisfy the intent of the special initiative.

The OSIRIS-project was a joint effort by Physics IV, Saab–Scania in Gothenburg, the Swedish Space Corporation and the camera manufacturer Hasselblad AB to develop a mid-size image processing computer. Nils Åslund and his group at Physics IV had previously developed an image scanner, manufactured by Saab–Scania.[12] The scanner and the complementary research and development regarding image processing at Physics IV were moulded into the concept of OSIRIS, a low-cost computer with sufficient capacity for image processing. The image processing technology of Physics IV, the production capacity of Saab–Scania, the user experience of the Swedish Space Corporation and the marketing capability of Hasselblad were combined into the OSIRIS-project. It looked perfect. The OSIRIS-project bridged the gap between scientific research and industrial production, or at least preconditions for bridging did exist. What were the goals of the collaborating actors? The aim of Nils Åslund and Physics IV was undoubtedly to promote the development of OSIRIS. Saab–Scania probably perceived the project as an interesting complement to their engagement in the space program. Hasselblad was primarily motivated by an interest in digital image technology. The Swedish Space Corporation needed an image processing computer in their development of remote sensing technology. They were, however, dragged into the project at a rather late stage, when the concept of OSIRIS was already defined and specified and when it was difficult to adapt the system to user-specified needs.[13]

If we take a closer look at the projects which received funds from the special initiative, we see that seven of the nine projects were related to some of the founding members of the Swedish Association for Automatic Image Processing. The project leader of the eighth project, who in 1982 was appointed professor in image processing, was thought to be one of the leading image processing researchers in Sweden. The selection mechanism that was applied in the special initiative was technological innovativeness rather than industrial applicability. The projects supported within the program were all perceived as being at the cutting edge of Swedish image processing technology. Projects which were closer to having commercially viable applications did exist. Companies such as ASEA and Saab–Scania were well on their way to developing image processing for industrial automation and robotic vision. Since 1976 Saab–Scania had been selling image processing systems for edge detection in automatic sawing. Furthermore, the Department for Electrical Measurement at the Royal Institute for Technology (Sydat) had successfully installed several image processing systems in different industries.

The projects funded within the special initiative can be lumped together into five dominating research and development ventures, receiving 18 of the SEK 18.5 M. And, if the contributions from industrial partners are taken into account, the funds were equally distributed among the five projects. Thus, each project received approximately SEK 5 M over a five-year period. Three of the five ventures were closely linked. A triad consisting of the PICAP-group, the Image Analysis Laboratory in Uppsala and Semyre Electronics can be detected. The image processing computer used at the Image Analysis Laboratory in Uppsala was the predecessor to the image processing computer developed by the PICAP-group. The laboratory had previously also made use of a predecessor to OSIRIS. The automatic inspection of PC-boards developed by Semyre Electronics was a spin-off from research at the PICAP-group. And the patent rights to the original invention were held by three members of the PICAP-group.[14] The development of automatic cell analysis and automatic inspection of PC-boards can be regarded as being specific applications of the development of a general image processing computer pursued by the PICAP-group. The special initiative discloses three pillars of the development of image processing in Sweden, the PICAP-group, the GOP-group and Physics IV. Two of these, PICAP and GOP, were based at the University of Linköping and apart from these two groups the university also harboured a prominent research group in image transmission. Linköping had grown into a local centre for Swedish image processing technology. This was further accentuated in 1978 when a part of FOA including the image processing research group was relocated to Linköping. It is true that FOA had abandoned the civilian side of remote sensing and image processing research, but it retained its leading position in the development of methods and software.

Aiming for general solutions and total control

STU's special initiative was biased towards the development of image processing computer systems. In three cases, the GOP-group, the PICAP-group and Physics IV, the focus was on the development of general image processing computers and in two instances, the Image Analysis Laboratory in Uppsala and Semyre Electronics, the focus was on the adaptation of image processing computers to specific applications. This bias towards image processing computer systems was not characteristic only of STU. Almost every actor in Sweden interested in the processing of image information also developed potentially multi-purpose, image processing computer systems. ASEA Robotics, Saab–Scania, Kockumation and Sydat developed image processing systems for robotic vision and industrial automation. The Swedish Space Corporation developed a low-cost image processing computer for remote sensing. Like many others, the Swedish

Space Corporation had no particular interest in developing the hardware of image processing.[15] Its competitive advantage was in the methods of image processing related to remote sensing. Its development of image processing computers was primarily motivated by the non-availability of image processing computers. Not all research groups developed computer systems. Some, such as FOA and the image transmission groups at the University of Linköping and the Royal Institute of Technology, concentrated their efforts on the development of methods and software for image processing and transmission.

BRIDGING THE GAP BETWEEN SCIENTIFIC RESEARCH AND INDUSTRIAL INNOVATION

The special initiative of STU was successful in that it enforced Sweden's technological position in digital image processing. It was successful also in the sense that it spurred entrepreneurial activities. The gap between scientific research and industrial production was unintentionally bridged through the university researchers establishing business firms. Image processing companies started as spin-offs from the universities and the researchers leaped from being scientists to becoming business leaders. First out was Imtec AB, a spin-off from the PICAP-group, established in 1981. This was followed, in 1983, by Innovativ Vision AB, another spin-off from the PICAP-group, and Context Vision, a spin-off from the GOP-group. The availability of research and development funds directed towards the commercial application of image processing under market conditions was of course instrumental in the entrepreneurial process. To some extent STU demanded that commercial partners should be involved in the finance and the development of each and every project.[16] In some cases this meant that the research groups had to establish a business of their own. The argument that public support lured the actors to become commercial too early can therefore to some extent be validated. The recipients of the public support were, however, very eager to go commercial. Note, though, that Innovativ Vision was not established with direct public support.

The entrepreneurial activities of the early 1980s were not solely driven by the availability of financial resources from STU. The underlying computer technology had progressed, producing faster and faster computers with larger and larger memories. In 1981 Motorola launched a 32-bit microprocessor, the first in their 68 000 series. Intel was not slow to follow. The availability of more powerful microprocessors increased the economic potential of image processing. More powerful image processing computers could be developed and produced at lower cost. Increased accuracy and speed of computerized image analysis could be achieved at lower cost.

Compelling breakthroughs had also been made in the field of opto-electronics, especially with respect to the conversion of light into electronic signals. In 1969 the CCD (Charge-Coupled Device) – semiconductor was developed at Bell Laboratories. CCD is a light-sensitive semiconductor, through which light from an image can be directly converted to electronic signals. In 1981 Sony presented Sony Mavica, the world's first fully digital camera, which was based upon CCD-technology. The Sony Mavica was only one of many newly developed instruments producing and storing images in digital form. Computer aided tomography, magnetic resonance technology and ultra-sound technology are but a few examples of others. Digital technology was gaining headway in the battle of systems between analog and digital image technology.

Digital image processing was reaching a stage of technological maturity. The research and development had started more than twenty years previously, searching for solutions to very specific problems. Now, in the early 1980s, new image processing firms were established all over the world, advocating different technological solutions for more general sets of image processing problems. In Sweden, all of the groups in question had actively pursued research and development in digital image processing for more than ten years. Taken together, the research and development undertaken represented both similar and complementary components of the technological system of digital image processing.

Except for the absence of manufacturers of electronic components and the fact that the Swedish computer industry was struggling for its survival, the necessary components of the technological system of digital image processing were present in Sweden. Through the collaboration between different proponents of image processing the emerging Swedish network had coalesced, exhibiting a structure and rudimentary division of labour resembling that of the technological system. As one proponent of a component of this system established a business firm, proponents of complementary parts were motivated to merge with the new venture or to continue to collaborate, either in the previous institutional form or by following a similar evolutionary path and establishing another new business firm. Thus, in the establishment of Imtec, prompted by the interest of a publicly owned development company, the complementary research of FOA played a critical role. It would be safe to say that Imtec was established through the combination of the evolutionary path of the PICAP-group, focusing on computer systems, and the path of FOA, pursuing computer software development.[17] The establishing of Imtec opened up commercial opportunities for other image processing endeavours and in 1983 the automatic cell analysis project of the Image Analysis Laboratory, accompanied by the leading researcher, was transferred to Imtec for further commercial development.[18] In the PICAP-group the founders of Imtec had worked together with the founders of Innovativ Vision. The latter had also been collaborating extensively with the Image Analysis Laboratory and the timing of the start up of Innovativ Vision was prompted by a development assignment from Imtec.[19]

Imtec, Context Vision and Innovativ Vision were, if not the tip of the iceberg, at least only part of the story. The Department of Electrical Measurement had formed Sydat Automation AB; the image coding group at the University of Linköping had established Sectra AB; at Saab–Scania research and development was intensified and broadened to embrace industrial automation in general; the Swedish Space Corporation established a subsidiary for the receiving and processing of satellite images; and in 1981 ASEA reopened its mummified project concerning robotic vision.[20]

The research and development ventures that, independently of each other, had been initiated ten years earlier had evolved to become interdependent. Critical in the establishment of new companies were the complementary resources and competencies evolving within the network of image processing. The newly established firms were often comprised of mixtures of resources; researchers, students, knowledge and equipment, originating from different research groups. And the entrepreneurial activities of the early 1980s were not activated independently of each other.

The newly established firms continued to set the pace during the research years. The aim was to develop general image processing technology. The developed computer systems were to be able to process images of different origin, depicting different scenes generated by different methods. The computer systems were to be equally equipped for remote sensing as for industrial automation. Moreover, many of the new firms aimed to fulfil all functions of developing, manufacturing and marketing of image processing equipment. They strove for maximum control of their activities. Here, the newly established firms differed from the established ones. The established firms were directed more towards specific applications and they had better opportunities to utilize the existing organization to develop business related to image processing.

RECAPITULATING THE COALESCENCE OF THE SWEDISH IMAGE PROCESSING NETWORK

Propelled by the creation of a number of novel technological solutions and the identification of the proponents of image processing as something new and different, genesis had induced a number of competing and complementary ventures into research and development of digital image technology. A critical mass of research and development was present, which facilitated the legitimating of the development of the novel technological system. The paths pursued converged on, or diverged from, digital image technology and the emerging network coalesced, forming a closely knit core of proponents of image processing. The core was based around STU, the major source of public funding. The special initiative issued by STU was not, however, institutionalized independently from the research and development activities. The progress made in the establishment of the new technological system and the legitimating of its further development by the central actors were instrumental in the issuing of the initiative. The coalescence of the industrial network was driven by the legitimating of the network of research and development activities which attracted resources for the development of the technological system. The establishing of the technological system gave sustenance to the legitimating of the network. A critical element for the evolutionary process to transfer from the domination of genesis to that of coalescence was the existence of a critical mass of competing and complementary research and development activities.

The state-of-the-art of digital image technology as a system of loosely connected components and the nature of the STU-program encouraged the actors towards the adaptation of the components of the technology into functional systems, developing general image processing systems capable of processing almost any kind of images. The period 1976–83 was concluded with the spinning-off of firms from university research and from established firms, thus bridging the gap between scientific research and industrial innovation.

From 1976 image processing equipment was sold on a regular basis. It was primarily the established firms and the firms aiming at lower levels of technological sophistication that were able to market image processing equipment successfully. The first highly sophisticated systems to be sold were bought by actors in the focal network or by research organizations outside the focal network. The new technology had emerged through the needs of military intelligence and research laboratories for improved and automated analysis of image information. These institutions were also among the first to acquire image processing equipment. Unfortunately, these early adopters seldom contributed significantly to the further development. The problems they addressed were often highly specialized and they were often capable of adapting the equipment to their specific needs and their experience of this adaptation was rarely communicated back to the seller. Furthermore they often used the equipment in isolation and did not integrate it in the technological context in which the image processing technology was applied. The first sales were critical, however, to the survival of the development projects; badly needed financial resources were provided.

The swedish image processing network in 1983

The coalescence of the Swedish image processing network is characterized by the legitimating of the emerging network and by the development of a technological system for digital image processing. The particular components of the technology were integrated into systems, transforming specific solutions for specific problems to general solutions for general sets of problems. The proponents of the different components of the technological system coalesced into a close-knit community of actors representing the necessary components and competencies to pursue the development of the technology. The coalesced Swedish image processing network in 1983 is depicted in Figure 7.1.[21]

In 1983 the image processing network was comprised of one large block of proponents of digital image technology, a peripheral block – the metallurgy block found during genesis which did not follow suit as the core of the industrial network coalesced – and some unblocked actors. Basically, the heterogeneous blocks found in 1975 have coalesced into one homogeneous block of actors striving to establish the technological system of digital image processing.

Coalescence was dominated by the mobilization of resources for the development of digital image technology and, apart from university research groups, the public policy actors STU and the Swedish Space Corporation accumulated strength and became the central actors in the coalescing network.[22] FOA lost its central position as it abstained from pursuing the development of civilian-oriented remote sensing. The Swedish computer industry also lost its position in the development of digital image technology. The core of the network consisted of almost an equal number of research organizations and business firms.

It is interesting to note that the core of the image processing network is still dominated by Swedish actors. None of these had achieved self-sustained growth and they worked under the threat of the dismantling of the projects. Some of the actors survived only through reconstruction. To reach a more stable state, digital image technology had to be integrated with pre-existing technological systems. Strategically, individual actors had to establish viable positions in the emergent network. At the same time they had to contribute to the strengthening of the total network.

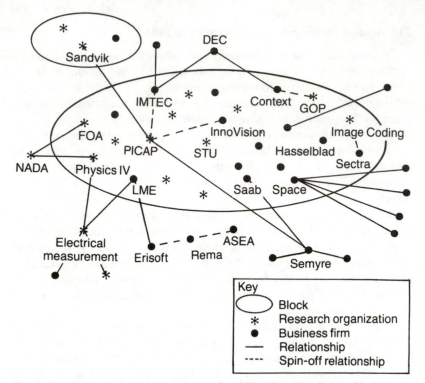

Figure 7.1 The image processing network in 1983. (Note that the graphical representation is not intended to depict the centrality of individual actors.)

8 Dissemination

In the late 1970s and early 1980s networks of actors had legitimated research and development into image processing and the technological system for digital image technology was developed. All over the world, new ventures into image processing were established and pre-existing firms extended their activities to develop, produce and apply digital image technology.[1] In Sweden the proponents of image processing technology coalesced into a tightly-knit homogenous network. Sweden was on the cutting edge of the technology. By 1985, different Swedish organizations had developed at least ten, more or less technologically sophisticated general image processing computer systems. Technologically the outcome of the development of image processing in Sweden was successful. Commercially, the results proved to be more disappointing.

INTEGRATING THE NEW TECHNOLOGICAL SYSTEM WITH PRE-EXISTING TECHNOLOGIES

In digital image technology, computer technology and opto-electronics had been transformed to produce technological solutions to the problems associated with the analysis of data contained in images or with the computerized production or communication of images.

The different computer systems for image processing produced in Sweden functioned well according to prior specifications, but sales were slow. The potential user's problems were rarely as well defined as they had been in the specification and development of the computers. The systems were, moreover, extremely expensive. The development cost had been higher than expected and the subsystems and components used were on the cutting edge of existing technology. The price of a general image processing computer therefore ranged from 200,000 to 2,000,000 SEK. An additional problem was the human–machine interface. Image processing computers represented the latest developments in computer related technologies, while most of the potential users still struggled to become friendly with personal computers. In most applications the machine had to be adapted to the environment in which it was to be used. And in some cases user friendliness proved to be even more important than technological power.[2]

The largest user groups were predominantly in the context of analog technology. The application of digital image technology thus required effective gateways between digital and analog technology. In certain areas of application, cartography, graphic production and industrial automation, some investments had been made in the transformation from analog to digital technology. The basic problem facing the proponents of image processing technology was therefore to adapt the technology to pre-existing technologies, integrating the system of image processing with the technological systems of the users.

Circumstances favouring early application of new technology

The development of image processing technology, from 1960 to the present day, is filled with examples of how image processing computers are used in different settings: remote sensing for military surveillance in the 1960s; analysis of non-metallic inclusions in steel in the metallurgy laboratories in the 1970s; and robotic vision in modern manufacturing in the 1980s. New technologies are often first adopted in contexts where economic performance is difficult to measure or is of minor importance; new technologies are consequently often embodied in medical equipment or in military weapons. Another circumstance which favours early adoption is when the new technology can be applied in isolation, unrelated to existing technologies or patterns of behaviour; the first micro-chips were used in modern, high-technology toys. Finally, the application of new technologies is favoured in contexts characterized by highly sophisticated users capable of and interested in the further development of the new technology; research laboratories and scientific institutions are thus not only important as generators of new technologies, but also, being on the technological frontier, represent important markets for new technologies.[3] The bulk of users are not, however, on the technological frontier and the fact that the new technology is adopted under favourable conditions does not mean that other users will follow suit automatically. And yet, to motivate the often enormous investments in research and development necessary to sustain a new industrial network, it is essential to reach a sufficiently large volume of users. The distance between the technological systems of the users and the producers has to be bridged. The major problem is rarely in the functioning of the new technological system, but rather in how it is adapted to the technological capabilities of the users.

No technology can persist in isolation

No technology can persist in isolation. The value of any technology is determined not by its static internal characteristics but by its dynamic relationship to other technologies. Any given technology is only an intermediary between other technologies. Its existence is based on its capacity to transform inputs from other technologies to produce solutions to problems in yet other technologies. A major theme in the advancement of bridge building is the recurrent changes in the materials used: wood, stone, iron, steel and concrete. The progress of the early chemical industry was closely connected to progress within ancillary industries; first the textile industry with the development of bleaching and dyeing techniques and later the prospering mining industry with the development of new explosives.[4] The economic value of a technology is thus determined by its relative efficiency in the transformation of inputs and the scope of the solution it produces.

The history of a technology can never solely be built upon single and isolated events and activities, on the heroic inventors of pieces of that technology or on the more spectacular utilization of the technology. The significance of a technology in social and economic evolution is determined by how it affects other technologies. Hence, a new technological system cannot be said to be established until it has reached a stage of widespread use. The *raison d'être* of a new technology typically lies far beyond its initial application. Flying today is quite different from the first attempt with Kitty Hawk. The critical contribution of the Wright Brothers was that they showed the world that flying with objects heavier than air was possible. But it was the huge number of minor improvements, the development or adoption of new technologies and, foremost of all, the evolution of systems combining aerodynamics, engine technology and petrochemistry with military and civilian systems of flying, that brought flying to what it is today. The genesis and continuance of a novelty are motivated by different sets of circumstances and require the solving of entirely different sets of problems. This suggests that genesis is propagated by certain factors and that coalescence and dissemination are breed by other sets of factors.

The origination of a new technology is typically motivated by the solving of specific problems. Radio technology was first expressed as wireless telegraphy and used as a means of communication between ships. The continuance of the technology was motivated, however, by the opportunity of broadcasting news and entertainment to the general public, which generated new sets of problems in the establishing of total systems for radio broadcasting.[5] The original invention, whether the Kitty Hawk of Orville and Wilbur Wright, the wireless telegraph of Guglielmo Marconi or the ENIAC of J. Presper Eckert, jun. and John W. Mauchly, did little more than hint at the promise of a different future.[6] Essential to the fulfilment of such promise was the composition and evolution of huge technological systems, in order to bring the new technology to the bulk of users and applications.

The revolutions promised by the initial inventions were set off by the need to link the novel technology with other technologies into interconnected technological systems. But once a system has been instigated, self-reinforcing mechanisms have often taken it well beyond the scope of the original invention. Steam technology, electricity and computer technology had no immediate impact on the society that prompted them but, as the technological systems of steam, electrical power and electronic computing evolved, the social and economic consequences went far beyond even the wildest dreams of the pioneers.[7]

Bridging gaps

The scope of a new technology must be extended, reaching towards other technologies and social structures; creating new interconnected technological systems, carrying the new technology from the research laboratories and development departments, bringing it into everyday life. In digital image processing the extension of the technology into other fields most typically implied that the gap between digital and analog technology had to be bridged. Image processing is only one of many new technologies focusing interest on overcoming or resolving the difference between analog and digital technology. The final chapter in the battle of systems between digital and analog image technology began as the proponents of digital image processing extended their activities to encompass other technologies.[8]

In 1984 STU's special initiative towards the development of digital image processing ended. The aim of the program had been to support the transition of image processing from scientific research to industrial production. The development had taken a somewhat unexpected turn in that image processing technology predominantly had been transferred from science to industry through the migration of scientists from university research to newly established firms. The path followed by the image processing researchers was, however, not unprecedented. Ever since Schumpeter the general notion has been that new technologies will primarily be embodied in new firms. The rise and development of computer technology is a striking example of how scientific research, industrial innovation and public policy coincided to foster the emergence of one of the most compelling technologies of our time.[9]

Research parks bridging the gap between science and industry

With the growth of the computer industry a new institutional form, the research park, materialized, connecting scientific research and industrial innovation. Stanford University Research Park, in what was to become known to the world as Silicon Valley, and MIT research laboratories, which brought about Route 128, were the pioneering research parks which set the standards for the rest of the world. In these research parks resources slowly accumulated, creating favourable conditions for entrepreneurial activities. Silicon Valley in particular evolved to become the single most important geographical location in the development of computer technology.[10] It attracted established computer and electronics firms, capital investments, and researchers and students from various fields, enthusiastically seeking to reap the benefits from years of research or studies by establishing new ventures or by participating in the entrepreneurial efforts of others. There are many stories of the heroic inventors and entrepreneurs of Silicon Valley: the Schockley Eight, William R. Hewlett and David Packard and the two Stevens – Wozniak and Jobs – carving for ever their names in the history of computer industry, making fortunes by turning their ideas into industrial realities.

Silicon Valley represented an increasing pool of resources and it functioned like an experimental economy with an excess of freely flowing resources. When perceived as agglomerations of resources for the development of new technologies, the institution of research parks is not a salient feature of the post-war era. The concentration of specific resources upon specific geographical areas has been the norm all through the industrialization process and the progress of society.[11] The question is to what extent these agglomerations of resources can purposefully be created.[12]

Silicon valley: a self-organizing system

The emergence and evolution of Silicon Valley was basically unplanned. A number of necessary preconditions were at hand, however, such as the presence of Stanford University, providing a steady flow of research-based technologies and graduate students, and the access to skilled manual workers. But these conditions were also present elsewhere. The fact that Silicon Valley happened to emerge where it did was purely accidental. The making of Silicon Valley was, however, paved with intentions. Stanford University officials intended to convert land to money when in 1951 they established the Stanford Research Park where companies were welcome to lease land. Hewlett and Packard intended to exploit the results of their research, a low-cost variable frequency oscillator, when they formed a partnership in 1938.[13] Frank G. Chambers, one of the pioneering venture capitalists, intended to increase the return on investment by investing in new ventures.[14] The actions of private firms, venture capitalists and entrepreneurs, all motivated by their specific intentions, forged the evolutionary path of Silicon Valley. But neither the officials of Stanford University, nor Hewlett and Packard nor Frank Chambers had Silicon Valley in mind when they formed their intentions.

The making of Silicon Valley can be described as a self-reinforcing process locked in by small historical events.[15] What if William Schockley had not returned to his hometown or if it had been in Texas? The self-reinforcing growth of Silicon Valley as the centre of microelectronics is comprised of two sets of interrelated processes. First, we have the techno-logical development of microelectronics and the rise of a mass-market for microelectronic gadgets, where highly sophisticated technology could be embodied in low-cost consumer products such as digital watches, pocket calculators and home computers. The consumers were effectively protected from the complexity of the underlying technology of these products and, if a gadget broke, repair costs were often much higher than the price of a new and better product. Thus, a huge market could be served even though most buyers did not know the difference between a transistor and a micro-chip and without the need to set up systems for repair and service. The electronics firms also produced more complicated products such as lasers and microprocessors. The cost of these was reduced through the existence of the mass-market for electronic products and the high-technology end of electronics fed back to the development of consumer products. Thus, the microprocessor was first used commercially in toys.

Second, turning closer to Silicon Valley, the settings were favourable and the success of the pioneering entrepreneurs served as an example for others. It also attracted resources enabling the would-be entrepreneurs to set up businesses on their own. Their success attracted more resources prompting even more entrepreneurial activity, making Silicon Valley the birthplace of microelectronics. The achievements of scientific researchers and graduate students setting up business in Silicon Valley and alongside Route 128 also served as role models for university researchers in Europe. Commercial exploitation of the fruits of years of scientific research ap-peared to be a financially rewarding alternative to continued research. From this perspective it should not have come as a surprise that the Swedish image processing researchers chose to bridge the gap between scientific research and industrial innovation by setting up businesses of their own. As in Silicon Valley, the pioneering entrepreneurs in Swedish image processing served as examples for the others, still striving at different universities. But, contrary to the entrepreneurs in Silicon Valley and along Route 128, the Swedish image processing spin-offs did not meet an infrastructure for high technology entrepreneurship.

Can the success story of Silicon Valley be repeated? Probably, but even if all the circumstances giving rise to Silicon Valley could be recreated, it is not certain that the outcome would be the same. The role of erratic events is too important for any process to be perfectly repeated. Nevertheless, the success story of Silicon Valley and Route 128 has echoed all over the world and policy makers not only in the USA but also in Europe have attempted to reproduce the making of Silicon Valley and Route 128 by setting up research parks in close proximity to major universities and institutes of technology.

Research parks in Sweden

In Sweden, as elsewhere, the dreams of a competitive edge in high technology prompted the establishment of research parks. In the middle of the 1980s research parks were instituted at most of the major universities: Ideon at the University of Lund, Technology Village at the University of Linköping, Technology Hill and Kista Valley at the Royal Institute of Technology and 'Glunten' at the University of Uppsala. Many of the recently established image processing firms were located or relocated in these research parks.[16] The Technology Village at the University of Linköping, in particular, became dominated by competing and complementary image processing firms. The University of Linköping had been lead scientific research in image processing so it was only natural that it also dominated the entrepreneurial activities in the field. Linköping, furthermore, had a history as a centre of Swedish high technology in that a major part of the Swedish computer industry had its roots in Saab–Scania in Linköping.

Technology Village in Linköping

A very special culture evolved at the Technology Village in Linköping. The village was comprised of individual firms, mainly spin-offs from the university but also more traditional Swedish firms. Also evolving was an invisible pool of personnel resources consisting of researchers from the individual firms and from the university. Whenever a specific actor had a problem or was at a critical point in the development process requiring more research personnel, that actor could draw on the pool of available personnel. When the problem was solved, the personnel called in returned to their normal duties. In this way the firms within the Technology Village were able to expand and contract depending on the phases of development of specific projects. Not all firms took part. Some firms, especially the traditional ones but also some of the spin-offs, did not participate in the sharing of resources.[17]

The research parks in Sweden have not yet prompted industrial progress in the surrounding area and most of them exhibit problems in attracting investments from established firms.[18] The evolving image processing network in Sweden was never supported by an ever-expanding computer industry. On the contrary, the emergence of image processing coincided with the decline of the Swedish computer industry. On the other hand this meant that the infant image processing industry never had to compete with the computer industry for resources. If the Swedish computer industry had been prosperous perhaps problems other than the analysis of images would have been more pressing and challenging, generating a totally different technological development.

THE DISSEMINATION OF THE IMAGE PROCESSING NETWORK

Instituted mainly for other reasons, the research parks indirectly prolonged the public support for the furtherance of digital image technology when STU's special initiative ended in 1984. Image processing had been legitimated scientifically and the evolving network was turning out technologically functional image processing computers. The Swedish image processing firms were, however, still struggling for survival. Contrary to the development of microelectronics in Silicon Valley a mass-market for image processing gadgets was neither available nor accessible to the Swedish actors. The dominant design and shape of the image processing equipment primarily satisfied the needs of men and women of science dressed in white robes and working in clean laboratories. The market represented by scientific laboratories was neither large enough nor sufficiently affluent to foster self-sustained growth for the large number of emerging image processing firms.

The actors outside the special initiative for the development of image processing

The development of image processing technology in Sweden and elsewhere had predominantly been financed through public funds or by publicly held companies: STU, the Department of Defence, the Swedish Space Program, different regional development funds or State-controlled companies. Private firms such as Saab–Scania and ASEA also invested in the technology but, at least initially, they were exceptions to the overall pattern. When STU's special initiative came to an end, the progress of the image processing network became increasingly dependent upon the actors' ability to attract support for technological development from sources outside the system. The emerging image processing firms had not been equally dependent on the availability of public funds. The growth of the actors outside STU's special initiative and the Swedish Space Program were to a greater extent contingent upon their ability to attract resources from the private sphere. Some spin-offs from university research, especially Sectra and Innovativ Vision both with their roots in the University of Linköping, were not directly included in the public policy programs towards the development of image processing.

Indirectly, both Sectra and Innovativ Vision could, as subcontractors, benefit from the overall progress of the technology, but their activities were more directly subject to a market evaluation. Innovativ Vision undertook development assignments on order. All development activities were thus directly connected with a user and they were also fully financed. When the assignments had been fulfilled Innovativ Vision retained the rights to further development of the instruments or systems in question and in these cases they naturally assumed a more independent role in the technological development.[19] Sectra was established to develop systems for computer and transmission security. As the requests for the development of systems and components for image transmission increased, the mission of the company shifted and development of image transmission and image coding became the central activity. Like Innovativ Vision, Sectra undertook technological development on direct order.[20] The first image-related project was to develop the image transmission component of Hasselblad's image transmitter. The commercial success of the transmitter secured the growth of both companies and the relationship between them became mutually beneficial. Sectra was not solely confined to the role of subcontractor to Hasselblad, other lines of development were also pursued. In one case, the development of image archives, this contributed substantially to the further progress of Hasselblad's development of digital image technology. In 1988 Hasselblad and Sectra established a jointly owned company, Image Server AB, to develop, produce and market digital image archives.[21]

The development projects within Innovativ Vision and Sectra were to a greater extent self-financed and both firms exhibited a smoother growth process than the actors involved in STU's special initiative. Other emerging proponents of image processing, actors within established firms competing for internally generated resources with other development projects and spin-offs from established actors in a quest for new sources of resources, were also more directly subject to the evaluation of their potential suppliers and users in their accumulation of resources.

Legitimating digital image processing as a problem-solving technique

When the flow of public policy motivated resources, predominantly development capital, tapered off, all actors became increasingly dependent upon their ability to attract resources from other sources. Some argued that STU should assume a greater responsibility: they had been instrumental in the emergence of the image processing network, now they ought to take the boat ashore. STU also continued to support the furtherance of digital image processing, particularly the research end of the development. They also followed the evolution of the image processing network with a keen interest but they did not issue a continued program directed towards the support of the commercialization of digital image technology, at least not immediately.

Many of the image processing firms were bleeding. The development had taken longer than projected and they needed more resources to realize the expectations of the new technology. The most urgent problem was the shortage of development capital. Naturally, other institutions, supporting the development of new technology apart from STU, could also be approached by the image processing firms. Digital image technology had been legitimated in the support system for technological development and it was comparatively easy to attract investments from other public sources, such as different pan-European, national and regional development funds. But increasingly the firms had to attract private investors. The future prospects of digital image technology were still promising and most actors were able to secure access to more money.

The public side of image processing

The need to attract new resources to the development of image processing required that the technology was also legitimated outside the institutions for the development of new technologies. The proponents of image processing attempted to establish that they had the capacity to solve a number of societal and individual problems, and image processing was increasingly featured in the press. One side of the publicity about the technology focused on how the digital image technology was invading the production of newspapers. Another side was more spectacular, presenting the technology in the most beguiling contexts. In the investigation of the assassination of the Swedish Prime Minister, Olof Palme, different modes of image processing were presented. First of all, computer generated images played a crucial role in the generation of phantom pictures of the alleged assassins. Second, the Swedish Airforce performed air surveillance in order to locate the murder weapon and Context Vision analysed the images produced. Other events also gave publicity to image processing. The Swedish Space Corporation and Satellite Image AB were the first in the world to show pictures of the nuclear catastrophe at Chernobyl. As a result of the Gulf War, Spotimage, partly owned by Satellite Image AB announced that it was no longer providing Iraq with satellite images.[22] In more bizarre circumstances image processing was used in a late-night, erotic, Swedish television production, where Innovativ Vision presented a system for generating phantom pictures of faces based on natural images. The system was used to produce artificial portraits of a man and a woman. Look-a like viewers were encouraged to send in pictures of themselves and the two with the greatest resemblance to the phantom faces were brought together in the next program. It seems that spectacular problems call for spectacular technological solutions.[23]

A more serious side of the legitimating of image processing in the business and public sphere has been the annual industry forecasts supplied by more or less scrupulous consultants. The general feature of these reports was that next year the market for image processing would explode and they were aimed more at encouraging potential financiers than at being a foundation for the everyday activities of the different proponents of image processing.[24]

The fundamental problem – the integration of image processing with the technologies of the users

The need to attract additional capital resources was in many cases urgent but yet only symptomatic of a more fundamental problem. The isolation of digital image technology had to be broken: the gap between the technological system of digital image processing and the technological systems employing the new technology had to be bridged. The proponents of image processing had to attract resources to integrate the new technological system with pre-existing ones and in this way connect the investments in the development of digital image technology with complementary investments made in other systems. In many technological systems, such as graphic production, map production, industrial automation and radiology, investments had already been made in the conversion to digital technology. The next challenge for the image processing actors was to connect their development activities to the development activities within these systems. Like most other network technologies, such as electricity and computers, the performance of the components of digital image technology – image reading instruments and image processing computers – were contingent upon the performance of the whole system. A complete industrial network for the development, production and consumption of image processing systems and of computer processed images was yet to be established.

The experience gained from the first installations of image processing equipment prompted the proponents of the technology to work more directly with some users, adapting the technology to the particular image analysis problems and preconditions of specific users. The focus gradually shifted from serving a generally defined market to serving specific user groups sharing common characteristics. Furthermore, the problem of insufficient capital prompted the image processing firms to cut costs and to establish a more viable resource structure. Many activities of development and production not vital to the subsistence of the emerging firms, which previously had been performed within the firms, were shifted backwards to suppliers of components and subsystems. The specialization and division of labour emerging from the image processing firms that were addressing urgent problems resulted in the dissemination of the coalesced image processing network.

The turning of OSIRIS from a blatant failure in image processing into a splendid success in image transmission

The first project within the special initiative to be abandoned was the development of OSIRIS, a low-cost image processing system. It was developed, in collaboration, by Physics IV, the Swedish Space Corporation, Saab–Scania in Gothenburg and the famous camera manufacturer Hasselblad. The project satisfied the aim of the special initiative and it was also in line with the ambition of STU to promote the formation of industrial networks. Nevertheless, the collaboration between the four crash-landed and the OSIRIS-project was abandoned. The reasons behind the collapse of the project were many. The technological design of the system proved to be less promising than had been anticipated. The market to be served proved hard to reach. The system was never used in the way that had been intended. More important, however, was probably the incompatability of the goals of the four actors. None of the actors, except Physics IV, the original inventor, had vested interests in the development of OSIRIS. The others participated in the project mainly for reasons other than the promotion of OSIRIS. Hasselblad was determined to follow the development of electronic image technology and the Swedish Space Corporation needed equipment to analyse satellite images.[25]

The project collapsed in 1982 but the actors continued on the path of digital image technology. Physics IV was determined to make a success out of OSIRIS; the Swedish Space Corporation initiated an internal project aimed at the development of a mid-size image processing computer; and Hasselblad continued to strive towards electronic image technology with the long-term goal of developing a still-video camera.

Connecting frontline users with frontline development

Hasselblad had been in contact with Agence France Presse, AFP, which had initiated the development of a digital picture-net for the newspaper industry. The basic components of this system were a digital image switch-board, image terminals and image transmitters. AFP had not yet commen-ced the development of image transmitters and they told Hasselbald of the need for an instrument capable of transmitting images digitally. In 1982 Hasselblad initiated the development of a digital image transmitter, thereby entering on the path which was supposed to lead towards an electronic camera. A former associate of the PICAP-group was appointed to lead the new venture. A first prototype of the transmitter was developed in collabo-ration with *Expressen* – one of the largest newspapers in Sweden – and one of its subsidiaries, which adapted the existing analog system for receiving images to digital technology. Sectra was engaged in the development of the transmission components and Hasselblad was also able to capitalize on its existing supplier structure: Carl Zeiss delivered the lens to the image transmitter. Technologically, the first image transmitter shared some common characteristics with the abandoned OSIRIS image processing computer. They both used a CCD-array, but the transmitter was a totally different instrument.[26] OSIRIS had been intended for the analysis of images, the transmitter was intended only for digital transmission.

The first phase of the development of the digital image transmitter was completed in time for the Summer Olympics in Los Angeles in 1984. Hasselblad measured up to the first challenge and at the Olympics the transmitter was exposed to the scrutiny of the assembled press. The primary advantage of the digital transmitter compared to the pre-existing analog system of image transmission was that it could transmit negative images. A photographer could thus develop a film at the sports arena and send the pictures directly to a newspaper using an ordinary telephone and without first having to produce a paper copy of the pictures. Important hours were saved, a deadline could be met and furthermore the editor was also given more discretion in selecting the final picture.

In order to modify the image transmitter even further according to the needs of the users, Hasselblad continued its discussions with AFP and other representatives of the global press. One element that was changed in the second generation of the transmitter was the film format. The transmitter was specified for the use of 35mm film only. This meant that the transmitter could not transmit photographs taken with Hasselblad cameras. But, more importantly, it also meant that the transmitter could be made portable and easier to operate. A 'dummy' of the new transmitter was presented to AFP and Hasselblad declared itself willing to complete the development within a certain time if AFP signed a letter of intent to acquire a specified number of transmitters at a fixed price. AFP agreed and Hasselblad had taken on a new challenge. Not only had the company promised to complete the development in time, it also set out to do it at a specified cost.[27]

Internal reorganization

To develop, produce and market the image transmitter Hasselblad established a subsidiary, Hasselblad Electronic Imaging AB. The new company could not meet all of the promises made in 1984. The project was delayed but so also was the development within AFP and the time schedule for the transmitter was still sufficiently close to the original plan. For the development of the optics, mechanics and electronics of the image transmitter Hasselblad drew upon the experience of around 25 subcontractors. Most important was the image coding and transmission expert, Sectra, which also produced the image compression elements of the final transmitter. Production of the image transmitter was organized internally through employing the resources of the mother company and by using the network of subcontractors, the most important besides Sectra being Carl Zeiss, producing the lens for the transmitter as well as for the Hasselblad cameras.

The first transmitter was delivered to AFP on 7 February 1986 and before the end of the year Hasselblad managed to turn out 28 systems. These went mainly to AFP but also to two Swedish newspapers and to the car manufacturer, Fiat. But it was too early to order champagne. The transmitter, marketed under the name 'Dixel 2000', was rarely used in active service: it was still impaired by some unsolved technical problems. Subsequently, Hasselblad was not only able to solve the problems but also, together with Sectra, took Dixel well beyond the specified performance levels. Delivered systems were recalled for revision and upgrading and Hasselblad attained a solid reputation as a producer of digital image transmission systems. Compared to its major competitor, Dixel was a real bargain. In 1987 the price of Dixel 2000, ranging from SEK 180,000, was less than half of the price of the Nikon transmitter, at SEK 450,000.[28] Dixel was sold through AFP and through the existing channels of the mother company.

Connecting digital and analog technology

Dixel 2000 was developed for digital image transmission but the bulk of the market was still within analog transmission. Apart from actors acquiring the AFP-system, the newspaper production system of Teragon Systems or some of the few other existing systems accepting digital signals, the transmitter was useless. The orders from AFP for digital image transmitters, close to 200 systems up till 1989, were of course vital for the growth not only of Hasselblad Electronic Imaging AB but also through it, of Sectra. However, it was essential to reach the users employing analog image technology. Thus, in order to make it possible to use Dixel 2000 without first having to invest heavily in digital technology, Hasselblad, still in collaboration with Sectra, developed an analog transmission module. In 1987 Hasselblad introduced Dixel for analog transmission and representatives of the Swedish press were enthusiastic. The analog module made it possible also to use Dixel in active service outside the AFP-sphere. The possibilities of analog transmission, through the use of Dixel by Swedish newspapers, substantially boosted the interest in the system. The first analog transmitter was developed according to the European telephoto standard. The next step in the development process was to adapt it to the American standard.

Spin-off effects

To promote digital image transmission even more, Hasselblad and Sectra developed a total system for digital transmission comprised of Dixel and a receiver-interface.[29] A digital system has certain advantages compared to analog transmission. It is safer, faster and the outcome is of higher quality. It has also proved to have certain qualities when it comes to the handling of colour pictures. A colour picture must be transmitted several times, one colour at a time. Before the editor can inspect the final result, the picture must first be reproduced, a costly process. In the digital system the picture could be recreated in the receiver-interface and displayed by connecting the receiver to a monitor. Colour separation could, of course, be performed directly with Dixel.

The growing number of colour pictures in contempoary newspapers revealed a hidden potential of Dixel. Newspapers found that the system could be used as a low-cost colour separation system. By transmitting colour pictures locally to the internal receiver, Dixel functioned as a colour separator which was affordable by almost every newspaper, especially since it also could be used for long-distance transmission. The A-Press, a large Swedish cooperative press organization, did initiate far-reaching tests of Dixel for colour separation.

An effective network for the development, production and application of digital image transmission

The successful collaboration between Hasselblad and Sectra has continued and in 1988 they began to develop a digital image archive. Together AFP, Hasselblad and Sectra have forged a network connecting traditional photography and digital image technology with the production of newspapers. What began as the development of a low-cost image processing computer has, through different critical events and through the establishment of a few critical relationships, evolved to become an effective system for the development, production and use of digital image transmission.

Physics IV: back to basics

Meanwhile, Physics IV did not rest easy. The department had a long history of developing scientific instruments for the measuring of data contained in images. Slowly their activities had crept closer to the evolutionary path of digital image technology. The first two systems developed at Physics IV, the spectral reader, IRIS, and the OSIRIS, had originally been designed for the reading of images. Gradually the instruments were adapted to the processing of images through the addition of computing capacity. Knowledge of computer technology was, however, never the motivation on which the department based its activities.[30] Their specific competence was more in the field of spectroscopy, image physics and optics. In the scientific endeavours which followed the OSIRIS-project, they turned back to basics, to the development of scientific instruments for extracting information contained in images. By combining laser and fluorescence technology Physics IV proved that it was possible to extract previously concealed information. Among other things it was found that the technology could be used for generating three-dimensional volumes from microscope slides, an observation that resulted in a collaborative research project between Physics IV and the PICAP-group.[31] This scientific venture was also manifested in the development of a scientific instrument, an opto-electronic microscope, PHOIBOS, patented in 1986. In this venture, Physics IV was able to establish fruitful co-operation with several research groups at major medical research institutes in Sweden. And in 1984 the first prototype was installed at one of these groups.[32]

While Physics IV wanted to exploit PHOIBOS commercially, they also firmly believed that OSIRIS deserved another chance. The experience gained from previous attempts to transfer projects to industrial partners, combined with the examples set by other university spin-offs, encouraged Physics IV to go it alone this time. In April 1985, Physics IV and a Swedish development company joined forces and established Sarastro AB. The mission of Sarastro was to develop, produce and market microscope-scanners, primarily PHOIBOS but also OSIRIS, to scientific institutes. The marketing of OSIRIS still proved problematic. Apart from a few systems installed at the image analysis laboratory at the Royal Institute of Technology, Sarastro did not manage to sell the system and eventually even Sarastro abandoned it. The prospects for PHOIBOS were much more promising. The microscope was adapted to conventional personal computers. A complete system was thus comprised of the microscope, any Intel-based personal computer and application software developed by Physics IV and Sarastro. For the production of PHOIBOS a number of suppliers were contracted. To foster usage, Sarastro established an applications laboratory where users were welcome to come and test the instruments. Collaboration with a group of users at the University of Philadelphia resulted in the establishment of a sales subsidiary in the USA. Future prospects seemed bright.

None of the instruments developed by Physics IV was motivated by market needs. IRIS, OSIRIS and PHOIBOS were all developed to satisfy the internal scientific needs of Physics IV. Contrary to the two previous instruments, PHOIBOS apparently had the capacity to solve more general sets of problems. In the development of PHOIBOS, Physics IV and Sarastro managed to establish a closer relationship to users than had been the case with the other instruments. The most significant difference, however, might have been the level of engagement devoted to the three projects. IRIS and OSIRIS never became more than minor undertakings in large companies, while the development of PHOIBOS was the sole purpose of Sarastro.

A network in space

The third participant of the OSIRIS project, the Swedish Space Corporation, needed an image processing computer to analyse satellite images. It had assumed a more passive role in the development of OSIRIS but it had also developed a sea surveillance system, containing digital image technology, for the Swedish Coastal Guard. The absence of functional image processing systems motivated the Space Corporation to develop a system internally.

The Swedish Space Corporation is a state-owned company and is the spider in the web of actors constituting the Swedish Space Program. Apart from remote sensing and digital image processing it is also active in every space-related activity in Sweden. It runs the rocket station at Esrange in northern Sweden and it coordinates the Swedish satellite ventures. The

Space Corporation coordinates the Swedish space effort and it controls, directly or indirectly, the resources devoted to space activities.

Internal needs urging the Swedish Space Corporation to develop image processing computers

At the same time as the Space Corporation became involved in the OSIRIS-project it developed its own low-cost image processing computer. In 1981 it launched 'EBBA', a micro-computer based image processing system in the price range 100,000–150,000 SEK. The system was based on the knowledge acquired in remote sensing and on the image memory developed in the sea surveillance project. Some 15–20 systems were produced and subsequently sold or leased mainly to research institutions, government authorities and companies active in the fields of remote sensing and cartography. EBBA was successively developed and upgraded and in 1984 EBBA II was launched. The second generation was internally financed and it represented an adaptation to the requirements of the potential users. Later, EBBA II was complemented by a larger, faster and more interactive image memory forming the basis for the third generation of low-cost image processing computer systems, named EBBA–GIS, developed by the Space Corporation. The sea surveillance system was subsequently also equipped with the new image memory. EBBA–GIS was an adaptation to specific users, namely those processing geographical information, hence the name GIS – an acronym for Geographical Information System. EBBA–GIS was developed to be used together with a host computer from Digital Equipment but it could also be used as a stand-alone system. In connection with making digital image technology more aligned to the needs of the users in geographic information systems, the Space Corporation acquired the rights to a PC-based cartographic software package, Strings, developed by Geo-Based Systems. The package was adapted to EBBA–GIS, which provided the Space Corporation with access to two computer systems, of different complexity, for the processing of geographical information.[33]

The line of EBBA-systems and the PC-based Strings-system represented a development of mid-size and low-cost image processing computer systems. The range of remote sensing activities performed within the Space Corporation, however, also called for an image processing computer system with an even higher capacity than the EBBA–GIS. To satisfy the need for a high-capacity image processing computer system the Space Corporation had outlined a new system, MIMA. To fulfil the specifications, higher image processing capacity was required and so the Space Corporation acquired the computer Teragon 4000 from Teragon Systems, one of two suppliers of general image processing computers in Sweden at that time. Teragon Systems and Context Vision had each developed a highly sophisticated computer system for image processing.

Teragon Systems and the development of a total digital production system for newspapers

Teragon Systems, originally a spin-off from the PICAP-group at the University of Linköping which was established in 1981 under the name of Imtec and one of the pioneering image processing firms, was the largest new venture in digital image technology. Teragon Systems developed the PICAP II-project to a commercially viable image processing computer system and they had anticipated serving all four major segments of image processing technology: industrial automation, graphic production, medicine and cartography.[34] They had started out with a project within industrial automation concerning automatic seed control and with a total digital production system for large newspapers. The medical segment was covered through the continuance of the collaboration with the Image Laboratory of Uppsala University, something that had been initiated earlier between the PICAP-group and the Laboratory. The relationship with the Space Corporation could be Teragon's entry ticket to cartography and remote sensing.

The development of the total digital production system, labelled the TIPS-system, soon became the dominant project. It was financed by the state-owned publisher Liber AB who considered the project to be a means of catching up with their competitors technologically. The TIPS-system was a desk top publishing system developed long before this concept was coined in the development of personal computing. But the TIPS-system was not intended for infatuated amateurs, it was supposed to satisfy the market for the professional production of large newspapers. It was to revolutionize newspaper production, which just recently had faced another such revolution, computerization. Like a young cuckoo the TIPS-system swallowed all of the resources the striving company could attract and in 1982 a subsidiary of Liber AB, Liber Systems Text and Image AB, acquired 91 per cent of the shares in Imtec. The remaining 9 per cent was still held by the original founding company, a state-owned development company, SUAB. It still proved difficult to pursue development outside the TIPS-project and they soon realized that they had to give up the aim of adapting the computer system to all four of the major applications. In 1984 Imtec was split into two parts according to the ownership structure. The major part of Imtec was transferred to Liber Systems Text and Image AB, which was to concentrate its efforts on developing digital image technology for newspaper production and for cartography and remote sensing.

The other segments, industrial automation and medicine, were to be served by the remainder of the company, initially under the control of SUAB. The spin-off consisting of one of the original founders and the leading researcher within the Image Laboratory retained the original name of the company, Imtec, and moved to Uppsala.[35]

Liber Systems continued to develop the TIPS-system and the general image processing computer system, then called Imtec 4000. The TIPS-project was developed in collaboration with a Finnish company, OY Typplan, a subsidiary of Nokia, producing computerized text-systems for newspapers. Liber Systems and Typplan were technologically compatible in that they both used the same host computer, a VAX from Digital Equipment. Others had also been involved in the project, especially related to the development of the human–machine interface of the system. The TIPS-system was developed to become a total digital system for the production of newspapers, integrating images, graphics and texts. An 'Application Support Package' with an open architecture, around which different application modules could be organized, was the heart of the interface between the hardware and the specific applications of digital processing. The original image and text modules were complemented by others to fit the needs and the specific technological vintage of the potential users. Some of these modules were supplied by different manufacturers; for example, the typesetting equipment was supplied by Monotype, Crossfield or Chemco, three traditional equipment manufacturers in the graphic industry.

Altogether three TIPS-systems were installed: at a small Finnish newspaper; at an American newspaper and at a Swedish newspaper. The first complete TIPS-system was installed at the Swedish evening paper *Aftonbladet* in 1985. With support from STU, *Aftonbladet* leased a TIPS-system for two and a half years. The system was tested during the time of the lease and Liber System continually upgraded the systems in accordance with the experience gained from using the system at the newspaper. The system was installed in a laboratory-like setting at the newspaper. It was placed in a separate room and five typographers were specially trained by Liber Systems to operate it. Apart from operating the TIPS-system, the typographers were also available if problems arose in normal production.

The TIPS-system was basically used to produce the images for the Sunday supplement of the Gothenburg edition and to compose one page containing the letters to the editor in the main edition. Why was the system not used to produce images for the other editions? The main reason was incompatible technology: the image technology of *Aftonbladet* in general was old and about to be replaced, while the Gothenburg edition was produced with more modern technology. There were no technological barriers to producing all of the images with the system, but the quality of the outcome was not deemed to be good enough for the main edition. Why, then, was only one page composed on the TIPS-system and why was it the letters to the editor? Letters to the editor was never an effective test of the capacity of the system: it offered few possibilities to use the 'goodies' incorporated in the system and it contained only a few, if any, images. In newspaper production failure is a catastrophe and the letters to the editor page was probably considered to be unimportant enough to be experimented with.

The TIPS-system could probably have been used to produce the whole newspaper or at least one of the supplements, but that would have required a total modification of production routines. As it is, all pages of a newspaper are produced simultaneously and they are all completed at the same time, just before deadline. The cost of a system and additional workstations suggested a more sequential completion of the pages in the paper.[36] The newspaper industry was not yet ready to take the giant leap into digital desk top publishing technology. It was not possible to change the routines of production and it could not afford to use the new technology in the traditional way. But it was slowly converting to digital image technology. *Aftonbladet* decided against acquiring the TIPS-system, but it did acquire both the AFP digital image system and Dixel 2000.[37]

New technology vs. traditional routines of production

The relative failure of the TIPS-system was a setback to the growth of Liber Systems. The American paper also returned its system but the Finnish paper continued to use the TIPS-system. The system had performed well technologically and the human–machine interface had proven to be well adapted to the preconditions and needs of the final users. The problem was that the TIPS-system challenged the traditional production routines within the newspaper industry. Liber Systems, still an emerging firm, could neither control nor attract the necessary resources to be the missionary of desk top publishing technology for the newspaper industry. Furthermore, OY Typplan had for different reasons left the collaborative venture. The difficulties encountered in the final stage of the development of the TIPS-system resulted in financial problems and the mother company announced an unwillingness to make up the deficiency. Liber Systems was put up for sale and was subsequently acquired by the independent venture capital firm, Connova Invest. The development of digital image technology could be continued, now under the name of Teragon Systems.

The restructured Teragon dismantled the TIPS-project and gave up or at least postponed the realization of a totally integrated production system for newspapers. Instead, they concentrated their efforts on developing one of the modules of TIPS, an electronic darkroom, and on the development of the image processing computer, renamed Teragon 4000.

Major competitors following different paths

The pursuit of the development of the automatic seed control system and the TIPS-system guided Imtec, Liber Systems and Teragon Systems along a specific path of development of digital technology: the evolutionary path of digital image technology for production systems. The major Swedish competitor, Context Vision, was ushered along a different path of development. Context Vision established relationships with research institutions and consequently the GOP image processing computer system was primarily adapted to the needs of the scientists. Context vision also established a collaborative venture with the French company Télécommunication Radio-électriques et Téléphoniques (TRT), to realize the processor architecture in VLSI-circuits.[38] Compared to Teragon Systems, Context Vision had a more pronounced European focus and it gave priority to the development of its European market organization. Context Vision followed the path of development of general image processing systems for research institutes and laboratories in Europe.

In the entrepreneurial stage of the evolution of the image processing network, the rivalry between Teragon and Context Vision had been fierce. They drew on the same resources; they competed for the same research and development capital; they used the same components and subsystem and finally they aimed to serve the same needs of the same customers. As they encountered and solved everyday problems of developing and producing image processing systems and of adapting them to the needs of the buyers, they established different relationships with other actors. Through the interaction within these relationships, Teragon with Liber and *Aftonbladet* and Context Vision with research laboratories, the two ventures were led on to different evolutionary paths: drifting apart competitively, but still remaining next door neighbours geographically. The two firms had, in a few years, passed from being relentless competitors to becoming potential partners.[39]

Connecting the space effort and the development of image processing computer systems

The Space Corporation had already initiated discussions with Imtec in 1982 regarding the possibilities of joint development of cartographic systems. They also ordered an image processing computer system from

Imtec. The discussions continued with Liber Systems when they where in the midst of the TIPS-project. The possibility of a collaboration with the Space Corporation was considered highly interesting. However, the TIPS-system was at a critical point of development and it swallowed all of the resources that Liber Systems could attract, so the Space Corporation attained a lower priority when it came to both the installation of the computer system and the plans for joint development.

The efforts to develop digital cartography and remote sensing in Sweden were to a large extent concentrated in the Space Corporation. It controlled, directly or indirectly, the resources allocated to the development of space technology and remote sensing and, as a consequence, came to be regarded as a most interesting partner in the development of digital cartographic technology and remote sensing and so attracted even more resources. In 1982 the Swedish Space Corporation established a subsidiary, Satellite Image AB, which was to receive and process satellite images. This was a natural extension of the Space Corporation's commitment to the development of European space technology and remote sensing capabilities. In 1978 the Space Corporation had, in collaboration with the European Space Agency, ESA, erected a data acquisition station for the Landsat-satellite at Esrange. The establishing and operating of satellite data acquisition stations and networks for dissemination of satellite data was considered to be an appropriate role for ESA in promoting the development of remote sensing.[40] In 1978, negotiations regarding the participation in the SPOT-satellite, a European remote sensing satellite, were concluded and the Swedish part was set at 4 per cent. The SPOT-satellite was, in contrast to Landsat, not experimental. SPOT was to be developed for commercially oriented remote sensing. The Swedish participation in the SPOT-project constituted the basis on which the Space Corporation's move into commercial exploitation of remote sensing was founded.

Approaching the launch of the SPOT-satellite, additional investments in resources for remote sensing were required in the modernization of the data acquisition stations, in the development of image processing capacity and in the enlargement of the networks for the dissemination of satellite data. Satellite Image was a part of the European investment in commercial remote sensing. The French board for space activity, CNES, had an equal interest in investing in an infrastructure for remote sensing and Spot Image, the French equivalent of Satellite Image, acquired 9 per cent of the stocks in Satellite Image. The remaining 91 per cent was held by the Swedish Space Corporation. Satellite Image was to be equipped for advanced acquisition, processing and refining of satellite data and fully functional by the time of the launching of the SPOT-satellite.[41]

Connecting the space effort and the production of maps

To be productive, raw satellite data had to be converted into geographic information and it also often had to be combined with other sources of information. To adapt the processing and refining of satellite images to the requirements of the users of geographic information, the Space Corporation initiated collaboration and joint projects with different actors active in the field of cartography: national, regional and local authorities, mineral prospectors and land survey institutes. The collaborative venture of most consequence was that with the National Land Survey of Sweden, SLS, which has the primary responsibility for the survey of the Swedish landscape and the subsequent production of maps, while the local authorities are responsible for more detailed surveying. Overall, a huge number of public and private organizations have a stake in the production and use of geographic information. The total cost of land surveying and map production in Sweden was in 1979 estimated at SEK 1.5 billion and 10,000–12,000 people were estimated to be engaged in surveying Sweden.[42] The position of SLS in the Swedish cartography industry can be compared to the position of the Space Corporation in the Swedish space effort.

Following the development of computer graphics a widespread conversion to digital technology was initiated decades ago in the field of cartography. Computer systems for digital map production had become increasingly available. In 1984 one-third of the Swedish 284 local authorities had acquired or had direct access to computer systems for map production.[43] The digital technology was primarily employed in the production process and was rarely used to produce new information. New sources of data, satellite images, were not employed. The conversion to digital technology signified that an increasing amount of geographic information would be stored digitally and would thus be accessible for further computer processing. The bulk of geographic information, accumulated during centuries, was of course still stored using analog technology.

Combining satellites, digital image technology and cartography

General computer systems dedicated to image processing were available at this time. These were, however, rarely used extensively outside the research institutions or the experimental workshops of the image processing firms. The production of maps was still dominated by analog technology, but digital technology had broken through the technological barrier and a few local authorities were mainly using digital technology in the production of primary maps. As remote sensing was reaching maturity, functional systems for remote sensing were being established. Thus, the aim of the collaboration between the Space Corporation and SLS was to develop and promote the development of digital geographic information systems, thereby interconnecting the emerging system for remote sensing and image processing with the emerging system for the digital production of maps.

The Space Corporation commenced the development of MIMA in 1982, but both the failure of Liber Systems to deliver the computer system on time and the internal development of EBBA–GIS produced substantial delays. Certainly, Teragon 4000 was not the only image processing computer available on the Swedish market, but Teragon was especially suited to be a partner in the development of MIMA. Teragon used the same host computer as the Space Corporation and it had specialized in the development of image processing for production systems. The most immediate competitor, Context Vision, used another host computer and it was becoming specialized in the field of image processing for scientific purposes. Several GOP-systems were also sold to organizations pursuing research in remote sensing and geographic information systems. When the development of the TIPS-system reached the final stage, Liber Systems was able to devote more resources to the joint development of MIMA and, after the change of ownership and name, MIMA was considered to be its most important project. In MIMA the computer and image processing technology of Teragon Systems was combined with the knowledge and experience of remote sensing and geographic information systems accumulated at the Space Corporation and SLS.

The first phase of the development of MIMA was completed in 1986 and the first system was promptly installed at Satellite Image. The characteristics of Teragon 4000, with its high interactive image processing capacity and extremely high user friendliness, were incorporated in the system. At the same time the experience of the Space Corporation was reflected in the software for geographic information. Not only was it possible to analyse single satellite scenes, it was also possible to process multi-satellite images and combine these with data from several other sources. Teragon and the Space Corporation continued to develop the MIMA-system after the first installation. The next challenge was to integrate the matrix based image processing with the vector based computer graphics.

Spin-off effects

The first installation was followed by others. MIMA was marketed internationally by Teragon but naturally the basic market consisted of users in the Nordic countries. SLS and its corresponding organizations in the other

Nordic countries acquired MIMA-systems. The successful completion of the MIMA-system also proved to be an entry ticket to another similar project. Ericsson Radio Systems had received an order for a processing system for meteorological satellite data, PROSAT, from the Swedish Meteorological and Hydrological Institute, SMHI. When the British supplier of the image processing computer of PROSAT had problems in fulfilling their part of the project, the order went to Teragon, who delivered. Teragon 4000 became the main feature of PROSAT. In conjunction with the MIMA and PROSAT projects, Teragon also made some minor adjustments of the CCD-flatbed scanner developed for the TIPS-system.[44]

Success fostered success and Teragon found a new opening into the newspaper industry. Parts of the abandoned TIPS-system were converted into an electronic darkroom and, together with the flatbed scanner, this constituted an effective system for the digital production of both black and white and colour images. The electronic darkroom was further adapted to accept images sent by Dixel 2000 and Teragon was also granted the rights to sell Dixel. One of the former potential suppliers to the TIPS-system, Chemco Europe, agreed to market the electronic darkroom in Europe. For the production of Teragon 4000 and the electronics of the flatbed scanner Teragon established a relationship with Saab Combitech. The systems are finally tested and connected to the host computer at Teragon.[45]

For the Space Corporation the collaboration with Teragon meant that they could abstain from further development of the hardware for image processing. The development of the line of EBBA-systems had primarily been motivated by the absence of reliable computer systems for remote sensing. Through the relationship with Teragon the Space Corporation had attained access to an image processing computer system adapted to remote sensing and cartography. Consequently the Space Corporation could concentrate on the development of methods for using satellite images as one component of geographic information systems and on the establishment and maintenance of infrastructures for connecting the acquisition, dissemination and processing of satellite images with the users of geographic information.

The Space Corporation and Satellite Image intensified the collaboration with SLS, which also located a branch office in Kiruna, in the vicinity of Satellite Image. Satellite Image alone or together with SLS sold satellite data of varying degrees of refinement in Sweden and all over the world. In the Western world the systems for geographic information are well established and satellite data can at most complement the existing amount of information. Consequently satellite data are of less economic value. Here the basic problem is to adapt the digital image technology to the existing digital and analog production technology. In the underdeveloped part of world the situation is different. An insignificant base of geographic information and systems for production of information have been accumulated. Here satellite data can constitute the sole basis on which geographic information is construed. The economic value of satellite data is in this case relatively higher. Together with Swedsurvey, a subsidiary of SLS, the Space Corporation has undertaken several projects regarding resource mapping in the Third World. A survey of the Philippines and an inventory of fire woods in Tanzania are two examples. Naturally, most projects concerning the Third World, including the two mentioned, are financed by different international aid organizations.

The network in space connecting complementary technologies

The sequel to Imtec, Liber Systems and Teragon was too small and too lonely to establish a digital system for the integrated production of newspapers. The new venture had neither the financial resources nor the endurance to be the pioneering firm in the development of desk top publishing systems for newspapers. The necessary resources could not be attracted, either through the establishment of relationships controlling critical resources or through internal growth. Together, Teragon, with its relationships to the emerging image processing network and to the computer industry, the Space Corporation, with its position in the European Space Program, and SLS, with its position in Swedish cartography, successfully connected the complementary technologies of digital image processing, space and satellite technology and cartography into a digital system for civilian land survey and production of maps. Through this collaboration the three firms established positions consistent with self-sustained growth in the development of remote sensing and cartography. But the system as such can probably not survive without public support for years to come. Even before the initiation of the transformation to digital technology, two-thirds of the total costs for land survey and map production in Sweden was paid for through government spending. The immense investments in an infrastructure for digital geographic information systems – satellites, ground stations, image processing computers and distribution networks – will take decades to recoup. And the volume of demand for satellite images is not yet substantial enough to sustain the system without public support.[46] But a digital system for land survey and map production has an economic advantage over the analog system in that geographical information once produced can be reproduced and used in other contexts at a much lower cost.[47]

Other chains of producer–user interactions in the dissemination process

The above constellations, Hasselblad – Sectra – AFP and Teragon – the Space Corporation – SLS, were not the only ones capable of transforming the general solution of digital image technology into a specific solution to a common set of problems.

The established companies

The established firms, Saab in Jönköping and ASEA, had an advantage in that they could embrace and control a relatively large part of the underlying technological system. The chains of producers and users connecting digital image technology with the application involved internal actors. Both Saab and ASEA could benefit from being both users and producers, which rendered them at an advantage in the commercialization of digital image technology. Saab in Jönköping had already in 1976 successfully completed the development of an edge detector for sawmills. Having no previous experience of solving problems in the sawmill industry, Saab acquired a firm which was active in the industry, in order to attain access to the resource and knowledge base necessary for the successful completion of the venture. The ambitions of Saab in digital image technology, however, went well beyond systems for efficient sawing. After some attempts at developing general systems for image processing in industrial automation, Saab specialized in systems for identification in logistic systems. Acting upon an order from the Swedish Postal Authorities, Saab developed a total system for the sorting of mail. Through this and other projects Saab developed strengths in digital image technology for identification in industrial automation systems. In 1988, they acquired the image processing department, C. E. Johansson AB, a remnant from a spin-off from ASEA, specializing in digital image technology for inspection and control in industrial automation systems.[48]

ASEA developed a vision system for industrial robotics. As ASEA was establishing itself as one of the largest manufacturers of industrial robots in the world, it benefited from the accumulated experience of the application of robotics and from the fact that its vision system could be perfectly integrated with the general guidance system for the ASEA-robot. The robotic vision system was taken to the international market through the marketing of the industrial robot. Like most other actors in the image processing network, ASEA also aimed at producing general image processing systems, but after an internal reorganization it once again concentrated its efforts on the development of robotic vision.

This does not signify that huge firms with immense financial strength can overcome all the problems associated with the development of new technologies. The new technology must compete for resources with the other activities of the firms and few firms can devote more than a minor part of their resources to the development of new technologies. Naturally, Saab and ASEA encountered ample sets of problems in their promotion of digital image technology. But both firms have a long industrial tradition and they have accumulated experience in industrial automation for decades. For both companies digital image processing was only a minor component in a larger system, and so the new component could be well integrated with the overall system. And the technological solution of image processing could be adapted to the problems. Contrary to the emerging firms, ASEA and Saab opted for less sophisticated technology.[49]

Innovativ Vision: a winning spin-off

Another firm that successfully adapted digital image technology to the users was Innovativ Vision. Originally a spin-off from the PICAP-group it went into business to solve the image processing problems of potential users. Contrary to Imtec and Context Vision it was not established to develop a specific image processing computer system. Innovativ Vision developed solutions to specific problems and as its clients increased in number so did the number of technological solutions. The primary aim became to discriminate between the projects and to choose solutions suitable for further development. As it solved specific users' problems, a line of general image processing computer systems evolved and Innovativ Vision set out to market these outside the initial producer–user relationship. In general it encountered similar problems to those of Hasselblad, Imtec and Context Vision. Digital image technology was not readily generalized to solve common sets of problems. But Innovativ Vision had the advantage of not being tied down to one specific solution and together with a few users it continued to develop systems according to user specifications. One such system was a document reader which scanned the relevant part of football coupons for the Swedish Tipstjänst. Systems for automatic correction of football coupons had been in service for some years. To be fully automated, however, the system had to be able, in addition, to read the names and addresses on the coupons. Innovativ Vision adapted one of their computer systems to this application and connected it to the existing system for automatic correction. The first document reader was delivered to Tipstjänst in 1986 and it has been followed by other orders. Initially the document reader was sold and installed by Innovativ Vision, but the company also entered into agreements with the producers of the systems for automatic correction and through them gained access to a much larger market. The development of the document reader was typical of the projects pursued by Innovativ Vision. The other projects show similar patterns of intensive collaboration with users. To secure production capacity Innovativ Vision – together with one of its major clients – acquired an electronic assembling firm.[50]

The cases cited above are some obvious examples of how the development and production of the image processing capability were connected and adapted to the use of the same capability. Through chains of close collaboration between users and producers, digital image technology was extended backward, towards the producers of computers and electronic components, and forward, towards the users of image processing. Through such collaboration a distinct specialization and division of labour evolved and the coalesced image processing network was disseminated.

Connecting the Swedish image processing network to the international market

The dissemination of the image processing network did not merely connect the production and usage of digital image technology. The dissemination was also an extension of the Swedish network into an international market. The Swedish market for image processing technology was far too small to sustain most individual applications of digital image technology and the relatively large image processing network. The Swedish image processing network had a relative geographical disadvantage. An added complication was probably the dismantling of the Swedish computer industry, implying the dismantling of the distribution channels for general computers from Sweden to an international market. In the absence of a functioning infrastructure for connecting the Swedish image processing network with users internationally, the Swedish image processing firms had not only to develop the technology but also to establish functioning international distribution channels. The Swedish image processing network was mainly disseminated to international users through the primary users' international relationships.

Failures to connect image processing with the user technology

Not all Swedish ventures into digital image technology were as successful as those reported above. The path to digital image technology in Sweden is strewn with temporary successes, futile attempts and failures, such as the picture phone, the OSIRIS-project and the TIPS-system. The TIPS-system collapsed and was abandoned owing to the system's incompatibility with the pre-existing routines of newspaper production. Other failures exhibit a similar pattern of inadequate connection between the system of digital image technology and the technological systems where it was to be applied.

The measuring of non-metallic inclusions in steel

One of the first applications of digital image analysis was in the measuring of non-metallic inclusions in steel, a highly standardized problem with high market potential for the technological solution. The proponents of an image processing solution to the problem in Sweden were mainly the research laboratories of two ironworks, Sandviken and Avesta, and their English supplier of image processing equipment, Cambridge Instruments. They did not follow the core of Swedish image processing actors as the latter coalesced into a tightly knit network, but they remained on the periphery of the evolving Swedish digital image technology. As they struggled to solve the problem of measuring the non-metallic inclusions in steel, the development of steel quality ran ahead of them. Within a few years the quality of steel, with respect to non-metallic inclusions, had improved 50 times. This implied that with the existing image processing equipment the errors would be greater than the factual inclusions. The linkages between digital image technology and the measuring of non-metallic inclusions in steel could not be upheld and so the proponents of the image processing solution to the problem had to turn elsewhere in the search for a solution. They turned back to the old, low technology, manual method, complemented it with the experience gained from image processing and came up with a new standard for the measuring of non-metallic inclusions in steel.[51]

Automatic inspection of printed circuit boards

The story was repeated in the development of a system for the automatic inspection of PC-boards. The development venture into the production of PC-boards for electronic components originated within the PICAP-group as an application of their first image processing computer system. The system was specified by a group of actors in the electronics industry and the PICAP-group developed a prototype for which they were later granted patent rights. In 1980 the project was transferred to Semyre Electronics in Gothenburg for commercial development and the project was granted funds from the special initiative for the commercialization of image processing technology. The system for automatic inspection of PC-boards, named Cavis 8500, was a combination of several technologies: electronics, image processing, laser technology, optics and mechanics. The first problem was to integrate the different technologies into a functional system.

Especially problematic was the development of the laser scanner component. The resolution and accuracy specified was on the edge of what could be achieved with existing laser scanner technology and Semyre devoted a tremendous amount of work to developing the scanner and to building up relationships with actors capable of producing it. A general discussion with representatives of the electronics industry was maintained, but owing to problems, primarily with the scanner, the system was never tested in existing production lines. Finally, in 1986, all of the problems with the scanner appeared to be solved and the future seemed bright and clear. Some additional adaptations were still required but the system was close to completion and ready to be marketed. Then a new blow fell. Owing to the delay in the completion of the project, the opportunity for the technology used in Cavis had been missed. The potential buyers had chosen competing systems and it seemed impossible even to have a reference system installed. What had happened during the development of Cavis? The Cavis system was specified for error detection for unitary conductor widths down to 0.25 mm. Meanwhile the technology for production of PC-boards had developed and the production of PC-boards with conductor widths down to 0.25 mm was relatively unproblematic. Quality problems arose primarily for conductor widths down to 0.1–0.05 mm. Furthermore, the PC-boards were increasingly made up of varying conductor widths. The new specification hit Semyre hard. The laser scanner technology used could not be taken further and at the end of 1986 further development of Cavis was halted.[52]

In the development of Cavis, Semyre had accumulated knowledge and experience regarding not only the development of digital image technology but also the integration of the technology with other technologies. The halting of the Cavis-project left a hole in the business of Semyre. It did not have other image processing projects with which to replace Cavis, so, instead of pursuing internal development of image processing systems, it became a subcontractor to other firms in the image processing network.

ASEA de-emphasizing robotic vision

ASEA's venture into image processing was not a complete success either. The vision system developed for the ASEA robot was functioning perfectly technologically and it was well integrated with the overall robotic system but, while the availability of the industrial robot was 99 per cent, the availability of the vision system was approximately 75 per cent. Thus, the vision system severely lowered the overall economic performance of the robotic system and for most applications suitable for robotic vision alternative solutions often proved more profitable. The market for robotic vision did not grow as projected and to achieve the level of resources required to be devoted to the development of image processing systems it was considered necessary to take the technology beyond robotic vision, and to cover industrial automation in general. Since the strength of ASEA was in industrial robotics and not in industrial automation in general, the company chose the opposite path: to decrease the amount of resources devoted to the development of image processing for industrial automation and thus to focus only on robotic vision. The foremost manufacturer of industrial robots could not abstain from the likelihood of providing its robots with vision systems, but it did not necessarily have to lead the development of robotic vision.[53] ASEA continued to dissolve the development of robotic vision and in 1988 the team responsible for vision was encouraged to set up operation on its own. Consequently, the robotic vision department was spun off from ASEA and a new image processing firm, Sensor Control AB, was established in Sweden. Naturally, ASEA will, for many years to come, remain the most important buyer of Sensor Control's vision systems.

Competence entrapment in the development of digital image technology

A common feature of the abandoned ventures into the development of image processing was the failure to integrate the systems for digital image technology with the pre-existing technological systems, unifying previously separated systems into one whole. This inability to integrate into one whole system may be considered as competence entrapment, which in its turn may be described on three different levels.[54] First, the problems of the TIPS-system and ASEA's robotic vision exemplify a situation where the individual systems could be adapted to the needs of the users, but where further learning and adaptation were disabled through the incompatibility of the different technological systems. This is a general type of competence entrapment, with non-convergence of the different paths of learning, and it will have a similar effect on all proponents of the technology in question. This type of entrapment can, however, be dissolved through the further development of the different systems. It can thus be a problem of timing: of being too early with an oversophisticated technology. The real competence trap arises when the pioneering actors do not have the endurance to wait for the paths to converge but instead abandon their ventures. One way of managing the problem is to look for early trends towards technological convergence and to establish relationships with actors active in this facet of the technological system. This seems to be what Teragon Systems did. It broke up the total system and went for a minor part of digital image technology, electronic darkrooms, which could be used without disrupting the normal production of newspapers. ASEA on the other hand saw few possibilities in further specialization: it was robotic vision or no vision at all. And it chose to let the venture survive in another corporate shape; an entrepreneurial firm which would be less bound by the ASEA-network.

A second type of competence entrapment is revealed in the development of both the Cavis-system and systems for measuring non-metallic inclusions in steel. Here, the paths of development pursued by the firms diverged from the development of the application area. Changes in the technological systems of the potential users made the application of digital image technology obsolete. This trap thus consists of diverging paths of learning. It can also be a problem of timing; in this case digital image technology was applied too late or the solutions were locked into specific paths of learning too early. Sufficient resources had not been accumulated and the relationships between the actors were not strong enough for the path of digital image technology to follow the paths of the application areas. The two cases handled the situation differently. Semyre Electronics persisted in the image processing network, aiming to benefit from the general knowledge and resource bases it had accumulated. In the case of non-metallic inclusions in steel, the actors held more peripheral positions in the image processing network and they turned back to the network of their origins.

Finally, a third type of competence entrapment, which is more firm specific, is shown in the development within ASEA, where the path pursued in research and development diverged from the development path of the company in general.[55] The going concern of a network actor is in general driven by a different logic than is its research and development. The former is concerned with the present and the latter with the future. Ideally these activities should in some way be linked. But research and development is frequently pursued down a path of exploiting a specific technology, which diverges from the path followed in the going concern. Most commonly it is the future that is sacrificed in favour of the present. This type of entrapment will predominantly appear within large and established actors; in entrepreneurial firms the present is the future. Actors can handle the possibility of firm-specific competence entrapment in different ways. It can either be avoided by making research and development totally contingent on the going concern or the problem can be addressed when it has arisen. ASEA handled the situation by spinning off the diverging development, giving it more leeway to establish relationships within the image processing network. Perhaps established firms could play a more important role in the industrial evolution of a nation if they not only accumulated strength in acquiring new technology, but also actively sought to sell or spin off some of its development ventures.[56]

Hence, competence entrapment is about diverging and non-converging evolutionary paths of development and learning. Individual actors cannot control the risk of falling into competence traps: research and development connotes genuine uncertainty. Actors can, however, reduce the risk by avoiding being locked into specific technological solutions and by more consciously taking advantage of the knowledge and resources accumulated in the surrounding network.

The surviving and prospering ventures exhibited a different pattern of evolution, where the image processing systems were adapted to and integrated with other technological systems. Through chains of producer–user relationships complementary investments in the development of new technological systems were interconnected. A new technological system slowly evolved, reinforcing emerging relationships into mutual interdependencies. The coalesced network of the proponents of digital image technology was disseminated, revealing explicit patterns of specialization and division of labour.

Powers countervailing dissemination

The credibility of the Swedish network for the development, production and application of digital image technology was struck a hard blow when it was announced in 1988 that Context Vision had fallen into an acute financial crisis. Image processing firms had balanced on the verge of bankruptcy before, but they had always managed to find last-minute solutions. This was the first time that someone had cancelled payments. The event was especially traumatic because it hit Context Vision, the flagship of Swedish image processing.

Context Vision was a spin-off from the GOP-group, one of the most prestigious research groups in Sweden. When the company was established the founders raised more working capital than any of the other image processing firms. These facts boosted expectations. Context Vision was also the image processing firm mentioned most often in the Swedish press. To a large extent Context Vision represented the public face of Swedish image processing. The expectations raised by the firm were not without substance. The technology of the GOP image processing computer system was regarded as being on the cutting edge of digital image technology. Furthermore, Context Vision had the most professional management and board of directors of all the image processing firms.

Context Vision did not fail to come through. But, as was also the case with most of the new ventures, it took more effort to realize the potential of digital image technology than had initially been expected. Technologically, Context Vision did meet expectations. Several systems were installed at research institutes all over Europe. They had also established a collaborative venture with the French company TRT to realize the processor architecture of GOP in VLSI-circuits.

The market for image processing computers in Europe, however, did not grow at the expected pace and problems arose in serving the European market. The situation in Germany was especially problematic. Context Vision was beginning to have problems in meeting the cost of the European expansion and, as the problems were piling up, it fell into an acute financial crisis.[57] The problems of Context Vision induced possibilities of horizontal co-operation in the image processing network. Negotiations regarding a horizontal merger with the major competitors, Teragon Systems and Imtec, were initiated. All three firms were heavily supported by the Swedish Industrial Development Fund, which recommended that the development of general image processing computers should be concentrated in one firm. The Swedish Industrial Development Fund had taken over the role of STU in supporting the commercialization of Swedish image technology and it now participated in the restructuring of the image processing network. The creditors in general were positive towards a reconstruction of Context Vision and they agreed to accept that only 25 per cent of the debt would be covered if the company were restructured. Both Teragon Systems and Imtec participated in the bidding for Context Vision. The final choice fell in favour of Teragon Systems and in the autumn of 1988 the two former competitors were merged into one large firm, in the hope of Swedish supremacy in digital image technology. The merger involved a changeover of the activities of the firms, moving towards a further specialization in the use of the different computer systems. The Teragon part was to serve the needs of image processing in production systems, while the Context Vision part was to be directed to the needs of science. The merger also brought a reduction in activities and the number of employees was cut from 110 to 70.

The discussions with Imtec were not ended by the merger. Negotiations regarding the possibility of establishing a trinity of Swedish image processing firms continued, under the assumption that together they could establish a leading position in the European market. This vision was not without precedent. A similar pattern was exhibited in the emergence of the Swedish computer industry. Major problems in the development were addressed by concentrating the emerging industry in one large company. Perhaps this is characteristic of the emergence of new technology in small countries with very limited resources for the development of new industries. To be productive it is often thought essential that limited resources are concentrated in the control of a few actors, who are then endowed with the power and capacity to steer the development. And it is quite natural that, when problems arise, these actors will attempt to increase the efficient use of resources by concentrating different development ventures into one. Differentiation and heterogeneity are sacrificed in favour of efficient use of limited resources. At the same time, when the future is uncertain, differentiation is more likely to be productive than is concentration. If it is very likely that one specific path of development will lead to a prosperous future, then a concentrated effort will be productive. If, on the other hand, the future is impossible to predict, as often is the case with technological development, the outcome of a concentrated effort will be purely incidental. The emergence of viable new industrial networks in small countries will, therefore, often be left to pure luck, or to the abundance of previously untapped resources, such as oil or minerals. To increase the return on investments in new industrial networks, a small country must strike a balance between the necessity of concentrating the limited resources and the need for a differentiated development.

The separation of science and industry

The Swedish digital image technology emerged from scientific research, mainly performed at the universities. University research was also instrumental in the early phases of the commercialization of the technology, in that most of the entrepreneurial ventures were spin-offs from the universities. The dissemination of the industrial network, on the other hand, was driven by the business firms primarily addressing the problems of adapting the new technology to, or integrating it with, complementary technologies. Meanwhile, the research organizations continued to address some of the basic problems of machine vision: three-dimensional vision and the processing of moving images. Thus, the dissemination of the image processing network conveyed the separation of the scientific research performed at universities from the technological development performed by business firms. The separation of science and technology was reinforced by the new program for the support of digital image technology issued by STU in 1987.[58] The previous special initiative was designed to promote the commercialization of image processing and it unintentionally resulted in the impoverishing of the scientific institutions. In the renewed initiative the scope is different in that it primarily is designed to promote basic research. One effect of the enterprise is that the development of scientific instruments, the activity on which the first wave of commercialization rested, has been banned and is no longer to be supported. STU also conducted an international evaluation of Swedish research in digital image technology. The evaluation confirmed the prominence of Sweden's scientific position. It specifically identified the Image Coding Group at the University of

Linköping as being on the scientific frontier. But it also pointed at some deficiencies in the Swedish system of scientific research in the field of digital image processing, suggesting collaboration and a concentration of efforts.[59]

One consequence of the reorientation of public support was that new research organizations emerged as winners in the competition for public funds. The Image Coding Groups at the University of Linköping and the Royal Institute of Technology and the Computer Vision and Associative Laboratory at the Royal Institute of Technology became the main beneficiaries in the new STU-program. None of these had previously been assisted within the realms of STU's support of image processing. Image coding was not even considered as being a part of digital image processing prior to the launching of the new program. The main beneficiaries in the special initiative, Physics IV, the Image Analysis Laboratory in Uppsala and the PICAP-group, received relatively less support in the new program. The funding for the GOP-group was, however, maintained at the same level as before.[60] An underlying cause behind the different orientations of the programs was the fact that the two program administrators at STU had different sets of relationships to the actors in the image processing network. While the first administrator was linked to Physics IV, the Image Analysis Laboratory in Uppsala and the PICAP- and GOP-groups, the administrator of the latter program became more closely related to the Image Coding Group.[61]

The beneficiaries within the new initiative were advised to abstain from the development of scientific instruments. As a consequence, the new STU program functioned as a barrier to a constant flow of new technologies from scientific research to industrial innovation. The new directions in the commercial development of digital image technology were to be founded not in scientific research but in industrial applications. As the network of actors spread and the problems in commercializing digital image technology became more apparent, some of the former scientists migrated back to the universities, which further underscored the separation of science and industry.

The separation of scientific research and industrial innovation was not absolute. Informal relationships were maintained between the researchers at the University of Linköping and the firms in the Technology Village. The Image Coding Group in Linköping retained a strong working relationship with the two spin-offs from the group, Sectra and Integrated Vision Products. The relationship between the Department of Electrical Measurement and its spin-off also remained intact, but they were never supported through the STU-programs for digital image technology. The separation of scientific research and industrial innovation in image processing accentuated the dissemination of the image processing network.

The re-entry of the computer industry

The image processing firms no longer stand alone in the fostering of digital image technology. Many technologies previously dominated by analog technology are being converted to digital technology: television, telecommunication, and synthetic speech are examples of this. Since the computer industry lost interest in digital image technology, the development of computer technology has reached new heights, continuously turning out less expensive gadgets of ever higher quality. The capacity of electronic components has increased tremendously, while the cost has decreased, and computer firms now have a new and stronger drive to re-enter into digital image technology. For reasons other than the processing of images, electronics firms in general have increased the processing capacity and memories of ordinary computers. The development of user friendly computer software applications has increased the demand for higher processing capacity. Simultaneously, the development of super-computers and image processing systems has shown that it is also possible to achieve much higher processing capacity in ordinary computers. Today, even personal computers are often equipped with co-processors. The increased capacity of personal computers has made them available for operations demanding high capacity, such as image analysis, and a volume market for image processing components is emerging, which provides new opportunities for self-sustaining growth. The pioneering image processing firms participated in the creation of a market for digital image technology; to what extent can they now reap the benefits? The traditional computer equipment firms, with stronger relationships with potential users, will be in a better position to exploit the new technology.

The re-entry of the computer industry into image processing has completely altered the conditions for the image processing firms. The competition has stiffened, especially in the low-end, fast-growing, consumer market (for instance, desk top publishing), where the computer industry is capturing the major part of the business. On the other hand, the total amount of resources devoted to the development of digital image technology has also increased, creating new opportunities for the image processing firms as specialized firms in an ever expanding digital technology. So far, only one of the Swedish image processing firms, Sectra, has developed image processing equipment for the growing volume market.

RECAPITULATING THE DISSEMINATION OF THE SWEDISH IMAGE PROCESSING NETWORK

Dissemination was characterized by the emphasis on the user side of the new technology and by the establishing of chains of producer–user relationships aiming at, and resulting in, the adaptation of digital image technology to pre-existing technological systems. The previously coalesced Swedish image processing network was disseminated. When the directed support of digital image technology petered out, the proponents of the technology increasingly had to go elsewhere to attract the necessary resources. The evolution of the industrial network had to be re-legitimated in a different context. The interconnection of the network to international networks, producing electronic components and subsystems, and to those applying digital image technology became of increasing importance in lowering the cost of production and in reaching applications which were sufficiently large to encourage further investments in the fine tuning of the computer systems and the development of application software.

In the successful ventures the actors were able to hook up to investments made in the development of complementary technologies: the image processing component was adapted to and integrated with larger technological systems. In the abandoned projects a contrary pattern was revealed, where the actors became trapped by their inability to attract sufficient resources to connect the development of digital image technology with the developments within the field of application.

The Swedish image processing network in 1989

The dissemination of the Swedish image processing network involved the interconnection, in two directions, of the technological system for image analysis: forwards, to the networks in which it was to be applied, and backwards, to networks for the production of the new technology. As actors committed themselves to specific producer–user interactions or else abandoned projects, the focus shifted from the development of image processing as a general solution to all image problems to the development of specific solutions to common sets of problems. The functions performed by individual actors were shifted backwards and forwards, resulting in increasing specialization and division of labour in the industrial network that was developing, producing and applying digital image technology. The proponents of digital image technology could not, however, transform the world on their own and the existence of a critical mass of investments in complementary technologies was a necessary precondition for the evolution to progress from the domination of coalescence to dissemination. The structure of the disseminated image processing network in 1989 is shown in Figure 8.1.[62]

The image processing network of 1989 exhibits a structure totally different from the network of 1983, but with some resemblances to the

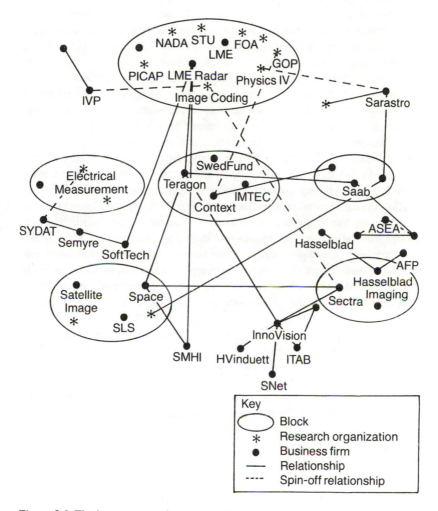

Figure 8.1 The image processing network in 1989. (Note that the graphical representation is not intended to depict the centrality of individual actors.)

network of 1975. The disseminated image processing network is comprised of six relatively homogeneous blocks of actors and several strongly inter-related, but as yet unblocked, sets of actors. The last observation suggests that these actors are becoming increasingly sequentially interrelated. The actors within each of the six identified blocks share some common characteristics. The largest block consists mainly of scientific research groups;

two of the blocks are composed of actors belonging to the same corporate structure; one block contains the pride of Swedish image processing and the remaining two blocks represent the successful venture into digital image transmission and the Swedish space effort. Contrary to the structure in 1975, the blocks are now notably interconnected. The blocks are primarily complementary, representing different components or functions in the network that is developing, producing and applying digital image technology. This pattern is even more apparent when the unblocked actors are taken into consideration. To some extent the dissemination process was contradicted by coalescence tendencies and the pattern from the earlier period was repeated. Parts of the network of actors coalesced and they coalesced towards financial resources. This time, however, these resources were controlled by the Swedish Industrial Development Fund.

The dissemination process has produced only minor changes in the positions of the most central actors. The actors accumulating strength during the coalescence phase retained their position also in the dissemination process. The Space Corporation is still the most central actor but, behind it, some minor changes can be detected. These include the declining importance of STU and the PICAP-group and the increasing centrality of Innovativ Vision and the Image Coding Groups, two of the previously more anonymous actors in the image processing network.[63]

Digital image processing is not yet fully established in our society and not all actors in the Swedish network have yet reached a position where self-sustained growth can be taken for granted. This study, however, shows that even in a small country like Sweden high technology can emerge. Whether this new technology can be transformed into viable economic structures that can persist in the international competition remains to be seen. The once promising Swedish computer industry did not survive increased international competition; will the Swedish ventures into image processing prove to be more viable?

THE EMERGENCE OF THE SWEDISH IMAGE PROCESSING NETWORK: AN EPILOGUE

The case study was introduced by the suggestion that digital image technology is slowly invading the prevalent structures of Western technology. This observation was further emphasized later in the text, where there were claims that the integration of digital image technology with other technological systems and the dissemination of the Swedish image processing network signify the beginning of the final battle of the systems between digital and analog image technology. Eventually digital technology will dominate analog but for centuries to come the systems will coexist. For the foreseeable future they will, side by side, constitute the predominant technological systems for image processing. And even after digital technology has won the battle, pockets will remain where analog technology can prevail, just as direct current is still used for some applications, even though alternating current won the battle of electrical systems several decades ago. The development of efficient interfaces and gateways between digital and analog technology will still be a major problem in the future.

The emergence of an industrial network for image processing in Sweden was the result of the interaction between the emerging new digital image technology and the emerging image processing network. This process, however, reflected the barriers to developing image processing within the computer industry. As these are now being dissolved, it must be assumed that the image processing network will continue to be restructured. And this is certainly what has happened. At the end of 1989 it became obvious that the merger between Teragon Systems and Context Vision, and the plans to integrate Imtec also in this constellation, had failed. A new crisis in Swedish image processing surfaced. This time the outcome had more of a restructuring character. The Context Vision part of the merger was acquired by a Danish firm, with a Finnish firm holding a minority interest, and the name was changed to Struers Vision. The Teragon Systems part was taken over by Innovativ Vision. Imtec has also been restructured but not to the same extent. It has been divided into two: one part, controlled by the founding researcher, has turned back to the roots of the venture, namely cytology; the other part, Imtec, is continuing on the path of digital radiology. At the beginning of 1994 Imtec was acquired by Sectra. Through this acquisition Sectra has built a solid foundation for exploiting the opportunities in digital radiology. Sarastro, the spin-off from Physics IV, has been acquired by the American firm Molecular Dynamics. Thus, the pride of the once promising Swedish image processing either has dwindled into more peripheral positions or is now controlled by foreign interests. Meanwhile, others such as Innovativ Vision and Sectra have emerged as the most prominent image processing firms.

The economic boom has come to an end: economic life is now dominated by a deep recession. The optimism of the 1980s has, in the early 1990s, been superseded by pessimism. The economic crisis is especially severe in Sweden. The bank system is falling apart. All larger banks, except one, have been or are facing the risk of becoming nationalized, this at a time when the winds of liberalization are blowing harder than ever. But Swedish banks are bleeding and the state is taking over to guarantee the depositors' money. During the 1980s the supply of capital seemed almost unlimited. Resources for development of, and investments in, new technology were readily available. Now the supply of development capital is strictly limited and actors are cutting down on investments in new technology. The public sector, which is one of the largest investors in new technology in general and in digital image technology in particular, is working under oppressive economic conditions. Hence, image processing ventures are squeezed from two directions: lower availability of resources for research and development and less demand for new technology. And the economic conditions are worse than ever. More ventures have been scrapped and yet others will follow. For instance, Saab Automation has dropped some of its ventures into digital image technology. Altogether, the re-entry of the computer industry and the less favourable economic climate will produce further restructuring of the Swedish image processing network.

Part IV

Critical revision of the emerging pattern

> The story is told. I think I now see the judicious reader putting on his spectacles to look for the moral. It would be an insult to his sagacity to offer directions. I only say, God speed him in the quest!
>
> Charlotte Brontë: *Shirley*

The story is told and the major findings lie in the storytelling itself and the judicious readers have probably already unpacked the moral of the story. Yet, I cannot resist the temptation of offering some directions as to how to interpret the emergence and evolution of industrial networks. So, let me close by repeating some of the results and giving a critical revision of the emerging pattern of the evolution of industrial networks. This final part is divided into two chapters. In Chapter 9 the major findings of the study are repeated, while in Chapter 10 the implications of the perspective laid before us are outlined.

9 In conclusion

This chapter begins with a recapitulation of the basic ideas resulting from the inquiry into the development of digital image technology and the emergence of the Swedish image processing network. This is followed by a discussion taking us beyond industrial evolution.

RECAPITULATING THE BASIC IDEAS

Technological and industrial development is a two-way road. One cannot be explained without the other. The emergence and evolution of a new industrial structure is a 'doubly dynamic' path-dependent process of accumulation. The process is 'doubly dynamic' in that it is driven by technological as well as social factors. Emerging and evolving are not groups of naturally selected firms, but rather sets of interconnected social activities, that is, industrial networks. The evolutionary process is not characterized, as in the population ecology school, by the growth in number of firms of that industry. Not only actors but also the technology and the industrial structure are emergent and the most interesting facet of industrial evolution lies beyond the sheer numbers of firms or innovations, it lies in how these are interconnected in time and place. Hence, to unravel the evolution of interconnected social activities, it is necessary to start off with a historic and contextual perspective. What is evolving is the industrial network and, to paraphrase Bruno Latour, it must be clearly stated that the industrial network is not what holds us together, it is what is held together.[1] What holds the industrial network together is the interplay of social action and its outcome in terms of a material world. To complicate the picture, both social action and its outcome in terms of a material world come as interconnected entities. Social action takes place in networks of inter-connected actors and the material world forms technological systems. Industrial networks are held together by the unity of networks of actors and technological systems. Or, as John Law and Wiebe Bijker say: 'Indeed, what we call the social is bound together as much by the technical as by the social. Where there was purity, now there is heterogeneity. Social classes, occupational groups, organizations, professions – all are held in place by intimately linked social and technical means.'[2] This also means that change is determined by neither purely social nor purely technical factors. The emergence and evolution of the Swedish image processing network does indeed result from the dynamic interplay between the emergence of a new network of actors and the establishment of a new technological system.

The emergence of image processing networks

Digital image technology bears the marks of many contemporary technologies in that it predominantly emanated from scientific research. In Sweden, the gap between science and industry was bridged not through the diffusion of ideas from science to industry but through scientists migrating to industry, setting up firms on their own. When the international computer industry lost interest in the new technology, its development became dominated by university spin-offs. University research, technological development in both university spin-offs and traditional firms and public policy coincided to bring Sweden to a leading technological position. The technological capabilities have not yet been transformed in to economic growth. Scientific and technological leverage alone is not a sufficient conditions for commercial success. Neither nations nor firms have an equal rate of return on investments in new technologies. Science, technology and industry are linked through institutional and technological structures and it is the historical evolution of these structures that determines the return on investments in research and development. In the case of Sweden, the return on investment in research and development would be higher in pulp and paper technology than in digital image technology. But, while pulp and paper promises only more of the same, digital imaging promised a new industrial future. Digital image technology did not forge a new industrial path; it never became Sweden's return ticket to the computer and electronics industry. Yet, resources were invested and transformed and without doubt the development boosted Sweden's scientific and technological capabilities. The first educational program in computer engineering was instituted by Professor Per-Erik Danielsson, one of the pioneers of digital image technology. The question is: to forge a new industrial path, how much in the way of resources must be invested and who should be making these investments and when?

The industrial network for digital image technology in Sweden emerged and evolved as the network of proponents of digital image technology incessantly developed and adapted pieces of a technological system and both were transformed. It emerged and evolved through actors striving to solve pressing, yet locally perceived, problems. Some of these problems prompted actors to search for new technological solutions. Once the problems were solved and solutions produced, new technological avenues opened up, which motivated the actors to search for more general technological solutions to image problems. In this way a new technological system was developed. The establishment of the technological system encouraged the actors towards rationalizations within the realms of the emerging system. In some corners of the industrial network, digital image technology was integrated with pre-existing technological systems, through actors interacting with leading users of image processing equipment. From a commercial point of view, Swedish digital image technology proved to be less viable than the technological capabilities had promised. This was not because Swedish firms were out-competed by international image processing firms but rather they were overcome by the inertia of the older analog image technologies.

Does the Swedish development constitute a special case: does the development of digital image technology in Sweden differ from that in other nations?[3] First of all, since different countries have different technological capabilities, digital image technology most likely emerged in different clothing in different countries. In the USA, digital image technology was nurtured by military problems and ambitions, while in Great Britain scientific instruments were likely to have been more impelling. Second, it is probable that industrial networks evolved differently in different nations. In the USA the largest image processing firm, Gould Imaging and Graphics Division, is relying heavily upon defence contracts. In Great Britain, Cambridge Instruments is one of the more important firms.[4] Hence, when it comes to specifics, such as the origin of digital image technology and the way in which the national industrial networks evolved, nations will most certainly differ. Yet, while the technological and industrial capabilities differ between nations, technological systems are global and universal: scientific laws know no national borders.

The underlying technological systems, from which digital image technology emerged, are global; the underlying industrial and scientific structures are also highly internationalized. It is therefore most likely that the industrial networks of different countries will show some similarities. Comparing digital image technology in the USA and in Sweden, Björn Wasell and Robert Forchheimer report some striking similarities. In both countries most image processing firms have their roots in university research and they have been established by leading scientists. Furthermore, while economic performance in general has been poor, these firms do not seem to have had any problems in securing additional financing. While public policy has been more important in the European development, Wasell and Forchheimer cite defence contracts as the engine of the American digital image technology.[5] Other sources report similar findings; firms in established industries showed less or no interest in participating in the development of the new technology. Also, on the international scene, the emergence of digital image technology was dominated by small entrepreneurial firms.[6] Today, when the underlying technologies have reached a capacity almost equal to that of specialized digital image technology, the international scene is becoming controlled by more traditional and well established firms. Thus, digital radiology is now dominated by the same firms that dominate traditional radiology and desk top publishing is promoted by computer firms and established suppliers of equipment to the graphic industry.

The emergence and evolution of the Swedish image processing network represents a special case. It was born out of certain scientific, technological and industrial capabilities and it is evolving in the direction set by the past. Yet, even though new industrial networks are connected differently in different nations, the technological system is of a more global nature and there are some striking similarities between the evolution of the image processing networks in different nations. Hence, even though the content of evolution is different, the process might be the same and, more importantly, it might be driven by the same set of factors.

The emergence of industrial networks

The emergence and evolution of a new industrial network has been depicted as occuring in three distinct phases: genesis, coalescence and dissemination. The evolution is 'doubly dynamic' in that the two levels of representation, networks of actors and technological systems, have their own evolutionary logics which occasionally are in harmony, but which most often create tensions and so crave action. The network and the technological system also feed upon each other, so that a change in one requires a change in the other. The industrial network is driven by concurrent socio-technical processes of creation, integration and expansion, where as the evolution of the technological system is promoted by creation of novelty, development and use. The evolution of networks of actors is promoted by three concurrent processes: identification, legitimation and adaptation. Each of these processes has its own values and intentions; they are omnipresent and they do not unfold in one over-arching sequence.

Genesis was characterized by the ascendance of interrelated clusters of innovations emerging from actors independently striving to solve everyday problems. The identification of a new technological system was instrumental in genesis rising from the normal surge of innovative activities. In coalescence the emerging development activities were legitimated and the actors diverged from their origins or converged towards a core of digital image technology, establishing a closely knit network of proponents of the technology and pushing it further towards the establishment of a technological system. The network coalesced and, it did so around the Swedish National Board for Technical Development (STU), the main source of financial resources. Dissemination was characterized by the establishment of different chains of producer–user interactions, adapting and integrating the new technology with the pre-existing technological systems. The primary chains of producer–user relationships, which developed Swedish image technology, were dominated by Swedish actors. But the extension of the Swedish network towards international users as well as the separation of science and industrial innovation were other salient features of dissemination. Ventures which were characterized by insufficient connections between the development of digital image technology and the development within the field of application were eventually abandoned. The actors involved in these ventures did not, however, vanish from the face of the network: they most often scaled down the venture, focusing on particular components of it, or they otherwise benefited from the competencies that had been developed by assuming a more peripheral role. Thus, dissemination resulted in increased specialization and division of labour in the evolving Swedish image processing network.

The three different phases were initiated and prompted by different sets of circumstances. Genesis was initiated by the development of complementary technologies, in this case primarily computer and television technology. This enabled actors to address new problems but more often to develop new, and hopefully more efficient, solutions to old problems. Instrumental in genesis were the changes in the social structure encouraging the search for new solutions and the addressing of new problems. The genesis of the Swedish image processing network produced a heterogeneous cluster of interrelated innovations around the use of computer technology for image analysis. One important precondition for the outcome of genesis was the heterogeneous Swedish industrial and research structure. Another factor stimulating the emergence of the image processing network was the barrier to developing digital image technology that faced computer firms.

The move from genesis to coalescence was propelled by the existence of a critical mass of actors pursuing both similar and complementary research and development. The existence of a critical mass was a necessary condition but not sufficient on its own. To attract the necessary resources to pursue research and development in image processing and thus to usher the evolutionary process into coalescence, the technology had to be legitimated.

The legitimation of technology is a political process and its outcome will most certainly affect the future development. In Sweden, the legitimation of digital image technology favoured the development of the scientific end of image processing. The resources attracted to the development of digital image processing prompted the researchers to move out from the scientific institutes and to establish new business ventures. The coalescence phase produced a closely knit core of actors striving to establish the technological system of image processing.

The transition from coalescence to dissemination was facilitated by the existence of a critical mass of investments in the development of complementary technological systems. Investments in the development of complementary technologies created opportunities for the establishment of producer–user relationships integrating previously separated technologies, thus bridging the gap between image processing and the pre-existing techno-logical systems. So far the dissemination process has resulted in increased specialization and division of labour and in the Swedish image processing network the new technology has in some applications been integrated with the pre-existing industrial structure. But, since the barriers to developing digital image technology within the computer industry have been dissolved, we can expect the international image processing network to continue to be restructured.

To sum up, the emergence and evolution of the Swedish image pro-cessing network can be described as being made up of three evolutionary phases: genesis, coalescence and adaptation. These in turn were given by both technological and social processes: by both creation of novelty, de-velopment and use and identification, legitimation and adaptation. Even if these processes are most commonly understood to happen in consecutive order, it should be stressed that they really must take place concurrently. Creation of novelty is not merely the starting point of a new technological system. Technological evolution is propelled by continuous streams of inventive activities. And even if the initial novelties might be of a more path finding nature, it is subsequent achievements that give the new system its character and specific technological style. Development and use must likewise be omnipresent and concurrent processes. It is in the use of technology that new problems occur and it is in the development that new solutions to these problems are tried and novelties are induced. The direc-tion of the evolution of the technological system is controlled by social processes. A new social group or network of actors often emerges as actors begin to adapt to new sets of actors, with whom they later identify them-selves as being parts of a whole. Only sets of novelties coherent with the interests of identified social groups can induce the birth of a new industrial network. If the proponents of the technological system were not continuously identified and legitimated there would be no force holding the industrial network together, as the network of actors adapts to the interests of actors embracing complementary technological systems, and the industrial network would be dissolved or abandoned. A necessary condition for genesis to be succeeded by coalescence is the existence of similar and complementary R & D ventures; and for coalescence to turn into dissemination, a critical mass of investments in complementary industrial networks is necessary. For a summary of the suggested framework, see Figure 9.1.

Characterizing industrial evolution as if it were composed of distinct phases is quite a common alternative to showing it as a series of ideal sequences, life cycles and trajectories. Several studies show similar results:

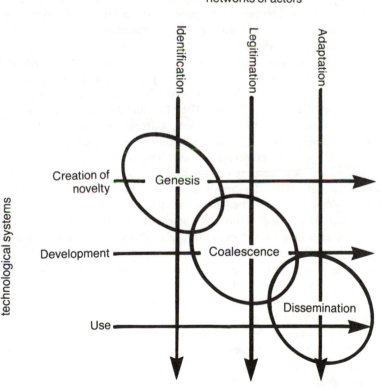

Figure 9.1 A framework for the understanding of the emergence of industrial networks

industries, or markets for that matter, unfold in phases or stages. The perceived view is that societies, economies, industries or markets move from less to more sophisticated levels of development through series of phases or stages; one learns how to sit, how to crawl and then how to walk. Walt Whitman Rostow generalizes the sweep of modern economic history into a sequence of five stages: traditional society, pre-conditions for take-off, take-off, drive to maturity and age of mass-consumption. Rostow furthermore states that all societies can be identified as lying within one of these five stages.[7]

Approaching market and industry evolution, Philip Kotler combines the idealized product life-cycle model with a model of phases through which markets evolve. He suggests that as the product moves along the life cycle, the market will move through five stages of evolution: crystallization, expansion, fragmentation, reconsolidation and, eventually, termination.[8] The pattern is clear: new markets emerge from everywhere as users build preferences for solutions to previously unsatisfied needs. In the expansion stage the market will be unified. Fragmentation and reconsolidation signify the splitting of the market into specific compartments. In other words, genesis, coalescence and dissemination could very well describe the same process. Addressing the issue of technological innovation and the emergence of industries from a social system perspective, Raghu Garud and Andrew H. Van de Ven search for particular sequences of events in the development of cochlear implants.[9] They find that the events can be grouped into four phases: gestation, initiation, start-up and take-off. Gestation represents a period of undirected search for general knowledge, which in initiation is given a specific direction. The industry start-up period is marked by the development of proprietary products by competing firms and by the institutional legitimation of the technology. Industry take-off, finally, seems to be governed more by demand pull factors. Even if the Minnesota study focuses on sequences of events rather than on the evolution of structures, the evolution of cochlear implants and of image processing exhibit some striking similarities. Initiation might result in genesis, start-up in coalescence and take-off in dissemination. It is interesting to note that both a technologically determined evolution of markets and a socially constructed emergence of industries can be interpreted as moving through similar phases of development.

Do business networks also evolve in identifiable stages or phases? In a dynamic evolutionary re-interpretation of the work of Alfred D. Chandler on business history in the USA, Mika Pantzar addresses the issue of network evolution. He suggests that business networks evolve from a dispersed structure into a unified structure, which is transformed into a compartmentalized structure. Unification discloses 'the rise of increasingly extensive systems of interdependence', whereas compartmentalization sig-nifies increased differentiation.[10] Hence, regardless of whether we observe a small business network in Sweden or a big business network in the USA, the results point in the same direction; industrial networks evolve through eras of inception, convergence and divergence.

What does this quest for phases of industrial evolution really prove? That genesis, coalescence and dissemination is a general model of how industrial networks evolve? Or does this prove only that it is possible to divide every process into a number of phases? If we look for general statements we are bound to end up with idealized trajectories or general-ized stage models. The result is often yet another false picture of evolution. In truth there is nothing inevitable about socio-technical evolution. To interpret the changing nature of technological innovation and industrial evolution it is essential that we understand the heterogeneous webs in which technologies and societies are embedded. At the same time we need the phases to structure our stories: to tell us how the stories unfold. This will not, however, help us in understanding the why and what of evolution. To reach this higher level of understanding we must focus on the unique-ness of historical processes.

When we observe a historical development process it is natural to try to interpret its changing character over time. We approach history by dividing it into periods or phases; by dividing it into periods of equal length or into phases which, independent of time, are determined by what characterizes the process. We seek the beginning and the ending of the process and its life there in between. It is in this way that the emergence and evolution of the image processing network in Sweden has been presented as a develop-ment process delineated by three characteristic phases: genesis, coalescence and dissemination. But are these phases merely the result of the observer's delimitation? Reality knows no periods or phases: it knows no beginning or end. It is fully absorbed in the happening. Of course, there is always a beginning, a living and an ending. But do these follow on from each other in one sequence? Do they not happen simultaneously?

In the primeval forest we find germinating seeds, powerful life and decay. Side by side they give the forest its character and they live off and for each other. A germinating seed is born out of potent life and it receives nourishment from decay. At the same time, it is the powerful life that impedes the germinating of seeds. The powerful life chokes its offspring and, in order for the forest to be renewed, infinitely more seeds than trees are required. Under favourable conditions seeds, life and decay will coin-cide and foster a new forest. In hindsight it seems natural that the new forest emerged when and where it did. What beforehand was only one of an infinite number of alternatives will *ex post facto* seem fully logical. If we are interested in the development of a single tree, this process can definitely be described as a sequence of phases: as birth, life and death. And we can answer the question of how a tree develops. However, the why of development – why was the tree born, why did it grow and why did it die – will be hidden in the shadows of the forest. To unravel the why of development, the perspective must certainly be broadened to encompass the whole forest. Although it will still be possible to describe the evolutionary process as a sequence of phases, we must remember that this sequence of phases is primarily a result of the observer's delimitation of time and place. We approach history by dividing it into periods or phases, but this can never be more than a descriptive tool. Neither periods nor phases explain history. Another period or another forest would most certainly produce another sequence of phases. Historical processes are unique. They are determined by the context of time and place and so the interpretation of the course of events can never be generalized. What we can and should do is to seek the why of development: what are the mechanisms and processes behind the course of events?

The evolution of the primeval forest is a natural process, which by definition is untouched by the human, often destructive, hand. It is striving onwards, without any goals or intentions, in a direction set by thousands of years of germinating seeds, powerful life and decay. The evolution of industrial networks, on the other hand, results from human endeavour and is filled with dreams, goals and intentions which are not pointing in just one direction but in many. Also this evolution will unfold in a direction set by achievements in the past. Industrial evolution is a social process controlled by what humans have done and will accomplish. At every point in time the possibilities are set by history. Which possibility is explored is, on the other hand, controlled by the present. Or, as the Swedish author Niklas Rådström puts it: 'The memory is the wind. Oblivion a pertinacious sea current. Without memory we are left drifting. Without oblivion the sea becomes a stagnant water with rotting seaweed.'[11] Evolution is thus controlled, not determined, by the past: it is controlled, not determined, by the present. It is path-dependent (see Figure 9.2).

In our attempts to understand the birth of new industrial networks, our interest lies far beyond the mere creation of novelty, in how that is related to the pre-existing. It is from the existing that the novelty is born, it is from here it is nourished and, until such time as the novelty has accumulated enough resources to generate a self-sustainable development, its future is controlled by the existing. When the novelty has reached this level it is already just another part of the pre-existing. Behind the genesis, coalescence and dissemination of new industrial networks, we have the more

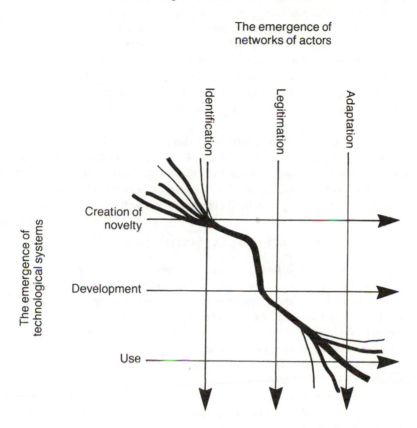

Figure 9.2 The path-dependence of the evolution of industrial networks

fundamental concurrent socio-technical processes of inception, convergence and divergence which incessantly reshape society from within.

The Swedish image processing was first observed as different networks of actors interested in optical character recognition, picture phones, radiology, scientific instruments and air surveillance. Some of these groups opted for general technology and the network converged towards computerized image analysis. This coherent network diverged into new networks of actors supporting the development of digital image archives, robotic vision, image transmission, geographic information systems and other areas. The path has been filled with temporary successes and failures, enclosed by futile attempts and unexplored routes, and paved as the industrial network emerged. There is nothing inevitable in this development. Will the industrial network endure or will it be broken into new, smaller parts that might set off the emergence of yet other, new industrial networks?

The digital image technology of today is neither optimal nor conclusive. Other solutions to the problem of analysing data contained in images might, if they had been legitimated, have guided the evolution of the technology along different paths. If the computer industry had also continued to develop image processing it would probably have affected the design of both the digital image technology and the computer technology. Technological development is path-dependent; the future development will be shaped by the past. In the evolution of the Swedish image processing network, it is interesting to note not only that the technology emerged from technologies where Swedish industry was traditionally strong but also that the image processing network has been unable to catch up in other fields.

LOOKING BEYOND INDUSTRIAL EVOLUTION

To come to terms with technological and social change, we must look beyond the evolution of industrial networks into the heterogeneous web in which it occurs. Understanding evolution means making palpable the heterogeneous networks of scenes and passages which constitute the reality of change. We must ask ourselves, why is change path-dependent? What changes the course of direction? What is the role of individual actors and of public policy? We will close this chapter with an inquiry into how the structures of past and present actions govern technological and social change. The discussion is centred around three themes: network technologies, system-building without system-builders, and the role of public policy and strategic action.

Network technologies

The roots of digital image processing can be traced back at least thirty years and yet the technology is still not fully established in the Western world. The impact of the new technology is far less than expected. The transfer of image processing from science to industry has taken much longer and it has been much more problematic than the proponents of the technology had reason to anticipate. The commercial development of digital image technology has advanced at a much slower pace than projected, and the economic outcome has in most cases been extremely disappointing. Furthermore, the evolution of digital image technology has not advanced at the same pace in all segments; the development in industrial automation has advanced at a much slower pace than the development of remote sensing and the number of scientific instruments produced has far outnumbered the production systems installed.

The technological interdependencies, the system qualities, of digital image technology are controlling the industrial evolution. They set the agenda of development and they constitute the major development problems. Technologies endowed with strong interdependencies are often called network technologies. This concept is most often associated with technologies where the network features are obvious, that is, with electricity, telecommunications and railroads. Two basic problems are associated with network technologies. First of all, given that technological interdependencies exist, there will also be a possibility of gaining from network integration. Network technologies are thus a market imperfection which requires re-allocation of resources. This is the basic problem addressed by economists: how should resources be allocated optimally under conditions of technological interdependencies?[12] The second problem is of a totally different nature; given that technologies are interdependent, how will this affect technological and industrial development? The interdependency of social and material life is not an aberration. It is a matter of fact and it represents the petrified structures on which the future is to be built. To a varying degree, all technologies embody network characteristics in that technological interrelatedness and network integration benefits are present. The first problem is only critical under conditions of strong interdependencies. The development problem is, however, present also under conditions of weak interdependencies. Since the issue here is development rather than resource allocation, the network feature of technology is a critical problem, regardless of the strength of the interdependencies.

In digital image technology, two sources of network externalities or effects are obvious. First, we have internal network effects in the interrelatedness of the components constituting the basic technological system of image processing and, second, we have external effects associated with the interrelatedness of the basic technological system and the surrounding technologies.[13] Technological interdependencies create a momentum, a stable and quiescent structure, which will affect the outcome of the efforts or strategies of change. The direction of change is controlled by underlying, often esoteric, structures. Getting a grip on technological and industrial evolution necessarily means getting a grip on technological interdependencies.

History shows that a common feature in the emergence of all technologies is the flourishing of rival systems, where the potential integration benefits (primarily the external but also the internal benefits) have been difficult or impossible to exploit.[14] The network effects or externalities function both as a driving force propelling further integration and as a barrier to the development of the new technology.[15] In this respect the emergence of an image processing technology in Sweden reveals a similar pattern of development. The coalescence phase saw the development of several rival and incompatible image processing systems. The systems were internally consistent, the components of the systems were adapted to each other and they functioned according to specifications. The choice of components was, however, determined by the functionality of the total system rather than by the cost or performance of the components. Internal integration benefits were difficult to realize. The difficulties were even worse when it came to exploiting the external network effects. Individual users could hardly benefit from the use of other systems. In cartography, one system was employed in the production of maps and another system was installed at the research institutes. The problems of exploiting the network effects encouraged some actors to collaborate in order to standardize image processing technology. AFP, Hasselblad and Sectra, on the one hand, and Teragon, the Space Corporation and SLS, on the other, were two constellations standardizing image processing in certain segments.

The existence of network technologies does not merely have an impact on how we should approach the study of the complex and messy problem of the emergence of new technologies. It also has a significant effect upon the nature of the emergence of new technological systems and upon the behaviour of individual actors. In the next section we will focus attention on network behaviour: on system-building without system-builders. But, before we continue, we will briefly discuss the nature of competition and co-operation in the presence of network externalities. It is often assumed that competition is a necessary prerequisite for change and development. Competition is certainly important, primarily since it indicates the existence of several alternative solutions.[16] Under the presence of network technologies there is, however, the question of how free the choice between existing alternatives can be. In nascent network technologies, freedom of choice is usually restricted by the non-existence of standards, or the risk of lock-in is at least greater when there are no standards. All existing alternative solutions are not equally suited to solve all existing problems. Competition can function both as a selection mechanism, selecting the most efficient solutions, and as a driving force, driving competitors to improve their solutions. The problem is, however, that in the presence of network technologies with no standards, alternative solutions are not interchangeable. Hence, even though alternative solutions might exist, competition functions neither as a selection mechanism nor as a driving force. To increase interchangeability among the alternative solutions, some form of collective action is necessary: standards must be established so that a potential user can choose freely among existing alternatives. Thus, given that we believe that competition has a significant effect upon the pace of development, collective action enabling it must be encouraged.

System-building without system-builders

Technology is never purely technological, it is also social and without human ingenuity and action there will be no technological change. Technological systems are not mere reflections of technologies, technology also directs human action. The notion that technologies or industrial activities are interconnected into systems is not a novel finding of contemporary research. Throughout history different authors have identified this specific quality of technologies and discussed its effect upon technological change. Thorstein Veblen, taking the systems for granted, wrote: 'In more than one respect the industrial system of today is notably different from anything that has gone before. It is eminently a system, self-balanced and comprehensive; and it is a system of interlocking mechanical processes, rather than of skilful manipulation.'[17]. The nature and complexity of the systems rendered Veblen and others such as Frederick W. Taylor and Henry Ford to believe that the systems could effectively be managed, but only by engineers, familiar with the intricacy of the systems.

Others, recognizing the existence of technological systems, have approached the issue differently and focused on the emergence of new systems. Two prominent authors studying industrial dynamics from the perspective of technological systems, Erik Dahmén and Thomas P. Hughes, present converging views on the nature of the emergence of new systems; they both challenge the view of Veblen and they refute the importance of engineers as managers of technological systems. Instead they both put forward entrepreneurs or system-builders as the propelling human force behind economic and technological progress.[18]

A third perspective on the emergence of technological systems, more aligned with the biological theory of evolution, is that they emerge and evolve, without entrepreneurs, system-builders or designers, as self-organizing systems.[19] In biology this would be achieved by the mechanism of natural selection. In industrial economics a similar process could be reproduced through mutual adaptation and self-reinforcement. This would imply that industrial networks could emerge without foresight and grand design through actors acting individually to satisfy internally determined objectives. That is, we would have system-building but no system-builders. But what distinguishes human evolution from biological is that, while biology is without intent, humankind is filled with intentions.

Even though industrial evolution might seem to be without foresight and grand design, it is not without intentions. We have previously argued that the agglomeration of resources around growth poles, such as Silicon Valley, in essence was a self-organizing process without foresight and grand design. Yet it was also suggested that this process was inflated with fulfilled and unfulfilled visions, dreams and intentions. The evolution of industrial networks is driven not by individual system-builders but by the expression and formation of individual and collective intentions. Understanding industrial evolution thus means understanding how intentions are formed and expressed. Of course there will always be system-builders, but they do not necessarily build the same system. And if everyone is striving in different directions a new industrial network will never emerge. Visions, dreams and intentions are not born in thin air. They are to some extent contingent upon the technological systems and to become fulfilled they must be coherent with the ambitions of other actors. Intentions are formed and expressed in networks of actors. This is a social inertia of industrial networks; the interconnections between actors and the intentions of these actors.

Digital image technology in Sweden emerged through actors acting individually to solve locally defined problems and the technological system was established through trial and error and mutual adaptation in the relationships between proponents of complementary components of the system. At first, no one had any intention of initiating a new scientific and technological field, or, if anyone had this intention, it was not shared by others. Some actors assumed the role of system-builders or coordinators and in some cases their activities had a significant impact upon development. One such actor was FOA which, from the late 1960s onwards, coordinated the diverse components of the emerging technological system. The most significant effort of FOA was in identifying image processing as a scientific field. Critical in forming the intention to develop image processing was the creation of the Swedish Association for Automatic Image Processing. This loosely maintained group of prominent researchers shared the dream of general machine vision and they legitimated the scientific end of the evolution of the Swedish image processing network. The special initiative of STU to commercialize image processing expressed the group's intentions and as such it qualifies as a system-building activity. As the number of actors in the network grew, other intentions were formed in specific segments of the technology. The Swedish Space Corporation intended to combine satellite technology, image processing and map production. Hasselblad and Sectra shared the intention of developing digital image transmission. The formulation and expression of intentions represent system-building activities. Despite these activities, the general conclusion must still be that digital image technology and the Swedish image processing network evolved without foresight and grand design: it was system-building without system-builders. This is not the same, however, as stating that neither public policy nor the acts of individual actors matter, an issue that will be discussed in the next section.

Public policy and strategic action matters

The perspective laid out here is rather discouraging, leaving no room for individual actors, planned action or public policy. In all of this continuity is there no room at all for deliberate action? Remember that the aim of most firms and individuals is simply to make a difference in an otherwise indifferent world! And they express their intentions and acts accordingly. Is this for no use at all, other than for the pleasure of sensing the freedom to act? The story told shows unequivocally that public policy and the activities of individual actors have significant effects on the path of development. Public policy and strategic action matter, that is, they make a difference. It is only against the backdrop of technological and social continuity that individuals, governments, firms and humans take measures and act. It is only against this backdrop that the outcome of individual action can be fully understood. The effort can always be directed, but the outcome can never be controlled. The aim of this concluding section is to discuss individual action and the effect of public policy and strategic action.

In the development of digital image processing public policy most certainly was effective. The outcome was not always what had been anticipated or even desired, but public policy mattered in that it pushed the path-dependent development in certain directions. The two major public policy institutes affecting the image processing network have been STU and the Swedish Space Program. The major part of the support for image processing by the latter was without question issued to or through the Space Corporation, hence the centrality of its position. The Swedish Space Program was a concentrated effort to develop Swedish remote sensing and the support was primarily concentrated in one actor. The question is whether this strategy produced a better outcome than alternative strategies would have done. This we will never know. For now, it is sufficient to observe that public policy was effective.

STU directed their support for image processing differently. After some initial years of passive support, STU issued a programmatic support of the technology. STU and the Space Program complemented each other in that, where the Space Program represented concentrated support for application development, STU offered widespread support for the development of digital image technology. This indicates that public activities aimed at the support of new technology interact: the effects of one activity can be strengthened or set off by other activities. The fact that one public institution supports a specific development can legitimate development at other institutions. STU's special initiative towards the commercial development of image processing technology supported the recipients not only directly but also indirectly through legitimating the projects in the eyes of other institutions, such as the Swedish Industrial Development Fund. Public support not only has an effect, it is also self-reinforcing. It is difficult or wellnigh impossible to make a truthful evaluation of endeavours in the development of new technology. A positive assessment from one direction will definitely mean that others will be more eager to participate in supporting the project. Support favours more support.

The formulation and direction of public policy programs towards the development of new technologies is not autonomous. It is very much affected by contemporary research and development. The leading Swedish image processing researchers had a significant impact upon the direction set in STU's special initiative. In the second program STU appointed a new program administrator, who had other connections in the network of actors and so also guided the public support in other directions. The outcome of the special initiative illustrates to the point that public policy is effective, but that the effects are not always the ones desired. The initiative was designed to promote the transfer of image processing from science to industry. No one had anticipated that it would be instrumental in the spin-off of university-based research firms, impoverishing the scientific institutes. Neither was the outcome of the ventures selected for support completely successful. This leads to the conclusion that public policy is effective in directing the efforts to develop new technology, but that it cannot control the outcome of this development. This leaves us rather ambivalent regarding public policy towards technological development. It is encouraging to note that policy measures are effective, but it is discouraging that the outcome cannot always be anticipated or is even desirable. Thus, a word of warning is required: directed public support of technological development ought to be issued with caution and with a certain degree of flexibility. That should not, however, be seen as a recommendation to abstain from experimenting with public policy. If public policy is to evolve it must be subject to variation. Industrial networks evolve as heterogeneous webs of technological and social interdependencies and public policy, if it is to be effective in more ways than in directing the efforts, must reflect this heterogeneity.

Most public policy programs are designed to pick the winners in the technological battle: the support is directed towards the producers of the 'best' technology. National and international evaluations are used to identify research and development projects at the scientific or technological frontier. The Swedish Space Program, rather than selecting the winner, designated it. The STU programs for the development of digital image technology did not differ from the norm. Both of the STU programs for development of digital image technology were designed to support projects at the cutting edge of the technology. The outcome of the special initiative displays the difficulty in selecting future winners. Half of the projects in the first program turned out to be failures and the others were not unquestioned successes. In the second program new actors emerged as scientific and technological leaders. Despite the self-reinforcing mechanisms embodied in the public support of technological development, unsupported actors did emerge as leading actors in the supported field. The designated winners, that is, the recipients of public support, were less successful than those who did not receive public financing. Why? One reason could be that public financing locked the development of the technological solutions into specific paths, while the unsupported actors continuously had to adapt to the changing demands of the users. Another reason is that public policy is effective. It is a structure that creates certain actors. 'Actors and structures are *both* products, and they are created and sustained together: to create an actor is also to create a structure, and vice versa.'[20] That is, policy programs for the development of new industries might create actors who are better at adapting to the requirements of the policy makers than to the changing needs of the users. Here again public policy is effective, it makes a difference. There is a self-fulfilling prophecy about public policy. Programs directed towards entrepreneurship will attract entrepreneurs who need the available resources to start a new business. These entrepreneurs will in time become experts in tapping the public source of support. The fact that a new venture is well adapted to the source of funding does not mean that it will be in line with what its users expect from it now and in the future. Policy directed towards entrepreneurship will foster the development of new firms; policy directed towards technological change will foster new technology. Will it also foster industrial and economic change?

In the special initiative, STU did try new directions in that the aim was to support constellations of both producers and users of new technology. The user–producer constellations were, however, rarely spontaneous, they were constructed in order to pursue specific research projects. The outcome of the constellations was almost catastrophic; when the public support was withdrawn the projects collapsed. On the other hand, the transfer of technology effects were significant. The more spontaneous constellations were much more profitable. In general, users are increasingly being supported as a part of policy programs. If we look at the direct effects of support of users, this policy can be even more problematic to apply than straightforward support of producers of new technology. Picking winning users might prove as difficult as picking the winning innovators.

The public support of image processing technology has generally had a positive effect on the emergence and evolution of the Swedish image processing network. The question, however, is whether a more positive outcome would have followed from a differently directed policy. I do not purport to have the answer to this question. But the critical issues in supporting the development of new technologies are: how much money should be devoted to it, to whom should it be distributed, and when? Perhaps public policy is more effective when it comes to the generation of variety, than when it comes to selection.

What about the impact of individual actors? Implicit in the discussions above has been the tension between the development of the parts and the development of the whole. The outcome of the whole is dependent on the outcome of the parts, which in its turn determines the outcome of the whole. Thus, the outcome of the development pursued by individual actors is dependent on the outcome of the development pursued by all actors. The relationships between actors in an emerging industry are critical and, as Van de Ven and Garud state, 'Each firm competes to establish its distinctive position in the industry; at the same time, firms must cooperate to establish the industry infrastructure.'[21] The strategy of an individual actor should therefore be geared towards both the establishing of a strong position and the strengthening of the whole network. The most successful actors in the Swedish image processing network, the Space Corporation, Hasselblad, Sectra, Innovativ Vision and others, all managed to combine the establishment of a strong position with the establishment of fruitful relationships with others. None of these actors broke the technological frontier; their products were not marked by exceptional technological innovativeness. Instead they managed to link their internal competencies and resources to other actors with complementary competencies and resources. The actors on the scientific and technological frontier, the winners in the hunt for public financing, the nominated winners of the technological battle, the proponents of the 'best' technology, did not live up to the expectations raised by their technological competencies and resources. It does not matter if one can build a better mouse-trap if there are no more mice to be caught; it does not matter if one can build a computer that is 100,000 times faster if users are struggling to learn how to use an ordinary computer. The issue is not what one can do but what one can do in relation to others. The critical question in technological entrepreneurship is not the competencies and resources with which a firm is endowed but how this is linked to related firms. The critical issue is not the innovator but the relationships. Actors are created by the structure and the structure is created by the actors.

Is it competition or co-operation which is most effective in fostering technological and industrial development? In the emergence of image processing in Sweden, competition seems to have induced imitative behaviour, which has fostered similarities, resulting in the coalescence of the network of exchange relationships. Co-operation, on the other hand, seems to have induced innovation, which has fostered dissimilarities, resulting in the dissemination of the network.[22] Competition promises more of the same; it fosters efficiency. Co-operation promises adaptation and change; it fosters effectiveness. Once again the recommendation would be that both co-operation and competition are necessary in the development of new technologies.

The presence of network externalities implies that economic benefits are to be gained from network integration and actors can exploit the network benefits by assuming the role of system-builder or coordinator. The classical economic problems of external economies – indivisibility, uncertainty and appropriability – are obvious.[23] How large are the potential benefits and who can appropriate the profits from integration? Can individual actors appropriate the total benefits from their coordination of the network? Will the prospects of appropriating at least some of the potential benefits be sufficient to motivate actors to engage in the integration of the network? The traditional answer to this type of question is that, in the presence of external economies, individual actors will invest less than is socially desirable in network integration. Thus, the role of public policy should be to support network integration directly or indirectly by encouraging collective actions.

In conclusion, there is certainly room for individual action and actors will behave as if they were autonomous. Individual action is, however, reflected against the social and technological structures of past collective behaviour. Actors can direct their efforts, but they cannot control the outcome. If we are to understand the outcome of action we must understand the heterogeneous web of social and technological activities in which it is implicated.

In international competition, where most industrial nations cherish public institutions for the development of new technology, it is difficult to see how Sweden would be able to maintain and develop a strong position in high technology without resorting to public spending on research and development. The capability of establishing viable positions in emerging technologies – assuming this is desirable, which is not as self-evident as it might seem – rests upon the building of vital and potent public policy towards research and development.[24] This is especially apparent if the technologies of tomorrow will increasingly be emerging from basic research, an activity in which a market economy will under-invest. But how can the gaps between science, technology and industry be bridged? In the final chapter, the inquiry into technological innovation and the evolution of industrial networks will be concluded with a discussion of the implications of the framework outlined.

THE END IS THE BEGINNING

We are living in one world, filled with humans and with human-made objects. There is nothing pure in this world of ours. Objects and people hang together in intricate ways. Intertwined and heterogeneous social and technological structures, which were formed in the past, will affect the present. If we want to understand how our world changes, we must begin with how the structures are intertwined and how they change.[25] On my journey of discovery concerning how the world changes, concerning the emergence and evolution of heterogeneous industrial networks, I have passed many obstacles and I have learned a lot. Yet, somehow, it does not seem enough. There are so many questions unanswered and so many issues that I have not raised. Perhaps I knew more in the beginning than I do now. I have tried to approach industrial evolution from many angles. I have tried structures, phases, paths and, at the end, time sequences. I have not painted one but many images of evolution and maybe this is the answer: to start with a multitude of perspectives and to paint many images.

In the end I have tried to escape from my own preconception, which had led me to the path-dependence of change. If the industrial network is heterogeneous, how can I assume that it will evolve along one path? The alternative would be to search for the particular processes of change. One way of doing this is to begin with what is continuous, what does not change or what changes only in the very long run; second, is to look at what changes only slowly; and third, is to consider what attempts are made to make a difference. The third is only reflected in the first two and it is only effective in terms of the others. What I propose is that change is stability and to understand change we must grasp how the three different sequences with different time horizons hang together. The deep process was referred to as network technologies and it corresponds to use and adaptation. The midrange process was about system-building and it can be linked to development and legitimation. The surface process was about human action and it coincides with creation of novelty and identification. Do not focus on the words used, look at the meaning of what I am trying to say. The world will change not as one structure but as many, not as one process but as many. The task is to unravel social and technological change and we should never allow ourselves to rest in our quest for knowledge of change. Given the observed reality we should always question our interpretations. 'The world was never made; . . . Nothing was born; Nothing will die; All things will change.'

10 Implications

The emergence and evolution of a new industry is a complex and heterogeneous process with many facets. It is enigmatic as change always is. What drives change and how can it be fostered? Why are some ventures successful, while others, once more promising, are failing? We know very little of the forces behind change. Developing new technology is problematic; the room for novelty will always be limited. Resources are not free floating, awaiting to be employed in the development of every new idea that crops up. The room for change and resurrection is squeezed between traditional industries and growing public sectors consuming all available resources. Room must be made or taken for new technologies and industries. The need for new industries is urgent. Can our present society feed its future population and can it provide meaningful employment for everyone? But, how do we foster new technologies and industries? Our knowledge is limited. The truism states that new industries are built upon great heroes and their inventions, which only need sufficient financial backing. We have known this for a hundred years, but still we face change only in confusion. We do not know much at all about the nature of change.

The heroes do not slay the dragons, the great inventions do not go past the scientific journals and more and more money is spent on research and development and less and less is coming out in terms of economic growth. The problem is not a shortage of inventors, innovators and entrepreneurs, nor is it a shortage of knowledge, ideas and inventions or of financial resources. Normally when the need for industrial change comes up in public debate, inventors, firms and policy makers rise up as one and point out the need for more money. How much money should be spent on research and development? From one perspective we might conclude, that since the outcome of the spending is poor, we should increase the spending. On the other hand, before investing more, should we not try to increase the return on the existing investments? I firmly believe that the available financial resources are sufficient. The resources might be misspent, but more money will not solve that problem. We obviously need to address the issue of how to organize the distribution of the spending.

Organized human behaviour, knowledge and ideas and financial backing are necessary but not sufficient conditions for change. The problem lies elsewhere, in the heterogeneous industrial networks in which technological innovation and industrial evolution are embedded. Here we will not find any simple answers. The challenge is not to identify the 'best' actors and the 'best' technologies and to decide how much should be invested. The challenge lies in building public and private policy directed towards the creation and endurance of both actors and structures: to foster the evolution of the whole rather than of the parts.

Fostering technological innovation and industrial evolution is more about building history than about aiming at the future. It is about building industrial networks rather than about supporting spectacular individual actors. It is about building a vital and potent public policy. In passing it was stated that the rate of return on investments in research and development varies. The variation in the rate of return is determined by two factors: prior investments, that is, history, and access to investments in complementary research and development, that is, industrial networks. This means that all actors, industries, regions or nations do not have equal opportunities in transforming research and development into economic benefits. It also means that there is nothing inevitable in technological innovation and industrial evolution. The rate of return on investments in research and development is not absolute and fixed. It can be influenced. The building of history and of industrial networks can substantially raise the capacity to procreate and sustain specific new technologies and industries.

BUILDING HISTORY

The dynamics of technological innovation and industrial evolution are not concealed in the future, they rest in the past. Change is not about en-visioning bright futures, but about building history. History matters and the possibilities are set by the past. The present controls only what possibilities will be explored. Development is about creating possibilities, hence, about building history.

Confining the issue of change to the present and to images of brighter futures yet to come fails to recognize the delimitations set by the past. It treats technological development as if it were only a question of choosing the 'best' alternative, with no attention given to the availability of this alternative. Development is about breaking with the past to establish a new future: a new technology, a new industry and new firms. The future has no history. Its history must be made on the way. Prior investments determine the rate of return on future investments. The accumulation of investments is thus more critical than the absolute level of a specific investment. The logic of this would be to build investments gradually. In building history, small wins and so the creation of traditions would be more critical than innovativeness. The new future must be built on the old and the question should be how to exploit the past in escaping from it.

Different nations and firms have different histories and their capacity to build new histories also differs. The problem in computer technology and electronics in Sweden is the lack of a past. The traditions are, however, strong in other fields such as mechanical engineering, steel, pulp and paper and telecommunications. The rate of return on investments in research and development should also be higher in fields where traditions are strong. This does not mean that new ground cannot be broken in fields were the industrial traditions are less accentuated. Sweden could reach a technologically leading position in digital image technology. The return on investments in technological development seems to vary less than in commercial development. Even if the capacity to generate new technology is equal, the ability to exploit it differs. The nation or firm with the strongest industrial traditions will have a great advantage in appropriating the economic benefits from technological innovation. This is one reason why Japanese firms are tapping into the international scientific and technological community. From the investors' point of view this is clearly problematic, but, if we believe that history matters, we should perhaps encourage more trade in science and technology.

In industry, established firms always have a past, to which the new development can be related. The problem can be the opposite: the past holds such a strong grip over future development that specific endeavours are disabled. The only way round this problem is to create strong links between the past and the new project. Expressing development as an extension of the past makes it more legitimate. The spin-off from a university has a specific problem: the establishing of the firm signifies a break with the past. A new history must be made and some resources must be devoted to building a past. How do we build a past that produces possibilities of making a difference in the future? The critical issue is not what we can do but what we can do for others. Others should thus be brought into the development process as early as possible. Developing new technology should be aimed at making an improved mouse-trap for users to benefit from, not at developing the best possible.

Firms fostering new technology must put all their efforts into finding pockets of the new technology where revenues can be generated today. Two advantages come out of this. Generating revenue is a first important step towards self-sustained growth and it necessitates access to users and suppliers, which enables adaptation; it forces the firm to adapt to the stable structures of the industry. The extreme implication of this is that only firms capable of generating revenues on their own should be candidates for public as well as private support of technological development. A newly established firm developing new technology should never rely solely upon external financing. Financial support of innovation and entrepreneurship is somewhat problematic. Money does not carry history. The investors behind the money might have grand and bright pasts and the financial support might be an opportunity for the recipient to tap into the past of the investors. There is thus a great difference between public and private spending on research and development. Public financing rarely carries history: it only provides money. And money is not sufficient to develop future technologies. Without a past there will be no future.

Fostering the emergence of new technologies and new industries requires the making of a past. This means that business managers, policy makers and scholars of technological and industrial change must have a clear sense of the meaning of history. They must also put effort into understanding the past. It is the past that sets the possibilities. Without a past there can be no sense of direction. Embedded in history are the collective actions of the past. History is not only individuals and events, it is also stable structures, of both inertia and change. Actors create structures and structures create actors. History is the past of the whole. Building history means connecting to the past of others: building history means building networks.

BUILDING NETWORKS

Nations and firms are not equally equipped in developing new industries. The rate of return on investments in research and development varies with investments in complementary technologies. The outcome of technological development depends on the accumulation of investments in research and development, but it is not only the investments in the technology in question that determine the outcome. Critical also is the accumulation of investments in complementary technology. Tapping into complementary investments increases the possibilities of successfully completing the development of new technology. To tap into these investments we must build relationships with the firms developing the complementary technology. Development hinges upon the ability to build relationships and networks. Both firms and nations have an interest in building networks. A firm has to rely upon its network in order to reap the benefits from its activities. The firm's strategy would be to build and manage its relationships. Nations are spending heavily in the support of new technology and industries. Building networks is an essential means to increasing the return on the efforts to create favourable conditions for a dynamic economy.

The problem of technological innovation and industrial evolution lies not in what humans, firms or governments can do but in what they can do for each other. Innovations come in clusters; they come in the shape of technological systems or they must be adapted to the pre-existing system. Technology is reflected in industrial structures, where actors are parts of a greater whole of organized collective behaviour. Changes in the technological system necessitate adaptation in the networks of actors and developing new technology necessitates the building of new networks. No actor can singlehandedly control technological and industrial change. The Thomas Alva Edison of the modern industrial era is not a heroic individual developing great inventions but a network of actors advancing the development of technological systems. Fostering technological innovation and industrial evolution thus means the building of networks.

Building history entails adapting to the stable structures of technology and collective behaviour: it entails the building of networks. Actors can direct their efforts, but they do not control the outcome. It is always mediated through the stable structures of the past and present, through the industrial network. Actors do, however, like to believe that they are in control. Actors perceiving themselves as atomistic, that is, as if they could control both efforts and outcomes, will always be taken by surprise by the unexpected and unintended outcomes of technological change. Their aim would be to minimize the unexpected. However, the problem in innovation and industrial change is not to avoid making mistakes but to learn from mistakes and to take advantage of them. The challenge is to learn to take advantage of unexpected and unintended outcomes.

It is the network rather than the actors that controls the outcome of research and development. The success or failure of technological development is determined by how the actor is related to its network. From a single actor's point of view the management challenge is to learn to exploit the network. In development, the individual actor must learn how to exploit the network. Networks contain both seeds for change and fertilizers: they will induce change, but they also provide the ground for realizing change. Networks are, however, stable structures and if the actor goes against the network nothing will be accomplished. Standing before a development of new technology, the actor must either adapt it to the network or change the network. Changing the network is hard, so the only possibility is to mobilize the network to participate in the development.

Building networks eventually means connecting production and consumption. Our understanding of technological and industrial change is biased towards the production side. The assumption is that if we get the technology right, users will rise and cheer. The experience of change speaks a different language. There is no right technology and the problem of change is on the consumption side. One of the greatest misconceptions in innovation theory is that there exist markets for new technology, that users are only waiting for the opportunity to be overwhelmed by the new opportunities. Markets do not exist, they must be created. Creating markets means building relationships with the users. It means learning from users how to develop technology, which can only be right in the eyes of the beholder. The beholder in this case should be the user and not the producer.

From a societal point of view, building networks is creating an infra-structure for resurrection and change. Most governments take an active role in the fostering of technological innovation and industrial evolution. We know that public policy is effective: it affects the direction of change. The question is: can it be made more productive? A basic problem with subsidies for research and development is that money does not carry networks. Financial support is probably more effective when it targets the enhancement of knowledge. In the development of new industries the structure of the industry, the network, becomes more critical. Public inter-vention is more appropriate in setting off development, in creating variety. In taking variety to the market, the state should assume a less active role. Yet, bridging the gaps between science, technology and industry means building history and networks.

BUILDING PUBLIC POLICY

In thinking of technological innovation and industrial evolution we must ask ourselves: do we need it? Furthermore, do we need public policy to foster it? What has happened to the invisible hand of the market, should we not abstain from intervening in natural processes? Looking at social life, do we really need more technology? Is the time not right to question tech-nology? On the other hand, development will always seem to be the best solution to any problem and, as there are always problems, there will always be advocates for more technology. The urgent problems of over-consumption, over-employment and economic decline can also be addressed through the development of new technologies and new industries. The advocates of development will cry out for more support and they will win. Politicians will claim interest in future development and, since we know that they will affect development, we need also to discuss how to design public policy.

How should a national system for the support of science, technology and industrial innovation be organized? To begin to answer this question I should like to go back more than 350 years, long before the industrial revolution, to the origin of modern scientific thought, to the dark streets of London and to the chambers of Sir Francis Bacon (1561–1626).[1] Long before any apparent connection between science, technology and economic progress, Bacon advocated the pursuit of science in the interest of society. Knowledge is power and so, for efficient production of knowledge, he proposed an organization for the quest of knowledge, a dreamt-of research institute, a Solomon's House of Science. The aim of the foundation was 'the knowledge of Causes, and secret motions of things; and the enlarging of the bounds of Human Empire, to the effecting of all things possible.'[2] The House was to be furnished with all known kinds of instruments for the pursuit of knowledge and there was a distinctive place for persons of science with various capacities. It allowed 'for all grades of ability and varieties of skills in a complex division of scientific labour'.[3] Solomon's House of Science was to harbour: 'Merchants of Light', who were to bring from foreign countries: books, abstracts and patterns of experiment; 'Depredators', who were to collect from books all experiments; 'Mystery-men', who were to collect earlier experiments in science and the mechanical arts; 'Pioneers or Miners', who were to 'try new experiments, such as themselves think good'; 'Compilers', or lesser theorists, who were to examine the accumulated materials, to draw inferences from them; 'Dowry-men' or 'Benefactors', who were to seek to apply this knowledge; the 'Lamps', who, 'after divers meetings and consults of' the whole number, were to undertake to 'direct new experiments, of a higher light, more penetrating into nature than the former'; 'Inoculators', the technicians who were to 'execute the experiments so directed and report them'; and finally, his 'Interpreters of Nature', who would 'raise the former discoveries by experiments into greater observations, axioms and aphorisms.'[4]

Sir Francis Bacon's vision of a scientific community devoted to the gathering of useful knowledge was to be realized in the Royal Society of London, established 1660.[5] The emergence and diffusion of modern scientific thought in most countries was accompanied by the inauguration of academies of sciences, modelled after Solomon's House of Science. The work and philosophy of Sir Francis Bacon was not the only source of the organization and growth of modern science. He was, as he himself would probably have put it, only a child of his time and the time was right for the organization of the pursuit of modern science.

The thoughts underpinning the outline of Solomon's House of Science are as valid today as they were 350 years ago. Indeed, had Sir Francis Bacon been alive today, experiencing the increasing reliance of industrial change upon basic research and being interested in the usefulness of science, he would probably have extended Solomon's House to include technology and industry.[6] He might have added a few capacities and put more emphasis upon the roles of users of scientific discoveries. The people would perhaps be actors, profit motivated companies, and institutions of science and the House might be an industrial network. But, most importantly, and even though the problem is of a different magnitude, he would have incessantly repeated his vision: the pursuit of scientific research, technological development and industrial innovation calls for instruments of various kinds and for actors with various abilities and capacities and with different skills. The degree of heterogeneity affects the likelihood of reaching solutions to perceived problems and effective communication or collaboration can reduce the scale of difference of the produced outcome.[7]

If Sweden, besides its traditional industry, is to maintain and develop a vital and potent national system for the emergence and evolution of new technologies and industries, that is a Solomon's House of Science, Technology and Industrial Innovation, room must be made for scientific organizations and business firms with various abilities and capacities and with different skills, and they must be encouraged to communicate and collaborate. No country can thrive on concentrated efforts on frontier science, technology and industry. Behind the frontier there must exist a viable infrastructure of complementary actors with different capacities. Second rank science might be of greater importance than frontier science in transferring science to industry. Problems should be defined by the inhabitants of the House and they should also decide where to search for solutions. The role of public policy should be to establish and maintain the House: to support communication and collaboration within and between science and industry and to encourage collective action.

There is nothing pure and simple in our industrialized world. Technological and social structures are interwined and inseparable. Taking on the challenge to understand technological innovation and industrial evolution means that we must face the heterogeneous whole. There are not one but many paths to fame and glory. Success is built upon a number of factors and different endeavours might have been successful for different reasons. It is impossible and also dangerous to single out specific factors determining success. Every historical process is unique and, in fostering a specific process, we must look into the nature of the process. No statement regarding how to foster technological innovation and industrial evolution should be made general. Industrial networks are heterogeneous and so too should be the attempts to foster their development. Creating public policy should thus be geared towards building a repertoire of activities and structures to support science, technology and industry. And it is worth remembering that what is true in one case might prove to be false in another.

Notes

INTRODUCTION

1 Two of the first books on industrial networks were Hammarkvist, K-O., Håkansson, H. and Mattsson, L-G., *Marknadsföring för konkurrenskraft* (Marketing for Competitiveness), Malmö: Liber Förlag, 1982; and Hägg, I. and Johanson, J. (eds) *Företag i nätverk* (Firms in Networks), Stockholm: SNS, 1982. Two studies associated with the pioneering years in the development of the network perspective were Benndorf, H., *Marknadsföringsplanering och samordning mellan företag i industriella system* (Market Planning and Coordination between Firms in Industrial Systems), Doctoral Dissertation, Stockholm: Stockholm School of Economics, 1987; and Liljegren, G., *Interdependens och dynamik i långsiktiga kundrelationer: Industriell försäljning i ett nätverksperspektiv* (Interdependence and Dynamics in Customer Relationships), Doctoral Dissertation, Stockholm: Stockholm School of Economics, 1988.

2 In the 1970s three doctoral dissertations focusing differently on new products were presented at the Marketing Department at the Stockholm School of Economics: Valdelin, J., *Produktutveckling och marknadsföring* (Product Development and Marketing), 1974; Brodin, B., *Produktutvecklingsprocesser* (Product Development Processes), 1976; and Hammarkvist, K-O., *Köpprocessen för nya produkter på byggmarknaden* (The Buying Process for New Products in the Construction Industry), 1976. The two first studies represent only minor deviations from the contemporary marketing view on product development. The third study is in this sense much more interesting in that it looks at new products in a larger context, where the adoption of new products is primarily explained by the product's degree of dependency on a system and the interdependencies of the social system of adopters.

3 Freeman, C., 'Networks of Innovators: A Synthesis of Research Issues', *Research Policy* 20(5): 499–514 (1990); pp. 511–12.

4 Usher delineates the process of cumulative synthesis as the sequential order of perception of an incomplete pattern, the setting of the stage, the act of insight and critical revision and full mastery of the new pattern (Usher, A. P., *A History of Mechanical Inventions* [rev. edn 1954], New York: Dover, 1982, pp. 57–83).

1 THE BIRTH OF A NEW INDUSTRIAL NETWORK

1 For an excellent review of the relationship between science, technology and economic growth, see Mowery, D. C. and Rosenberg, N., *Technology and the Pursuit of Economic Growth*, Cambridge: Cambridge University Press, 1989.
2 Landes, D. S., 'Introduction: On Technology and Growth', in Higonnet, P., Landes, D. S. and Rosovsky, H. (eds) *Favourites of Fortune: Technology, Growth, and Economic Development since the Industrial Revolution*, Cambridge, Mass: Harvard University Press, 1991, pp. 1–29; p. 4.

2 SETTING THE STAGE FOR DIGITAL IMAGE TECHNOLOGY

1 For a thorough description of digital image technology see, for instance, Dyring, E., *Nolla etta bild: Den nya bildrevolutionen* (Zero One Image: The New Image Revolution), Stockholm: Prisma, 1984; and Davies, D., Bathurst, D. and Bathurst, R., *The Telling Image: The Changing Balance Between Pictures and Words in a Technological Age*, Oxford: Clarendon Press, 1990. For a discussion of one specific application of the technology, machine vision, see Zuech, N. and Miller, R. K., *Machine Vision*, New York: van Nostrand Reinhold, 1989.
2 Freeman, C. and Perez, C., 'Structural Crises of Adjustment, Business Cycles and Investment Behaviour', in Dosi, G., Freeman, C., Nelson, R., Silverberg, G. and Soete, L. (eds) *Technical Change and Economic Theory*, London: Pinter 1988, pp. 38–66; pp. 45–7.
3 Federation of Swedish Industry, Stockholm, *Industry in Sweden*, Uppsala: Almqvist & Wicksell Boktryckeri AB, 1928, p. 68.
4 Atlas Copco 1873, Ericsson 1876, ABB 1883, Alfa–Laval 1883, Stal–Laval 1893, AGA 1904 and SKF 1907 are some of the firms dominating Swedish industry which were established around the turn of the century. See Hult, J., Lindkvist, S., Odelberg, W. and Rydberg, S., *Svensk teknikhistoria* (Swedish History of Technology), Hedemora: Gidlunds Bokförlag, 1989, p. 244.
5 Some of the inventors and the firms associated with their names are presented in Table 2.3.

Table 2.3 Major Swedish inventors and the firms they established

Inventor	Lifetime	Firm
Gustaf Dalén	1869–1937	AGA
Gustaf de Laval	1845–1913	Stal-Laval
Lars Magnus Ericsson	1846–1926	Ericsson
Alfred Nobel	1833–1896	Nobel Industries
Jonas Wenström	1855–1893	ABB (ASEA)
Sven Wingquist	1876–1953	SKF

Source: Hult, J. *et al.*, *Svensk teknikhistoria* (Swedish History of Technology), p. 245.

6   Kuznets, S., *Modern Economic Growth*, New Haven, Conn: Yale University Press, 1966, p. 9.

7   Ohlsson, L. and Vinell, L., *Tillväxtens drivkrafter – En studie av industriers framtidsvillkor* (The Forces of Growth: A Study of the Future of Industries), Stockholm: Industriförbundets Förlag, 1987.

8   Sölvell, Ö., Zander, I. and Porter, M. E., *Advantage Sweden*, Stockholm: Norsteds Bokförlag, 1991, pp. 59–60. The authors also include a heterogeneous cluster of civil engineering products, centrifugal pumps, gas-related equipment, etc., which they label multiple business.

9   Hultén, S., *Vad bestämmer de svenska exportmarknadsandelarnas utveckling* (What Determines the Development of the Swedish Market Shares), Stockholm: Stockholm School of Economics, 1988, pp. 115–17.

10 Two major national efforts to enhance Sweden's position in high technology are the development of a Swedish fighter aeroplane and the information technology program, modelled after the Japanese national programs.

11 See, for instance, *Ny teknik, teknisk tidskrift* (New Technology, Technical Journal), 1991: 5, pp. 16–21 and *Ny teknik, teknisk tidskrift*, 1991:6, pp. 14 – 17.

12 The section on computer technology in Sweden is primarily based upon Lund, J., *Från kula till data* (From Abacus to Computer), Värnamo: Gidlunds Förlag, 1988, pp. 99–118.

13 In sense parallel data processing does not signify a major break with respect to the computer architecture suggested by von Neumann. The only really non-von Neumann-architecture explored is neural networks.

3   PERSPECTIVES ON TECHNOLOGY AND INDUSTRY

1   Mainstream economics has very little to say with respect to economic growth or technological change, but it has never purported to address these issues. The aim here is not to criticize mainstream economics. For an excellent review of the place of growth and change in mainstream economics, see Nelson, R. R. and Winter, S. G., *An Evolutionary Theory of Economic Change*, Cambridge, Mass: Harvard University Press, 1982.

2   Abramovitz, M., *Thinking About Growth*, New York: Cambridge University Press, 1989, p. 1.

3   Landes, D. S., 'Introduction: On Technology and Growth', in Higonnet, P., Landes, D. S. and Rosovsky, H. (eds) *Favourites of Fortune: Technology, Growth, and Economic Development since the Industrial Revolution*, Cambridge, Mass: Harvard University Press, 1991, pp. 1–29; pp. 1–2.

4   Abramovitz, *Thinking About Growth*, pp. 4–5.

5   Landes, 'Introduction: On Technology and Growth', p. 4.

6   Abramovitz, *Thinking About Growth*, pp. 8–9.

7   Ibid. p. 80.

8   Ibid. p. 11.

9   The economic historian David S. Landes discribes this as three shocks of reality shaking analytical economists. The shocks in his words, are: (1) the pain of growth; (2) the discovery of the so-called residual; and (3) the so-called Japanese miracle of the 1950s and 1960s (Landes, 'Introduction: On Technology and Growth', pp. 8–10).

10 Two representatives of early growth accountants are Abramovitz, M., 'Resource and Output Trends in the United States since 1870', *American Economic*

Review, Papers and Proceedings, May 1956, pp. 5–23; and Solow, R., 'Technical Change and the Aggregate Production Function', *Review of Economics and Statistics*, August 1957, pp. 312–20.

11 Abramovitz, *Thinking About Growth*, pp. 14–15.
12 Ibid. p. 17.
13 In this context 'our' refers to the Western world. Whether humans are the masters or slaves of technology – whether technology is socially constructed or society is technologically determined – is a complex issue of a philosophical nature, which (without any ambition to produce a conclusive answer) will be addressed later. The perspective maintained throughout this work is, however, that technology evolves in interaction between social and technological systems.
14 Veblen, T., *The Engineers and the Price System* [1921], New Brunswick: Transaction Books, 1983, pp. 65–6.
15 Usher, A. P., *A History of Mechanical Inventions* [rev. edn 1954], New York: Dover, 1982, p. 2.
16 Rosenberg, N., *Perspectives on Technology*, Armonk, NY: M. E. Sharpe, 1976, p. 61.
17 Abramovitz, *Thinking About Growth*, p. 116.
18 Schumpeter, J. A., *Capitalism, Socialism and Democracy* [1942], New York: Harper Torchbooks, 1975, p. 84.
19 Schumpeter, J. A., *The Theory of Economic Development* [1934], New Brunswick: Transaction Books, 1983. It is interesting to note that both Marx and Schumpeter praised the inventors and that they both suggested that the outcome of the achievements of the inventors wase determined by the capitalistic system; where Marx criticized the negative effects of the capitalistic society, Schumpeter praised its ability to motivate inventive activities.
20 Rutherford, M., 'Introduction [to the Transaction Edition]', in Commons J. R., *Institutional Economics: Its Place in Political Economy* [1934], New Brunswick: Transaction Books, 1990, p. xxii.
21 Commons J. R., *Institutional Economics: Its Place in Political Economy* [1934], New Brunswick: Transaction Books, 1990, p. 629.
22 Ibid. p. 634.
23 This is consistent also with the three main features of modern economic growth put forward by Moses Abramovitz:

1 The integration of science, technology and business.
2 The discovery, application and exploitation of new knowledge is the outcome of costly and risky investments.
3 The outcome of investments in new knowledge is contingent upon conditions peculiar to individual firms, industries, technologies and countries.

24 Myhrman, J., *The Process of Economic Growth*, Working Paper, Stockholm School of Economics, January 1990.
25 Some of the thoughts of the group are published in a recent book, *Technical Change and Economic Theory*. In the introductory chapter, Cristopher Freeman summarizes the essence of the group's approach to the problem (Dosi, G., Freeman, C., Nelson, R., Silverberg, G. and Soete, L. (eds) *Technical Change and Economic Theory*, London: Pinter, 1988, p. 2).
26 Lindqvist, S., 'Vad är teknik?' (What is Technology?), in Sundin, B. (ed.) *I teknikens backspegel* (In the Mirror of Technology), Stockholm: Carlsons Bokförlag, 1987, pp. 11–33.

27 Lindqvist, S., *Technology on Trial*, Stockholm: Almqvist & Wiksell International, 1984, p. 14.
28 Merton, R. K., 'Singletons and Multiples in Science', in Merton, R. K., *The Sociology of Science*, Chicago, Ill: Chicago University Press, 1973, pp. 343–70; p. 352.
29 Schumpeter, *The Theory of Economic Development*, p. 3.
30 Kuznets, S., *Economic Development, the Family, and Income Distribution*, Cambridge: Cambridge University Press, 1989, pp. 8–9. In general the proponents of technological development cite the positive economic effects of increased employment, increased wealth or improved competitiveness. The critics, on the other hand, often discuss the social consequences of new technology, such as alienation, unemployment or inequality.
31 Braudel, F., *Civilization and Capitalism 15th – 18th Century, 1: The Structures of Everyday Life*, London: Collins, 1981, p. 306.
32 Ibid. p. 306.
33 Utterback, J. M., 'The Dynamics of Product and Process Innovation in Industry', in Hill, C. T. and Utterback, J. M. (eds) *Technological Innovation for a Dynamic Economy*, New York: Pergamon Press, 1979, pp. 40–65.
34 Rosenberg, N., 'Technological Interdependence in the American Economy', in Rosenberg, N., *Inside the Black Box: Technology and Economics*, Cambridge: Cambridge University Press, 1982, pp. 55–80; p. 59.
35 This sequence of development can take different forms. An example elaborate presumed to be valid for the development of technological systems, is:
    invention --> development --> innovation --> transfer -->
    growth --> momentum --> style.
    The same logic, as discussed earlier is also, used to describe the link between science and industry, where the imaginary line is drawn from science to technology to industry. This relationship will be discussed later at the end of the chapter.
36 See, Usher, *A History of Mechanical Inventions*.
37 Schumpeter, *Capitalism, Socialism and Democracy*, p. 110. He finishes the sentence by stating that the former, the capitalistic enterprise, was the propelling force of the latter, the technological progress.
38 Braudel, *Civilization and Capitalism 15th – 18th Century, 1: The Structures of Everyday Life*, p. 334.
39 Ibid. p. 431.
40 Ibid. p. 335.
41 Ibid. p. 435.
42 Hughes, T. P., 'The Evolution of Large Technological Systems', in Bijker, W. B., Hughes, T. P. and Pinch, T. J. (eds) *The Social Construction of Technological Systems*, Cambridge, Mass: MIT Press, 1987, pp. 51–82; p. 51.
43 The perspective on innovation and technological change suggested here is not as novel as it might seem. Francis Bacon had argued for the necessity of perceiving innovations as products of time and place. In his essay 'Of Innovations' he stated: 'As the births of living creatures at first are ill-shapen, so are all innovations, which are the births of time. ...All this is true, if time stood still, which contrariwise moveth so round that a froward retention of custom is as turbulent a thing as an innovation; and they that reverence too much old times are but a scorn to the new. It were good therefore that men in their innovations would follow the example of time itself, which indeed innovateth greatly, but

quietly and by degrees scarce to be perceived.' (Bacon, F., 'Essays', in Robertson, J. M. (ed.) *The Philosophical Works of Francis Bacon, Ellis and Spedding*, London: George Routledge and Sons 1905, pp. 733–814; pp. 764–5).

44 Scherer, F. M., *Industrial Market Structure and Economic Performance*, 2nd edn, Boston, Mass: Houghton Mifflin, 1980, p. 408.

45 Kamien, M. I. and Schwartz, N. L., *Market Structure and Innovation*, Cambridge: Cambridge University Press, 1982.

46 Ibid. p. 22.

47 Bain, J. S., *Industrial Organization*, New York: Wiley, 1959, pp. 6–7 and 110–12.

48 Schumpeter, *Capitalism, Socialism and Democracy*, p. 83.

49 Van de Ven, A. H. and Garud R., *A Framework for Understanding the Emergence of New Industries*, Discussion paper 66, Strategic Management Research Center, University of Minnesota, February 1987, p. 6.

50 Elster, J., *Nuts and Bolts for the Social Sciences*, Cambridge: Cambridge University Press, 1989, pp. 75–7.

51 Dawkins, R., *The Blind Watchmaker*, London: Penguin Books, 1986, p. 21.

52 Darwin, C., *The Origin of the Species* [1859], London: Penguin Books, 1968, pp. 459–60.

53 Sandemose, A., *Varulven* (The Werewolf), Stockholm: Forum, 1986, p. 102.

54 Dawkins, R., *The Selfish Gene*, Oxford: Oxford University Press, 1978, p. 36.

55 Nelson and Winter, *An Evolutionary Theory of Economic Change*, pp. 134–6.

56 Dawkins, *The Selfish Gene*, p. 39.

57 I am arguing against the population ecology perspective on the emergence and evolution of populations of firms, that is, industries. See Hannan, M. T. and Freeman, J., 'The Population Ecology of Organizations', *American Journal of Sociology* 82(5): 929–64 (1977).

58 Later, in Chapter 5, we will provide a more elaborate definition of industrial networks; meanwhile it is sufficient to perceive them as interconnected exchange relationships.

59 Rosenberg, N. and Birdzell, L. E., jun., 'Science, Technology and the Western Miracle', *Scientific American* 263(5): 18–25 (November 1990).

60 Håkansson, H. (ed.) *Industrial Technological Development: A Network Approach*, London: Croom Helm, 1987, p. 4.

61 Hayek, F. A., von, 'The Use of Knowledge in Society', *American Economic Review* 35: 519–30 (1945); pp. 519–22.

62 Ibid. p. 530.

63 Ibid, p. 523 – 524. In this context von Hayek also discusses the relationship between day-to-day adjustments and technological innovation, concluding that the growing interest in the role major changes was inappropriate; stating that the whole economic picture is made up by the constant number of small changes secluded in the statistical aggregates exhibiting a greater stability than the micro-dynamics.

64 I refer here to the theoretical tradition introduced in Nelson and Winter, *An Evolutionary Theory of Economic Change* and also represented by Dosi, G., Freeman, C., Nelson, R., Silverberg, G. and Soete, L. (eds) *Technical Change and Economic Theory*, London: Pinter, 1988.

65 Dosi, G., 'The Nature of the Innovative Process', in Dosi *et al.* (eds) *Technical Change and Economic Theory*, pp. 223–4.

66 Winter, S. G., 'Knowledge and Competence as Strategic Assets', in Teece, D. J.

(ed.) *The Competitive Challenge: Strategies for Industrial Innovation and Renewal*, New York: Harper & Row 1987, pp. 159–84.

67 Michael Polyani, quoted in Nelson and Winter, *An Evolutionary Theory of Economic Change*, p. 76.

68 A similar perspective on knowledge is conveyed by Karin D. Knorr-Cetina in her inquiry into the nature of the manufacture of knowledge. She argues that the manufacture of knowledge is a social process, marked by local, contextual, and social action, situated in time and space. She claims also that this scientific knowledge is manufactured and sustained in resource-relationships constituting the webs of social relationships in which the scientist acts. See Knorr-Cetina, K. D., *The Manufacture of Knowledge: An Essay on the Constructivist and Contextual Nature of Science*, Oxford: Pergamon Press, 1981.

69 The following illustration is solely based upon Lindqvist, *Technology on Trial*.

70 It is interesting to note the contrast between the promptness in trying out the Newcomen engine in Sweden and the delay in the adoption of the subsequent and more efficient Watt engine.

71 Rosenberg, N., 'Why Do Firms Do Basic Research (With Their Own Money)?', *Research Policy* 19(2), 1990.

72 See, for instance, Cantwell, J., 'The Technological Competence Theory of International Production and its Implications', Paper presented at the European International Business Association, 16th Annual Conference, Madrid, 12–15 December 1990.

73 Rosenberg and Birdzell, 'Science, Technology and the Western Miracle', p. 21.

74 We can note that multiplicity, variety and ambiguity are prerequisites for evolutionary modelling of any kind. That is not only in models employing natural selection. For the evolution of society, see Jantsch, E., *The Self-Organizing Universe*, Oxford: Pergamon Press, 1980, pp. 253–62; and for the evolution of technology, see Basalla, G., *The Evolution of Technology*, Cambridge: Cambridge University Press, 1988.

4   A CONTEXTUAL AND HISTORICAL PERSPECTIVE

1 Pettigrew, A. M., *The Awakening Giant: Continuity and Change in ICI*, Oxford: Basil Blackwell, 1985.

2 Merton, T., *No Man is an Island*, Tunbridge Wells, UK: Burns & Oates, 1955, p. xxi.

3 An example of how the message conveyed by John Donne can be applied in business studies is provided in; Håkansson, H., and Snehota, I., 'No Business is an Island: The Network Concept of Business Strategy', *Scandinavian Journal of Management* 5(3): 187–200 (1989).

4 Veblen, T., *The Engineers and the Price System* [1921], New Brunswick: Transaction Books, 1983, p. 72.

5 On the American system of mass-production, see Rosenberg, N., 'Technological Change in the Machine Tool Industry, 1840–1910', in Rosenberg, N., *Perspectives on Technology*, Armonk, NY: M. E. Sharpe, 1976, pp. 9–31; or Hounshell, D. A., *From the American System to Mass Production: The Development of Manufacturing Technology in the United States*, Baltimore, Md: Johns Hopkins University Press, 1984. On Veblen, Taylor and Ford and the American System, see Hughes, T. P., *American Genesis*, New York: Viking Penguin, 1989, pp. 184–294.

6 Usher, A. P., *A History of Mechanical Inventions* [rev. edn 1904], New York: Dover, 1982, pp. 18–19.

7 Giedion, S., *Mechanization Takes Command: A Contribution to Anonymous History* [1948], New York: Norton, 1969; p. 714.

8 Mumford, L., *Teknik och civilisation* (Technics and Civilization; 1934), Göteborg: Vinga Press, 1984.

9 Ibid. p. 15.

10 Gilfillan, S. C., *Inventing the Ship*, Chicago, Ill: Follet, 1935; and Gilfillan, S. C., *The Sociology of Invention*, Chicago, Ill: Follet, 1935. See also Rosenberg, N., 'The Historiography of Technical Progress', in Rosenberg, N., *Inside the Black Box: Technology and Economics*, Cambridge: Cambridge University Press, 1982, pp. 3–33; pp. 7 and 13; and Kelly, P., Kranzberg, M., Rossini,. F., Baker, N., Tarpley, F. and Mitzner, M., 'The Individual Inventor: Entrepreneur', in Roy, R. and Wield, D. (eds) *Product Design and Technological Innovation*, Milton Keynes, UK: Open University Press, 1986, pp. 76–85.

11 Staudenmaier, J. M., S.J., *Technology's Storyteller: Reweaving the Human Fabric*, Cambridge, Mass: MIT Press, 1985, p. 12.

12 Ibid. p. 201.

13 Veblen, T., *Imperial Germany and the Industrial Revolution* [1949], New Brunswick: Transaction Books, 1990.

14 Erik Dahmén articulates the concept of development blocks in his dissertation published in Swedish in 1950. See Dahmén, E., *Entrepreneurial Activity and the Development of Swedish Industry 1919–1939*, American Economic Translation Series, Homewood, Ill: Richard D. Irwin, 1970. In his later work he has developed the concept. See Dahmén, E., 'Development Blocks in Industrial Economics', *Scandinavian Economic History Review*, 1988 (1): 3–14. Also available in Carlsson, B. (ed.) *Industrial Dynamics*, Boston: Kluwer Academic Publishers, 1989, pp. 109–122. The quotation is from the latter, p. 109.

15 Rosenberg, N., 'Technological Interdependence in the American Economy', in Rosenberg, N., *Inside the Black Box: Technology and Economics*, Cambridge: Cambridge University Press, 1982, pp. 55–80; pp. 58–9.

16 David, P. A., 'Some New Standards for the Economics of Standardization in the Information Age', in Dasgupta, P. and Stoneman P. (ed.) *Economic Policy and Technological Performance*, New York: Cambridge University Press, 1987, pp. 206–39; p. 208.

17 Hughes, T. P., 'The Evolution of Large Technological Systems', in Bijker, W. B., Hughes, T. P. and Pinch, T. J. (eds) *The Social Construction of Technology Systems*, Cambridge, Mass: MIT Press, 1987, pp. 51–82; p. 59.

18 In a study of cost reduction of process innovation in the petroleum industry, John Enos divided the innovation process into two phases: the alpha-phase, cost reduction owing to the introduction of the basic innovation, and the beta-phase, cost reductions owing to subsequent improvements. He found that the alpha-phase had much less impact on cost reduction than the beta-phase. Actually the basic innovation accounted for approximately 5 per cent of the cost reduction and subsequent improvements accounted for 95 per cent (Enos, J., *Petroleum, Progress and Profits*, Cambridge, Mass: MIT University Press, 1967) Similar results are reported by Håkansson, H., 'Product Development in Networks', in Håkansson, H. (ed.) *Industrial Technological Development: A Network Approach*, London: Croom Helm, 1987, pp. 84–127; Hollander, S., *The Sources of Increased Efficiency: A Study of Du Pont Rayon Plants*,

226   *Technological innovation and network evolution*

Cambridge, Mass: MIT University Press, 1965; and Wibe, S., 'Change of Technology and Day-to-Day Improvements', *Umeå Economic Studies*, 78, Umeå University, 1978.

19 Hansi Kobes, statement made in the Swedish environmental TV-program, *Miljöbilder*, Channel 2, Sunday 3 February, 1991. See also Fridlund, H., 'Snabb elbil för 75 öre milen', (Fast Electric Car for 10 ¢ /10 km), *Expressen*, Sunday 3 February 1991.

20 Hunter, L., *Steamboats on the Western Rivers: An Economic and Technological History*, Cambridge, Mass: Harvard University Press, 1949.

21 Hughes, T. P., *Networks of Power: Electrification in Western Society, 1880–1930*, Baltimore, Md: Johns Hopkins University Press, 1983, pp. 404–60.

22 Pevsner, N., *Pioneers of Modern Design: from William Morris to Walter Gropius*, Harmondsworth, UK: Penguin Books, 1960, pp. 198–9.

23 Rosenberg, N. and Birdzell, L. E., jun., 'Science, Technology and the Western Miracle', *Scientific American* 263(5): 18–25 (November 1990).

24 Lindqvist, S., *Technology on Trial*, Stickholm, Almqvist & Wiksell International, 1984.

25 Hindle, B. and Lubar, S., *Engines of Change: The American Industrial Revolution*, Washington, DC: Smithsonian Institution Press, 1986, pp. 68–9.

26 Usher, *A History of Mechanical Inventions*, p. 2.

27 The fruitfulness of applying a network perspective to technological development is shown in several studies: Håkansson, H. (ed.) *Industrial Technological Development: A Network Approach* London: Croom Helm, 1987; Håkansson, H., *Corporate Technological Behaviour: Cooperation and Networks*, London: Routledge, 1989; Laage-Hellman, J., *Technological Development in Industrial Networks*, Department of Business Studies, Uppsala University, 1989; and Waluszewski, A., *Framväxten av en ny massateknik: En utvecklingshistoria* (The Emergence of a New Mechanical Pulp Technology: A Development Story), Department of Business Studies, Uppsala University, 1989. None of these studies addresses the issue of the emergence of new technologies and new industrial networks.

28 Veblen, *The Engineers and the Price System*, p. 110.

29 Häkansson, *Corporate Technological Behaviour*, p. 37.

30 I am indebted to Ulf Olsson, Professor in Economic History at the Stockholm School of Economics, for this particular expression of how history matters.

31 David, P. A., 'Computer and Dynamo: The Modern Productivity Paradox in a Not-Too-Distant Mirror', Paper presented at the OECD International Seminar on Science, Technology and Economic Growth, Paris, France, 5–8 June 1989.

32 Gould, S. J., 'The Panda's Thumb of Technology', in Tushman, M. L. and Moore, W. L. (eds) *Readings in the Management of Innovation*, 2nd edn, Cambridge, Mass: Ballinger Publishing 1988, pp. 37–44; p. 37.

33 Glete, J., *ASEA under hundra År 1883–1983: En studie i ett storföretags organisatoriska, tekniska och ekonomiska utveckling* (ASEA Hundred Years 1883–1983: A study of a Large Corporation's Organizational, Technological and Economic Development), Stockholm: Economic History Research Institute, Stockholm School of Economics, 1983, p. 168.

34 Ibid. p. 196.

35 David, P. A., 'Clio and the Economics of QWERTY', *American Economic Review* 75: 332–7 (1985). See also Arthur, W. B., 'Competing Technologies

and Economic Prediction', IIASA, *Options* 2: 10–13 (1984); and Gould, 'The Panda's Thumb of Technology'.

36 Gould, 'The Panda's Thumb of Technology', p. 44. 'The last quirky juxtaposition of uncongenial carnivores' is held to be the shortest English sentence that contains all twenty-six letters.

37 David, 'Clio and the Economics of QWERTY', p. 332.

38 David, P. A., *Path-Dependence: Putting the Past into the Future*, Stanford University, Institute for Mathematical Studies in the Social Sciences, Economic Series, Technical Report 533, November 1988.

39 Ibid. pp. 12–13.

40 Ibid. p. 14.

41 Ibid. p. 17.

42 Arthur, W. B., 'Competing Technologies: An Overview', in Dosi, G., Freeman, C., Nelson, R., Silverberg, G. and Soete, L. (eds) *Technical Change and Economic Theory*, London: Pinters 1988, pp. 590–607; and Arthur, W. B., *Industry Location and the Importance of History*, Centre for Economic Policy Research, No. 84, Stanford University, 1986.

34 David, *Path-Dependence: Putting the Past into the Future*, p. 20.

44 The list presented here is to a large extent similar to the one presented in Arthur, 'Competing Technologies: An Overview', p. 591.

45 These different modes of learning are discussed in David, P. A., 'Learning by Doing and Tariff Protection: A Reconsideration of the Case of the Ante-bellum United States Cotton Textile Industry', in David, P., *Technical Choice, Innovation, and Economic Growth*, Cambridge: Cambridge University Press, 1975, pp. 95–168; and in Rosenberg, N., 'Learning by Using', in Rosenberg, N., *Inside the Black Box: Technology and Economics*, Cambridge: Cambridge University Press, 1982, pp. 120–140.

46 Katz, M. and Shapiro, C., 'Network Externalities, Competition, and Compatibility', *American Economic Review* 75: 424–440 (1985).

47 David, *Path-Dependence: Putting the Past into the Future*, p.16.

48 This is an example of an unfortunate peculiarity that occasionally happens in the pursuit of social science, where one is obliged to quote a source at third hand. The words of Croce are originally quoted in Salvenni, G., *Historian and Scientist*, Cambridge, Mass: Harvard University Press, 1939, p. 88, and quoted again in David, *Path-Dependence: Putting the Past into the Future*, p. 15.

49 Here a fair word of warning is necessary. Criticizing historicism, Karl Popper argued that the search for a general law of evolution would be futile and impossible. He saw the idea that society can move as a whole along one singular path as merely a holistic confusion. According to Popper, social change is made up of numerous independent or interdependent paths of development. Hence, 'history is characterized by its interest in actual, singular, or specific events rather than in laws and generalizations.' Popper is suggesting an institutional and technological analysis of the conditions of progress (Popper, K., *The Poverty of Historicism* [1957] London: Ark Paperbacks, 1986, pp. 105–144; quotation from p. 143).

50 David, *Path-Dependence: Putting the Past into the Future*, p. 16.

51 Schumpeter, J. A., 'Letter to Miss Edna Lonegan, 16 February 1942', in Swedberg, R., *Schumpeter: A Biography*, Princeton, NJ: Princeton University Press, 1991, pp. 229–30; p. 230. This was not, however, a standpoint that he expressed in his earliest writings, where he argued for theoretical economics

and against the use of history and sociology in economics. In his later writings, where he set out to explain dynamic economics, he argued for the necessity of studying dynamic economic processes in their context of time and place.

52 Bloch, M., *The Historian's Craft* [1954], Manchester: Manchester University Press, 1992, p. 29. To make his case Bloch quotes an Arab proverb: 'Men resemble their times more than they do their fathers.'

53 Ibid. p. 48.

54 Schumpeter, J. A., *The Theory of Economic Development* [1934], New Brunswick: Transaction Books, 1983, p. 3.

55 Bloch, *The Historian's Craft*, p. 163.

56 Giedion, *Mechanization Takes Command*, p. 4.

57 Lindgren, H., 'Business History, Historical Economics and Economic Theory: The Bridge-Building Function of Business History', in *The Network of Financial Capital: Essays in Honour of Ragnhild Lundström*, Uppsala Papers in Economic History, Working Paper 9, Uppsala University, 1990, pp. 45–64; p. 53.

58 Quoted in Lewis, B., *History: Remembered, Recovered, Invented*, New York: Touchstone Books, 1975, p. 71.

59 The whole passage including the quote attributed to T. S. Ashton is from David, *Path-Dependence: Putting the Past into the Future*, p. 23.

60 Lindgren, 'Business History, Historical Economics and Economic Theory', p. 53.

61 Popper, *The Poverty of Historicism*, p. 150.

62 Ibid. p. 150.

63 The word choice has been put within quotation marks to indicate that the choice is not a choice in the traditional meaning. We rarely, objectively, set alternative theories against each other, choosing the one best fitted to solve the actual problem. Rather we are socialized into schools of thought, focusing our attention on specific problems and segments of the reality, and the theory adopted is more or less given by the context within which the investigator works.

64 Lindgren, 'Business History, Historical Economics and Economic Theory', p. 60.

65 Popper, *The Poverty of Historicism*, pp. 146–151.

66 Both quotations are from Cipolla, C. M., *Between History and Economics: An Introduction to Economic History*, Oxford: Basil Blackwell, 1991, p. 17.

67 Commons, J. R., *Institutional Economics: Its Place in Political Economy* [1934], New Brunswick: Transaction Books, 1990, pp. 98–102.

68 Ibid. p. 102.

69 Weick, K. E., *The Social Psychology of Organizing*, 2nd edn, New York: Random House, 1979.

70 Feyerabend, P., *Against Method*, rev. edn, London: Verso, 1988, p. 14.

71 There is only one reality and understanding this reality necessarily craves a total perspective. Regardless of disciplinary affiliation it is the whole that counts. Lucien Fevbre, one of the pioneers behind the French Annales school, tells his fellow historians: 'Historians, be geographers. Be jurists too, and sociologists and psychologists.' (Quoted in Burke, P., *The French Historical Revolution: The Annales School 1929–1989*, Cambridge: Polity Press, 1990, p. 2.)

72 Lundgren, A., *Datoriserad bildbehandling i Sverige: En fallstudie* (Computerized Image Processing in Sweden: A Case Report), Working Paper, Stockholm: Stockholm School of Economics, 1985.

73 Lundgren, A., *Datoriserad bildbehandling: Analys av framväxten av ett nytt teknikområde* (Computerized Image Processing: Analysis of the Development of a New Technology), Thesis Proposal, Stockholm: Stockholm School of Economics, 1986.
74 These attempts have been reported in Lundgren, A., 'Coordination and Mobilization Processes in Industrial Networks', in Axelsson, B. and Easton, G. (eds) *Industrial Networks: A New View of Reality*, London: Routledge, 1992, pp. 144–165; and in Easton, G. and Lundgren, A., 'Changes in Industrial Networks as Flow Through Nodes', in Axelsson, B. and Easton, G. (eds) *Industrial Networks: A New View of Reality*, London: Routledge, 1992, pp. 88–104.
75 This basic model has many similarities with some of the theories proposed by the sociologist Anthony Giddens, encompassing a materialistic and a social system put in their particular context of time and place. See Giddens, A., *The Constitution of Society*, Cambridge: Polity Press, 1984. See also Sellstedt, B., *Samhällsteorier: Vad har Giddens, Habermas m fl att säga ekonomer?* (Social Theories: What Have Giddens, Habermas and Others to Tell Economists?), Lund: Studentlitteratur, 1992.
76 Similar ideas are also set forth in Swedberg, R., and Granovetter, M. (eds) *The Sociology of Economic Life*, Boulder, Colo: Westview Press, 1992, pp. 16–19.

5 INDUSTRIAL NETWORKS: NETWORKS OF ACTORS AND TECHNOLOGICAL SYSTEMS

1 I am indebted to Ivan Snehota for this specific expression of network theory.
2 A basic problem, which will not be resolved here, is of course how to delimit the network. In general it can be suggested that network boundaries should be set in accordance with the specific outcome in focus. The network will probably be delimited differently if the outcome is corporate strategies or technological change.
3 For a comprehensive overview of studies related to interactions, relationships and networks, see Ford, D., *Understanding Business Markets: Interaction, Relationships and Networks*, London: Academic Press, 1990. For an overview of contemporary network theory, see Axelsson, B. and Easton, G. (eds) *Industrial Networks: A New View of Reality*, London: Routledge, 1992.
4 Hughes, T. P., *Networks of Power: Electrification in Western Society 1880–1930*, Baltimore, Md: Johns Hopkins University Press, 1983, pp. 38–42.
5 Hughes, T. P., *American Genesis*, New York: Viking Penguin, 1989, pp. 203–220.
6 Greenstein, S. and Ramey, G., *Product Inertia and the Incentive to Innovate*, Centre for Economic Policy Research, No. 149, Stanford University, 1988.
7 Chamberlin, E. H., *The Theory of Monopolistic Competition*, 3rd edn, Cambridge, Mass: Harvard University Press, 1938. He was not the only economist searching for new expressions of competition. It seems that the early 1930s was a ripe period in the field of imperfect competition. Several economists approached the problem independently and among Chamberlin's contemporaries we find Robinson, J., *The Economics of Imperfect Competition*, London: Macmillan, 1933; and Sraffa, P., 'The Laws of Returns under Competitive Conditions', *Economic Journal* 39: 41–57 (1929).
8 Products were differentiated through certain characteristics of their own and through conditions concerning the sale of these products. The sales of an

individual seller were limited and defined by the price of the product, the nature of the product and the advertising outlays.

9 Chamberlin, *The Theory of Monopolistic Competition*, p. 69.

10 This has of course created a decisive momentum favouring the orthodox view in the pursuit of research in industrial economics.

11 Harrod, R. F. and Hobson, J. A., *The Science of Wealth* [4th edn 1911], London: Oxford University Press, 1950, p. 25.

12 Schumpeter, J. A., *The Theory of Economic Development* [1934], New Brunswick: Transaction Books, 1983, p. 61.

13 Alderson was not alone. He represented a strong tradition in the early theory of marketing and he had many predecessors, contemporaries and successors. See Cox, R. and Alderson, W. (eds) *Theory in Marketing*, Chicago, Ill: Richard D. Irwin, 1950. See also Grether, E. T., 'A Theoretical Approach to the Analysis of Marketing', in Cox, R. and Alderson, W. (eds) *Theory in Marketing*, Chicago, Ill: Richard D. Irwin, 1950, pp. 113–24, and Grether, E. T., 'Pioneers in Marketing: Edwin Griswold Nourse', *Journal of Marketing* 22, 1958. A representative of Alderson's successors is Clewett, R. L., 'Integrating Science, Technology, and Marketing: an Overview', in Haas, R. M. (ed.) *Science, Technology and Marketing*, American Marketing Association, 1966 Fall Conference Proceedings, Indiana University, Bloomington, Indiana, pp. 3–20.

14 Alderson, W., *Dynamic Marketing Behaviour*, Homewood, Ill: Richard D. Irwin, 1965, p. 278.

15 Ibid. p. 259.

16 Since this is a study of technological and industrial change I cannot abstain from a further inquiry into Alderson's views on technology. His perspective on technology was as holistic as his approach to marketing theory. Technology constituted a subsystem completely integrated in the organized behaviour system. He expressed the changing technology in terms of the evolution of transactions as a part of the transactional network embraced by a transvection. Technological change was an inductor of changes in transactions which, through the transvection, would necessitate complementary changes to balance the system: a primary interest was how changes travelled through the system. His analysis of technology included the influence of technology in matching heterogeneous supply and demand as well as the sources, characters and dynamic effects of technological change. For a further discussion of how technology has entered into marketing theory, see Lundgren, A., *Technology and Marketing Theory*, Working Paper, Stockholm: Stockholm School of Economics, 1990.

17 It should, however, be noted that Alderson analysed both horizontal competition and vertical transformation.

18 For a discussion of how the need for control has prompted social and industrial change, see Beninger, J. R., *The Control Revolution: Technological and Economic Origins of the Information Society*, Cambridge, Mass: Harvard University Press, 1986. Also quoted in Hughes, *American Genesis*, pp. 298–9.

19 The development of integrated steel mills is an example of division of labour within an industrial system moving in the opposite direction, that is, from division of labour to integration. The problem for an individual firm is, however, the same: interaction with adjacent firms to increase the performance of the firms and the system.

20 The concept of flexible specialization is suggested as a path for economic

recovery by Piore, M. J. and Sabel, C. F., *The Second Industrial Divide: Possibilities for Prosperity*, New York: Basic Books, 1984, pp. 258–308.

21 Ibid. pp. 194–200.
22 Cyert, R. M. and March, J. G., *A Behavioral Theory of the Firm*, Englewood Cliffs, NJ: Prentice-Hall, 1963.
23 Ibid. p. 115.
24 Ibid. pp. 114–125.
25 Thompson J. D., *Organizations in Action*, New York: Mcgraw-Hill, 1967, p. 1.
26 Ibid. pp. 14–24 and 51–82.
27 Both quotations from ibid. p. 162.
28 Pfeffer, J. and Salancik, G. R., *The External Control of Organizations: A Resource Dependence Perspective*, New York: Harper & Row, 1978, p. 19.
29 Ibid. p. 72. Technology, the other basic source of uncertainty suggested by Thompson, is however treated as an integrated part of the environment.
30 Weick, K. E., *The Social Psychology of Organizing*, 2nd edn, New York: Random House, 1979, pp. 164–166.
31 Pfeffer and Salancik, *The External Control of Organizations*, p. 3.
32 Hägg, I. and Johanson, J. (eds) *Företag i nätverk* (Firms in Networks), Stockholm: SNS, 1982, pp. 18–22.
33 Ibid. pp. 14–15. See also Williamson, O. E., *Markets and Hierarchies: Analysis and Antitrust Implications*, New York: Free Press, 1975. Note that even if we can perceive exchange relationships as being on a continuum between price and authoratative control, this does not imply that the aggregated markets, networks and hierarchies are on the same continuum.
34 Håkansson, H., *Corporate Technological Behaviour: Co-operation and Networks*, London: Routledge, 1989, pp. 16 and 27.
35 Ibid. p.16.
36 Ibid. p. 25.
37 Three themes seem to dominate this line of research in industrial networks.

1 Strategic action in industrial networks. See, for instance, Mattsson, L-G., 'Management of Strategic Change in a "Market-as-Networks" Perspective', in Pettigrew, A. (ed.) *The Management of Strategic Change*, Oxford: Basil Blackwell, 1987, pp. 234–256.
2 Internationalization in industrial networks. See, for instance, Johanson, J. and Mattsson, L-G., 'Internationalization in Industrial Systems: A Network Approach', in Hood, N. and Vahlne, J-E. (eds) *Strategies in Global Competition*, London: Croom Helm, 1988, pp. 287–314.
3 Technological development in industrial network. See, for instance, Waluszewski, A., *Framväxten av en ny massateknik: En utvecklingshistoria* (The Emergence of a Mechanical Pulp Technology: A Development Story), Department of Business Studies, Uppsala University, 1989.

38 A few examples do, however, exist. Håkan Håkansson has studied product development in the wood saw and metal drill network. See Håkansson, H., 'Product Development in Networks', in Håkansson, H. (ed.) *Industrial Technological Development: A Network Approach*, London: Croom Helm, 1987, pp. 84–127. Phil Smith has studied the industrial network within a geographic area, the Morecambe Gasfield. See Easton, G. and Smith, P., 'The Formation of Interorganizational Relationships in a Major Gasfield Development', *Proceedings of the International Research Seminar on Industrial Marketing,*

Stockholm School of Economics, 29–31, August 1984. Jens Laage Hellman has studied the pattern of cooperation in R&D networks. See Laage-Hellman, J. and Axelsson, B., *Biotechnological R&D in Sweden – Research Volume, Direction of Research, Pattern of Cooperation: A Study of the Biotechnological R&D Network 1970–1985*, STU-Information 563–1986, Stockholm: Styrelsen för Teknisk Utveckling, 1986.

39 This metaphor regarding change processes accords with the five footnotes to organizational change suggested by James March:

1   Organizations are continually changing, routinely, easily and responsively.
2   Changes in organizations depend on a few stable processes.
3   Theories of change in organizations are primarily different ways of describing theories in action in organizations, not different theories.
4   Although organizational response to environmental event is broadly adaptive and mostly routine, the response take place in a confusing world.
5   Adaptation to a changing environment involves an interplay of rationality and foolishness.

See March, J. G., 'Footnotes to Organizational Change', *Administrative Science Quarterly* 26: 563–77 (1981); p. 563.

40 Håkansson, (ed.) *Industrial Technological Development*, p. 3.
41 Ibid. pp. 4–6.
42 Three other representatives of the increasing interest in innovation as interactive processes are Lundvall, B-Å., 'Innovation as an Interactive Process: From User-Producer Interaction to the National System of Innovation', in Dosi, G., Freeman, C., Nelson, R., Silverberg, G. and Soete, L. (eds) *Technical Change and Economic Theory*, London: Pinter, 1988, pp. 348–69; Hippel, E., von, *The Sources of Innovation*, New York: Oxford University Press, 1988; and Carlson, B. and Jacobsson, S., 'What Makes the Automation Industry Strategic?', Paper presented at the European Association for Research in Industrial Economics, 17th Annual Conference, Lisbon, Portugal, 2–4 September 1991.
43 Lundvall, 'Innovation as an Interactive Process: From User-Producer Interaction to the National System of Innovation', p. 349; and Laage-Hellman, J., *Technological Development in Industrial Networks*, Department of Business Studies, Uppsala university, 1989, pp. 34–5. Laage-Hellman also suggests a third process underlying the increasing needs for technological cooperation: increasing technological complexity leading to the fact that the nature of research and development is becoming increasingly multidisciplinary.
44 Laage-Hellman, *Technological Development in Industrial Networks*, p. 35. Boeing reports the cost of developing new wings for existing aeroplanes as exceeding $US 3 billion. Volvo reports the cost of developing their latest car model to be slightly less than $US 3 billion. Finally, Gillette reports the cost of development of their new razor to be $US 500 million.
45 Håkansson, *Corporate Technological Behaviour*, p. 3. An excellent example of this is provided by Alexandra Waluszewski in her study of the emergence of a new mechanical pulping technique (Waluszewski, *Framväxten av en ny mekanisk massateknik).*
46 Håkansson, *Corporate Technological Behaviour*, p. 37. Compare also with Cantwell, J., 'The Technological Competence Theory of International Production and its Implications', Paper presented at the European International

Business Association, 16th Annual Conference, Madrid, 12–15 December 1990; pp. 11–12.

47 Håkansson, *Corporate Technological Behaviour*, p. 4.

48 The sequential accumulation in industrial networks can be compared with the particular systems of events proposed by Abbot Payson Usher in Usher, A. P., *A History of Mechanical Inventions* [rev. edn 1954], New York: Dover, 1982. Waluszewski, *Framväxten av en ny mekanisk massateknik*, p. 249.

50 Rosenberg, N., 'Why Do Firms Do Basic Research (With Their Own Money)?', *Research Policy* 19(2), 1990.

51 Håkansson, *Corporate Technological Behaviour*, p. 89.

52 Ibid. pp. 88–9. Compare also with the previous discussion of the nature of technological change and with Cantwell, 'The Technological Competence Theory of International Production and its Implications', pp. 10–11.

53 The above mentioned texts on technological development in industrial networks are not the only ones studying this phenomenon. There is a strong tradition in this line of inquiry also in the Netherlands. On product innovation and development in industrial networks see Biemans, W.G., *Developing Innovations within Networks: With Application to the Dutch Medical Equipment Industry*, Doctoral Dissertation, University of Groningen, Groningen, 1989. For a discussion of technical co-operation in industrial networks see Hagedoorn, J. and Schot, J., *Co-operation between Companies and Technological Development*, Working Paper, University of Groningen, Groningen, 1988. Two studies under way regarding issues similar to those discussed in this work are Blauwhof, G., Rossum, van, W., and Zeldenrust, S., 'The Development of Technologies/Towards a Network Analysis', Paper prepared for the Dutch Workshop on Technology Research, Groningen, 31 May – 1 June 1990; and Hicks, E. K. and Rossum, van, W., 'The Developmental Process of Technologies: Combined Insights from Network and Systems Theory', Paper prepared for the Dutch Workshop on Technology Research, Groningen, 31 May – 1 June 1990.

54 Håkansson, *Corporate Technological Behaviour*, p. 18.

55 For a discussion of how network externalities affect the development of industrial networks see Hultén, S., 'On Network Externalities and the Evolution of Networks', Paper presented at the 8th IMP Conference, Lyon, France, September 1992. This conceptual paper suggests that, under norms of economic rationality, network actors will behave so as to reap the economic benefits of network externalities. Hence, the outcome of the evolutionary process would be a network structure contingent upon the network externalities.

56 Johanson, J. and Mattsson, L-G. 'Network Positions and Strategic Action: An Analytical Framework', in Axelsson, B. and Easton, G. (eds) *Industrial Networks: A New View of Reality*, London: Routledge, 1992, pp. 205–217.

57 Harrod and Hobson, *The Science of Wealth*, p. 26.

58 This means that the content of the concept of an industrial network is no different from that of the prevailing network model. What is different is how the concept is represented in lower layers of analysis.

59 David, P. A., 'Some New Standards for the Economics of Standardization in the Information Age', in Dasgupta, P. and Stoneman, P. (eds) *Economic Policy and Technological Performance*, New York: Cambridge University Press, 1987, pp. 206–39; p. 208.

60 A similar view was apparently held by Veblen. One of his interpreters writes:

'Reading Veblen, in contrast, makes us repeatedly conscious of the actually trivial fact that human beings live in a network of relationships of individual and institutional dependencies, which are constantly changing along with ideas and technological development. From this it can, however, also be deduced that this network of relationships can be changed by people.' (Mayer, O. G., 'Introduction [to the Transaction Edition]', in Veblen, T., *Imperial Germany and the Industrial Revolution* [1946], New Brunswick: Transaction Books, 1990, pp vii–xxviii.)

61 Schumpeter, *The Theory of Economic Development*, p. 9.
62 Ibid. p. 66.
63 Van de Ven, A. H. and Garud, R. *A Framework for Understanding the Emergence of New Industries*, Discussion paper 66, Strategic Management Research Centre, University of Minnesota, February 1987, p. 10.
64 See, for instance, Håkansson, *Corporate Technological Behaviour: Co-operation and Networks*; Håkansson, H., 'Evolution Processes in Industrial Networks', in Axelsson, B. and Easton, G. (eds.) *Industrial Networks: A New View of Reality*, London: Routledge, 1992; pp. 129–143; Hertz, S., 'Towards More Integrated Industrial Systems', in Axelsson, B. and Easton, G. (eds) *Industrial Networks: A New View of Reality*, London: Routledge, 1992; pp. 105–128; and Lundgren, A., 'Coordination and Mobilization Process in Industrial Networks', in Axelsson, B. and Easton, G. (eds) *Industrial Networks: A New View of Reality*, London: Routledge, 1992, pp. 88–104.
65 The product life-cycle is one of the most widespread models for the study of product innovation. An excellent inquiry into the nature of the product life-cycle can be found in Duijn, van, J. J., *The Long Wave in Economic Life*, London: George Allen & Unwin, 1983, pp. 20–32. This specific aspect of the life-cycle metaphor is criticized in Gherardi, S., *Development and Decline in Organizational Analogies: A Critical Review*, Working Paper, Dipartimento di Politica Sociale, Universita' Degli Studi Di Trento (no date). Svante Lindqvist criticizes it from another perspective, from the fact that it has focused our interest towards the early phases of the development (Lindqvist, S., 'Changes in the Technological Landscape: The Temporal Dimension in the Growth and Decline of Large Technological Systems', Paper presented at the conference, *The Development of Large Technical Systems*, at the Max Planck Institut für Gesellschaftforschung, Cologne FRG, 25–28 November 1987.
66 A recent and elaborated model of the basic life-cycle metaphor employed on an aggregated level, that is, for industries or technologies, can be found in Dosi, G., 'Technological Paradigms and Technological Trajectories', *Research Policy* 11(3): pp. 147–162, (1982).
67 Schumpeter speaks of discontinuous development propelled by the carrying out of new combinations of the productive means (Schumpeter, *The Theory of Economic Development*, pp. 65–6).
68 So far the suggested model is only slightly different from the perspective on the dynamic interplay between industrial innovation and industrial change proposed by James Utterback in 'The Dynamics of Product and Process Innovation in Industry', in Hill, C. T. and Utterback, J. M., (eds) *Technological Innovation for a Dynamic Economy*, New York: Pergamon Press, 1974, pp. 40–65. The difference basically pertains to the shift in focus from viewing the innovation and industrial change as a sequence of change processes to perceiving them as a number of parallel processes.

6   GENESIS

1 This presentation, entitled, 'The General and Logical Theory of Automata', has been published in John von Neumann's Collected Works (Taub, A. H. (ed.) *Colletced Works of John von Neumann*, Vol. 5, New York: Pergamon Press 1963, pp. 228–328). 'The General and Logical Theory of Automata' is an inquiry into the possibilities of artificial intelligence: into the possibilities of constructing a machine with self-regulating mechanisms. In his work on the theory of automata he suggests a construction of automata similar to that of the human brain. Curiously enough, not until recently have his ideas on automata borne fruit. Neural networks, which currently are presented as the future of computer technology, can be viewed as an extension of von Neumann's theory of automata. For the achievements of John von Neumann, see Aspray, W., *John von Neumann and the Origins of Modern Computing*, Cambridge, Mass: MIT University Press, 1990. In the mid-1960s, Bengt Wedelin and a small group of researchers at the department of Electric Circuits at Chalmers Tekniska Högskola worked on the construction of models of the human brain. The work of this group was to some extent explored in the development of the GOP-image processing computer (Personal interview, Prof. Gösta Granlund).

2 Neumann, von, The General and Logical Theory of Automata, p. 311.

3 Forester, T., *High-Tech Society*, Cambridge, Mass: MIT Press, 1987, p 124.

4 L. M. Ericsson, *Annual Report*, 1970.

5 Åslund, N., 'Digital bildteknik' (Digital Image Technology), *Kosmos*, Svenska Fysikersamfundet, Stockholm, 1984, pp. 73–82; pp. 81–2.

6 Personal interview, Professor Nils Åslund, 10.12.1984.

7 Malmros, G. and Werner, P-E., 'Automatic Densitometer Measurements of Powder Diffraction Photographs', *Acta Chemica Scandinavia* 27: 493–502 (1973); p. 493.

8 Braggins, D. W., 'The Evolution of Quantitative Image Analysers 1963–1981', in Proceedings of the Indian Statistical Institute Golden Jubilee International Conference, *Advances in Information Science and Technology, 1: Pattern Recognition and Digital Technique*, Calcutta, January 1992, pp. 298–315; pp. 298–9.

9 Unpublished list of Quantimet installations at Kjellbergs Successors AB.

10 Braggins, 'The Evolution of Quantitative Image Analysers 1963–1981', p. 300.

11 Yoxen, E., 'Seeing with Sound: A study of the Development of Medical Images', in Bijker, W. B., Hughes, T. P. and Pinch, T. J. (eds) *The Social Construction of Technological Systems*, Cambridge, Mass: MIT Press, 1987, pp. 281–303; p. 292.

12 The official name of the report was; 'Preliminary Design of an Experimental World Circling Space Ship', (Klass, P. J., *Secret Sentries in Space*, New York: Random House, 1971, pp 71–2).

13 It proved to be possible to orbit at lower altitudes and to produce images of higher quality than had initially been expected (ibid. pp. 79–80).

14 Orhaug, T., Eklundh, J-O. and Strand, L., 'Dator kan förvandla bilder till siffror' (Computers Can Change Images into Numbers), *FOA-Tidningen* 7(2): 12–14 (October 1969); p. 12.

15 The fact that Sweden is a neutral country restricts the possibilities of military intelligence directed towards other countries. This does not, however, mean that Sweden is not spying on other countries. A recent book on the history of

Swedish military intelligence reveals both an interest in spying on other countries and a willingness to employ the latest technology in doing so: Ottosson, J. and Magnusson, L., *Hemliga makter: svensk militär underrättelsetjänst från unionskrisen till det kalla kriget* (Secret Powers: Swedish Military Intelligence from the Union Crisis to the Cold War), Stockholm: Tidens Förlag, 1991.

16 Orhaug, T., Nyberg, S. and Granberg, E., 'Optisk "restaurering" gör suddig bild skarp' (Optical Restoration Makes Blurred Images Sharp), *FOA-Tidningen* 6(1): pp. 13–15 (May 1968) Personal interview, Torleiv Orhaug, 10.1.1985.

17 Orhaug, Eklundh and Strand, 'Dator kan förvandla bilder till siffror', pp. 13–14.

18 The group conducted and reported the results of several international study trips to France, Great Britain, the USA and Japan. In 1967 they gave a course in optical signal processing and among the participants in the course we find some of the researchers who were to become pioneers in Swedish image processing: Per-Erik Danielsson, Sten Ahlbom and Gunnar Brodin (source: list of participants course 161, Optisk signalbehandling [Optical Signal Processing], 5–7 April 1967). Orhaug also published a textbook on image processing; see Orhaug, T., *Bilder, bildinformation, bildbehandling* (Images, Image Data, Image Processing), FOA 2 Rapport A2538–51, March 1971.

19 Personal interviews, Per-Erik Danielsson, 17.9.1984, Gösta Granlund, 19.9.1984 and Ingemar Ingemarsson, 12.12.1984.

20 Personal interview, Lars Olsson, 2.10.1984.

21 Personal interview, Lars Dahlström, 25.10.1984.

22 Merton, R. K., 'Singletons and Multiples in Science', in Merton, R. K., *The Sociology of Science*, Chicago, Ill: Chicago University Press, 1973, pp. 343–70; p. 356. The historian Marc Bloch criticizes the preoccupation with origins. He firmly states: 'So in many cases the demon of origins has been, perhaps, only the incarnation of that other satanic enemy of true history: the mania for making judgements' (Bloch, M., *The Historian's Craft* [1954], Manchester: Manchester University Press, 1992, p. 26).

23 For a review of social network analysis, see Knoke, D. and Kuklinski, J. H., *Network Analysis*, Beverly Hills, Ca: Sage, 1982; and Scott, J., *Social Network Analysis: A Handbook*, London: Sage, 1991.

24 Everett, M., 'EBLOC: A Graph-Theoretic Blocking Algorithm', *Social Networks* 5: 323–46 (1983).

25 Sprenger, C. A. J. and Stokman, F. N. (eds) *GRADAP, Manual, version 2.0*, Groningen: iec ProGAMMA, 1989, pp. 327–75.

7   COALESCENCE

1 Morison, E., *Men, Machines and Modern Times*, Cambridge, Mass: MIT University Press, 1966.

2 See, for instance, Fischler, M. A. and Firschein, O., *Intelligence: The Eye, The Brain and The Computer*, Reading, Mass: Addison Wesley, 1987. How this was represented in Sweden is shown in Orhaug, T., *Bilder, bildinformation, bildbehandling* (Images, Image Data, Image Processing), FOA 2 Rapport A2538–51, March 1971; and in Danielsson, P-E., 'Bildbehandling som disciplin och teknik' (Image Processing as Discipline and Technology), in *Bildbehandling inom forskningen* (Image Processing in Science) FRN Rapport 83:10, Stockholm: Forskningsrådsnämnden, 1983, pp. 7–28.

3 Hughes, points out that a salient characteristic of the great inventors of the turn of the century was their freedom to choose problems (Hughes, T. P., *American Genesis*, New York: Viking Penguin, 1989, pp. 53–4).

4 Abrahamsson, S., *Från kristall till molekylstruktur* (From Crystal to Molecular Structure), Datasaab, Linköping, undated. This paper by the inventor of the drum-scanner is an introduction to its usage in X-ray crystallography. The paper also hints at how the scanner can be connected to Datasaab's D21 computer and the available software on this computer.

5 Personal interviews, Torleiv Orhaug, 10.1.1985, and Per-Erik Werner, 11.9.1987.

6 Personal interview, Lars Dahlström, 25.10.1984.

7 Between 1960 and 1970 Imanco Ltd supplied the Swedish market with rudimentary image processing computers and Saab sold a few drum-scanners. Between 1970 and 1980 Saab sold an image reading instrument system to the original inventor, the Department of Electrical Measurement sold one experimental system to ASEA and Saab began to market an image processing system for saw mills.

8 The initiative to establish the Swedish Association for Automatic Image Processing came from Torleiv Orhaug, FOA. The other founding members were Per-Erik Danielsson, the PICAP-group, Nils Åslund, Physics IV and Björn Stenkvist, the Image Laboratory in Uppsala. The fifth leading researcher associated with the rise of image processing in Sweden was Gösta Granlund, representing the GOP-group.

9 Chronhjort, B., 'Datoriserad bildbehandling, kort presentation av insatsområdet' (Computerized Image Processing, Short Presentation of the Special Initiative), STU-internal memo, 13 February 1980.

10 Åsell, P. and Backström, B., 'Industrirelevanta effekter av STUs långsiktiga insatser för kunskapsutveckling, *Preliminär utvärdering, STU* (Preliminary Evaluation), 1 October 1985. This is an evaluation of the effects of STU's special initiatives. It looks at the effects of the special initiative on different areas, such as education, diffusion of knowledge, commercial applications, international networking and development of resources.

11 Table 7.1 (p. 238) presents the groups that received grants within STU's special initiative for digital image processing.

12 The scanner did not become a commercial success. It was only sold to the Image Laboratory at the University of Uppsala and to Lund's Medical Hospital. Personal interview, Nils Åslund, 10.12.1984.

13 Personal interview, Claes-Göran Borg, 28.11.1984.

14 Danielsson, P-E., Pääbo, M. and Kruse, B., 'Automatisk avsyning av mönsterkort: Förslag till prototyp konstruktion (Automatic Inspection of PC-Boards: Prototype Construction), Internal Memo, Linköping University *Lith–ISY–I–0111*, Linköping, 27 September 1976. See also Danielsson, P-E. and Kruse, B., 'Distance Checking Algorithms', *Computer Graphics and Image Processing* 9(12), December 1979.

15 Personal interview, Claes-Göran Borg, 28.11.1984.

16 That the initiative required continuous support to be given to University based research was labelled as presenting too much of a barrier (Chronhjort, 'Datoriserad bildbehandling, kort presentation av insatsområdet').

17 Personal interviews, Björn Kruse, 28.9.1984, and Torleiv Orhaug, 10.1.1985.

18 Personal interviews, Ewert Bengtsson, 6.12.1984, and Sven Olofsson, 26.9.1984.

19 Personal interviews, Lars-Erik Nordell, 17.9.1984, and Sven Olofsson, 26.9.1984.

Table 7.1 Recipients of grants from STU's special initiative for digital image processing

Group	Person responsible	Content	Amount	Partner
GOP-group	Gösta Granlund	Development of image processing computer.	5,229,000 SEK	No industrial partner.
PICAP-group	Per-Erik Danielsson Björn Kruse	Development of image processing computer. Seed-control.	5,219,000 SEK	Initially no industrial partner, later partly Imtec AB.
Image Analysis Laboratory, Uppsala	Björn Stenkvist Ewert Bengtsson	Automatic cell analysis with TV and computer technology	2,691,000 SEK	Privately held, small, medical company.
Semyre Electronics AB	Göran Åsemyr	Automatic inspection of PC-boards.	2,463,000 SEK	PICAP-group.
Physics IV	Nils Åslund Sonny Lundin	Development of a smaller image processing computer, OSIRIS.	2,348,000 SEK	Swedish Space Corporation, Saab–Scania, Gbg, and Hasselblad AB.
Swedish Forest Products Research Laboratory	Staffan Rydefalk	Image analysis of paper fibre.	311,000 SEK	

Note:
A tenth project, under Lars Dahlström, Kockumation AB, concerning robotic vision received 250 000 SEK. But as Dahlström firmly believed that this was far from enough he did not accept the grant.

Source: Chronhjort, 'Datoriserad bildbehandling, kort presentation av insatsområdet'.

20 Personal interview, Hans Skoogh, 27.9.1984.
21 For a discussion of the procedure used to generate the image of the network, see Appendix 1 in Chapter 6.
22 The Katz index for the image processing network in 1975 and 1983 is shown in Table 7.2. For a discussion of the measure of centrality, see Appendix 1 in Chapter 6.

Table 7.2 The Katz index for the image processing network in 1975 and 1983

Year	Min.	Max.	Mean	Median	Var.	Spread	b
1975	0.139	1.284	0.386	0.341	0.061	0.898	0.11111
1983	0.084	1.383	0.374	0.249	0.099	1.009	0.07143

The Katz index of the eight most central actors in the image processing network in 1983 and their ranking for 1975 are given in Table 7.3.

Table 7.3 Katz index for the eight most central actors in 1983

Ranking	Actor	Katz index	Ranking 1975
1	Space Corporation	1.383	10
2	Imtec	1.243	_a
3	PICAP-group	1.117	19
4	STU	1.054	15
5	Physics IV	0.958	4
6	Innovativ Vision	0.877	_b
7	Context Vision	0.831	_c
8	Image Coding Group	0.830	33

Notes:
a. A spin-off from the Image Analysis Laboratory and Teragon System.
b. A spin-off from the PICAP-group.
c. A spin-off from the GOP-group.

8 DISSEMINATION

1 Braggins, D. and Hollingum, J., *The Machine Vision Sourcebook* (Berlin: Springer-Verlag, 1986) reports 268 firms and research organizations in 13 countries in machine vision alone, a sub-category of image processing. The concept of machine vision primarily includes image processing for industrial automation. Two of the major applications, radiology and remote sensing, are therefore excluded from these numbers.

2 In one evaluation between three Swedish (Context Vision/Gop 300A, Imtec/ Epsilon and Teragon 4000) and one American (Gould/IP 9000) image processing computers, Teragon 4000 was ranked first on the basis of user friendliness and technological completeness even though some systems were ranked higher in technological power (Gustavsson, T., *Upphandling av Bildanalyssystem för Medicinska Fakulteten vid Göteborgs Universitet* [Procure- ment of Image Processing System for the Medical Faculty at Gothenburg University], Ärendenummer nr 1/23, Gothenburg University, February 1987).

3 The outcome of basic research is the development of new scientific instruments is discussed in Rosenberg, N., 'Scientific Instrumentation and University Research', Paper presented at the annual meeting of the American Economic Association, New York City, 30 December 1988.

4 Bernal, J., D., *Science and Industry in the Nineteenth Century*, Bloomington: Indiana University Press, 1970, p. 31–3.

5 In recent years the vision of wireless telegraphy has been fulfilled in the guise of cellular phones.

6 Here only a few pioneers are mentioned, bearing in mind that they all had their predecessors, contemporaries and successors.

7 See, for instance, Bernal, *Science and Industry in the Nineteenth Century*, pp. 31–3; Hughes, T. P., *Networks of Power: Electrification in Western Society, 1880–1930*, Baltimore, Md: Johns Hopkins University Press, 1983; and David, P. A., 'Computer and Dynamo: The Modern Productivity Paradox in a Not- Too-Distant Mirror', Paper presented at the OECB International Seminar on Science, Technology and Economic Growth, Paris, France, 5–8 June 1989.

8 A battle of systems seem to be a recurring phenomenon in the progress of society and many lessons are to be found in history. See, for instance, David P. A. and Bunn, J. A., '"The Battle of the Systems" and the Evolutionary Dynamics of Network Technology Rivalries', High Technology Impact Program, Center for Economic Policy Research, Working Paper 15, Stanford University, 1987; and David P. A., 'The Hero and the Herd in Technological History: Reflections on Thomas Edison and the "Battle of Systems"', Center for Economic Policy Research, Technical Paper 100, Stanford University, 1987.

9 For an overview of the emergence of computer technology, see Flamm, K., *Creating the Computer: Government Industry and High Technology*, Washington DC: The Brookings Institution, 1988. The development of computer technology in Sweden is described in Lund, J. *Från kula till data* (From Abacus to Computer), Värnamo: Gidlunds Förlag, 1988.

10 The culture in the growing Silicon Valley is excellently depicted in Rogers, E. M. and Larsen J. K., *Silicon Valley Fever: Growth of High Technology Culture*, London: George Allen & Unwin, 1984.

11 Håkansson, H., *Corporate Technological Behaviour: Cooperation and Networks*, London: Routledge, 1989, pp. 8–9.

12 The question has in no way lost its actuality. The Swedish public policy towards bridging science and technology was in 1993 aimed at recreating the success of Stanford Research Park.

13 Rogers and Larsen, *Silicon Valley Fever*, pp. 32–6.

14 Ibid. pp. 73–4.

15 A theoretical discussion of the evolution of Silicon Valley as a self-reinforcing process is found in Arthur, W. B., *Industry Location and the Importance of History*, Centre for Economic Policy Research, No. 84, Stanford University, 1986.

16 Table 8.1 lists the image processing firms located within research parks.

Table 8.1 Image processing firms located in research parks

Company	Scientific origin	Research park
Teragon Systems	PICAP-group	Technology Village at the University of Linköping
Innovativ Vision	PICAP-group	Technology Village
Sectra	Image Coding Group	Technology Village
Integrated Vision Products	Image Coding Group	Technology Village
Context Vision	GOP-group	Technology Village
Sarastro	Physics IV	Technology Hill at the Royal Institute of Technology
Imtec	Image Analysis Laboratory	'Glunten' at the University of Uppsala

17 Personal interview, Robert Forchheimer, 17.11.1987.

18 None of the research parks has had the anticipated dynamic effects. They have neither renewed nor encouraged regional development. An example of another Swedish research park, which was set up differently but which still did not match expectations, is Novum Research Park. Novum was supposed to be a

centre for biotechnology in Sweden and it was established in the vicinity of Huddinge Medical Hospital. Here the idea was that the research park would attract the establishment of a full university. Novum is an example also of how the establishment of the research park comes to over shadow the reason why it was established: to bridge the distance between science and industry and to induce industrial change. See Sahlin-Andersson, K., *Forskningsparker & företagsrelationer* (Research Parks and Relationships between Firms), Stockholm: RTK, 1990.

19 Personal interview, Lars-Erik Nordell, 17.11.1987.
20 Personal interview, Jan-Olof Brüer, 17.11.1987.
21 *SIND 1988: 1*, 'Sverige: Drivhus för internationell konkurrenskraft?' (Sweden: Hot-house for International Competitiveness?), p. 108.
22 *Expressen*, Thursday, 31 January 1991.
23 The public side of a new technology might seem to be no more than anecdotal; entertaining but still insignificant. But if technological development is not a rational process striving towards optimal solutions, we would end up with a incomplete picture of the process if we overlooked the influence of public politics. Many of our heroic inventors knew the value of good publicity and they were resourceful when it came to playing the publicity game. Edison, for instance, used the fact that New York State executed a man with alternating current to promote for the less harmful direct current, in which he had a vested interest. See Hughes, *Networks of Power*, pp. 106–9.
24 An example of the annual optimism regarding the prospects of image processing is provided by Jonathan B. Tucker, stating that 'growing at a fast-paced 90% annual rate, the vision market was worth $42 million last year (1983) and is expected to exceed $342 million by 1987.' By 1987 as many as half of all of the industrial robots would be sold with vision capabilities (Tucker, J. B., 'Business Outlook: Robot Applications Enhance Vision Sales', *High Technology*, June 1984, p. 61).
25 Personal interviews, Lennart Stålfors, 11.9.1984, and Claes-Göran Borg, 28.11.1984.
26 Personal interview, Lennart Stålfors, 11.09.1984.
27 Personal interview, Lennart Stålfors, 23.11.1987.
28 Personal interview, Lennart Stålfors, 23.11.1987.
29 Personal interview, Jan-Olof Brüer, 17.11.1987.
30 This was also pointed out in an international evaluation of the group. See *STU Information no. 544–1986*, 'Report of Visiting Committee on Swedish Research in Image Processing and Analysis'. This principal weakness has, however, been compensated for by the collaboration with the Computer Vision and Associative Laboratory (NADA), also at the Royal Institute of Technology.
31 Personal interviews, Nils Åslund, 10.12.1984, and Per-Erik Danielsson, 17.9.1984.
32 Personal interview, Nils Åslund, 25.11.1987.
33 Personal interviews, Claes-Göran Borg, 28.11.1984 and 10.11.1987.
34 Personal interview, Sven Olofsson, 26.9.1984.
35 Personal interviews, Björn Kruse, 28.9.1984 and Sven Olofsson, 26.9.1984.
36 The cost of a complete TIPS-system, with work-stations, was SEK 2–3 million. Additional work-stations would cost SEK 100,000–200,000. The total cost would thus be beyond the means of any newspaper (Personal interview, Roger Cederberg, 5.4.1988).

37 Personal interviews, Ingvar Hall, 28.1.1987, Björn Sporsén, 28.1.1987 and Lennart Berg 28.1.1987.
38 Télécommunication Radioélectriques et Téléphoniques is a company within the Philips sphere and the collaborative venture was supported through the Pan-European project for technological development, EUREKA (*SIND 1988: 1*, pp. 110 and 122).
39 Personal interview, Roger Cederberg, 5.4.1988.
40 Grahn, S., and Borg, C-G., *The Sky is Not the Limit: SSC and the Swedish Space Effort*, Swedish Space Corporation: Stockholm, 1982, p. 41.
41 Alstermo, S., 'Satellitbild: Ett Företag i Rymdbolagskoncernen' (Satellite Image AB: A company within the Swedish Space Corporation), *Fjärranalys*, no. 10, November 1983.
42 *Nordisk Kvantif: Subreport 2*, Digital kartans ekonomi (The Economy of Digital Maps), Stockholm: The Economic Reserach Institute at Stockholm School of Economics, 1987.
43 Ibid.
44 Personal interview, Roger Cederberg, 5.4.1988.
45 Personal interview, Roger Cederberg, 5.4.1988.
46 The privatization of Landsat 4 and 5 would not have been sustainable without additional support from the American government.
47 *Nordisk Kvantif: Subreport 1*, Status i Norden beträffande digital, storskalig karta (Digital Maps: Status in the Nordic Countries), Stockholm: The Economic Research Institute at Stockholm School of Economics, 1986.
48 *SIND 1988: 1*, p. 108.
49 Personal interviews, Hans Skoogh, 27.9.1984, Jörgen Lindgren, 5.12.1984, Gösta Erikson, 16.11.1987, and Johan Halling, 18.4.1988.
50 Personal interview, Lars-Erik Nordell, 17.11.1987.
51 Personal interviews, Stig Johansson, 11.3.1987, and Lars Svensson, 26.1.1987.
52 Personal interviews, Göran Åsemyr, 11.9.1984, and 11.11.1987.
53 Personal interviews, Hans Skoogh, 27.9.1984, and Johan Halling, 18.4.1988.
54 For a discussion of competence traps, see Levitt, B. and March, J. G., 'Organizational Learning', *Annual Review of Sociology* 14: 319–40 (1988); and Blichner, L., *Competency Traps and Successful Experimentation*, Working paper, LOS–Senteret, Bergen, Norway, 1990.
55 A similar case, not mentioned before, is the telephone company Ericsson's engagement in digital image technology. At one point it aimed to exploit the connection between computer technology and telecommunication. Then it also got involved in digital image technology. One of its subsidiaries, Erisoft, took over the development at Kockumation, which previously had been developing the first robotic vision system at ASEA. Ericsson, however, encountered severe problems on the computer side of the vision technology and so, to resolve the acute situation, it decided to concentrate on telecommunication. The development of digital image technology, however promising, was pushed aside and it was subsequently sold to C. E. Johansson, an international giant in industrial measurement and control. One part of the venture was, however, spun off into a new image processing firm, Dikon Recognition AB (Personal interviews, Lars Dahlström, 25.10.1984 and 24.11.1987, and Roland Lans, 25.10.1984 and 18.11.1987).
56 When it comes to spin-offs the large firm should ideally participate in the financing of the new venture.

57 *SIND 1988: 1*, pp. 123–4.
58 Wasell, B., 'Ramprogram i datoriserad bildbehandling' (A Program for the Support of Digital Image Technology), *STU Internal Memo 1987–04–23*. In this memo the new 6-year initiative is outlined. The budget for the program is shown in Table 8.2.

Table 8.2 The six-year budget of the digital image technology program

Year	87/88	88/89	89/90	90/91	91/92	92/93
Million SEK	7	10	11.5	12.5	13.2	14

59 *STU Information no. 544–1986.*
60 'Datoriserad bildbehandling, projektkatalog 1990' (Digital Image Technology: Project Catalog 1990), *STU Information no. 769–1990.*
61 The latter program director wrote a report on image processing in the USA, together with the leading researcher in the Image Coding group. See Wasell, B. and Forchheimer, R., 'Bildbehandlingssystem för industrin: En studie av leverantörsföretag i USA' (Image Processing Systems for Industry: A Study of Suppliers in the USA), *Sveriges Tekniska Attachéer, Utlandsrapport, USA U2 8702*. The program administrator later left STU and became the president of Integrated Vision Products, a spin-off from the Image Coding group.
62 For a discussion of the procedure used to generate the image of the network, see Appendix 1 to Chapter 6.
63 The Katz index for the image processing network in 1975, 1983 and 1989 is given in Table 8.3. For a discussion of the measure of centrality, see Appendix 1 to Chapter 6.

Table 8.3 The Katz index for the image processing network in 1975, 1983 and 1989

Year	Min.	Max.	Mean	Median	Var.	Spread	b
1975	0.139	1.284	0.386	0.341	0.061	0.898	0.11111
1983	0.084	1.383	0.374	0.249	0.099	1.009	0.07143
1989	0.100	1.285	0.347	0.236	0.075	0.938	0.08333

The Katz index of the eight most central actors in the image processing network in 1989 and their ranking for 1975 and 1983 are given in Table 8.4.

9   IN CONCLUSION

1 Bruno Latour says: 'society is not what holds us together, it is what is held together'; Latour, B., 'The Powers of Association', in Law, J. (ed.) *Power, Action and Belief: A New Sociology of Knowledge?*, London: Routledge, 1986, pp. 264–79; p. 276.

Table 8.4 Katz index for the eight most central actors in 1989

Ranking	Actor	Katz index	Ranking 1983	Ranking 1975
1	Space Corporation	1.285	1	10
2	Teragon Systems	1.118	2[d]	_[a]
3	Innovativ Vision	1.117	6	_[a]
4	Image Coding Group	1.072	8	33
5	Context Vision	0.943	5	_[b]
6	Imtec	0.855	2[d]	_[c]
7	Sectra	0.775	10	_[e]
8	PICAP-group	0.718	3	19
9	STU	0,699	4	15

Notes:
a. A spin-off from the PICAP-group.
b. A spin-off from the GOP-group.
c. A spin-off from the Image Analysis Laboratory and Teragon Systems.
d. In 1983 Teragon Systems and Imtec were one company under the name of Imtec.
e. A spin-off from the Image Coding Group.

2 Law, J. and Bijker, W. E. (eds) *Shaping Technology/Building Society: Studies in Sociotechnical Change*, Cambridge, Mass: MIT Press, 1992, p. 290.
3 We might ask ourselves if this geographical delimitation is fruitful: technological systems and networks of actors know no national borders. But as long as nations pride themselves on national programs for science and technology, the outcome of these efforts must be discussed. Here it should be distinguished between national programs for the improvement of scientific and technological knowledge and those aiming at developing new commercial opportunities. A critical question when it comes to the latter type of program is: to what extent can the results of the investments in science and technology be appropriated within the nation?
4 Braggins, D. and Hollingum, J. *The Machine Vision Sourcebook*, Berlin: Springer-Verlag, 1986, pp. 168–9; and Wasell, B. and Forchheimer, R., 'Bildbehandlingssystem för industrin: En studie av leverantörsföretag i USA' (Image Processing Systems for Industry: A Study of Suppliers in the USA), *Sverges Tekniska Attachéer, Utlandsrapport, USA U2 8702*, p.18.
5 Wasell and Forchheimer, 'Bildbehandlingssystem för industrin', pp. 66–9.
6 Braggins and Hollingum (*The Machine Vision Sourcebook*) show that on the international scene, digital image technology was dominated by entrepreneurial firms and research and development actors.
7 Rostow, W. W., *The Stages of Economic Growth: A Non-Communist Manifesto*, 3rd edn, Cambridge Mass: Cambridge University Press, 1990, pp. 1–4. The purpose of conceptualizing economic growth as a sequence of stages was not only to build a dynamic, disaggregated general theory of production but also to illuminate specific problems of growth (ibid. pp. ix–x).
8 Kotler, P., *Marketing Management: Analysis, Planning and Control*, 5th edn,

London: Prentice/Hall International, 1984, pp. 375–81. Note that here it is the product that drives the market.

9 Garud, R. and Van de Ven A. H., 'Technological Innovation and Industry Emergence: The Case of Cochlear Implant', in Van de Ven A., Angle, H. and Poole, S. P. (eds) *Research on the Management of Innovation: The Minnesota Studies*, New York: Harper & Row, 1989, pp 473–516.

10 Pantzar, M. *A Replicative Perspective on Evolutionary Dynamics: The Organizing Process of the US Elaborated through Biological Metaphor*, Research Report 37, Helsinki: Labour Institute for Economic Research, 1991, pp. 186–204. Quotation from p. 192.

11 Rådström, N., *När tiden tänker på annat* (When Time Thinks of Something Else), Stockholm: Gedins Förlag, 1992, p. 11. Translation by the author.

12 Katz, M. and Shapiro, C., 'Network Externalities, Competition and Compatibility', *American Economic Review* 75: 424–40 (1985). To economists the critical problem is often the allocation of resources. If only resources are optimally allocated, development will take care of itself.

13 Of course the distinction between internal and external is arbitrary. In reality all effects are internal. The point is that we are facing at least two restrictions: the function of the part and the function of the whole.

14 Foray, D., *Exploitation of Networks Externalities vs. Evolution of Standards: Markets, Committees and the Dilemma of Efficiency*, Paper presented at the ITS-conference, Venice, Italy, March 1990.

15 This is along the same line of thought as the proposition made by the Swedish economic historian Erik Dahmén that structural tensions in development blocks work as driving forces to overcome the tension, but on the other hand if the tension cannot be resolved it can lead to the collapse of the whole development block.

16 The significance of competition thus lies more in the existence of alternatives, of variety, than in the contest between the alternatives.

17 Veblen, T., *The Engineers and the Price System* [1921], New Brunswick: Transaction Books, 1983, p. 72.

18 Dahmén, underscores the importance of entrepreneurs and Hughes, discusses the significance of system-builders. See Dahmén, E., 'Development Blocks in Industrial Economics', *Scandinavian Economic History Review* 1988(1): 3–14 (1988); and Hughs, T. P., *American Genesis*, New York: Viking Penguin, 1989.

19 See, for instance Jantsch, E., *The Self-Organizing Universe*, Oxford: Pergamon Press, 1980.

20 Law and Bijker (eds), *Shaping Technology/Building Society*, p. 293.

21 Van de Ven, A. H. and Garud, R., *A Framework for Understanding the Emergence of New Industries*, Discussion paper 99, Strategic Management Research Centre, University of Minnesota, February 1987, p. 28.

22 This is well in line with Schumpeter's thoughts on the static effect of price competition.

23 The external economies of scientific research are discussed in Arrow, K. J., 'Economic Welfare and the Allocation of Resources for Invention', in Universities – National Bureau Committee for Economic Research, *The Rate and Direction of Inventive Activity*, Princeton, NJ: Princeton University Press, 1962, pp. 609–25; and Nelson, R. R., 'The Simple Economics of Basic Scientific Research', *Journal of Political Economy* 65; 297–306 (June 1959). The 'simple' economic facts of inventive activities purported by Arrow and Nelson further underscore the role of public policy in generating variety.

24 Richard Nelson discusses the virtues of high-technologies in Nelson, R. R., *High-Technology Policies: A Five Nation Comparison*, Washington, DC: American Enterprise Institute for Public Policy Research, 1984. He raises the question: what special economic advantages do high-technology industries give?
25 Humans are part of the structures and in the end it is only humans that have the capacity to act. From a moral philosophy angle it is essential that we put the ultimate responsibility in the hands of individuals. Structures know no morality, it is only humans that can separate right from wrong and such responsibilty should at best be carried by each and every one of us.

10   IMPLICATIONS

1 Here I most definitely reveal one of my biases. To me, history prior to gas or electric light is without light. To me, dark history really means dark history.
2 Bacon, F., 'New Atlantis', in Robertson, J. M. (ed.) *The Philosophical Works of Francis Bacon, Ellis and Spedding*, London: George Routledge and Sons, 1905, pp. 710–32; p. 727. A fourth characteristic of Solomon's House of Science was the ordinances and rites that were to be observed.
3 Merton, R. K., 'Singletons and Multiples in Science', in Merton, R. K., *The Sociology of Science*, Chicago, Ill: Chicago University Press, 1973, pp. 343–70; p. 348.
4 Bacon, 'New Atlantis', pp. 731–2. Also quoted in Merton, 'Singletons and Multiples in Science', p. 348.
5 Frängsmyr, T. (ed.) *Science in Sweden: the Royal Swedish Academy of Sciences, 1739–1989*, Canton, Mass: Science History Publications, 1989, p. 1.
6 Actually, it seems that Francis Bacon's thoughts are enjoying a renaissance. 'New Atlantis' was recently translated into Swedish and the 75th Nobel Symposium was dedicated to the revisiting of Solomon's House of Science. See Frängsmyr, T. (ed.) *Solomon's House Revisited: The Organization and Institutionalization of Science*, Nobel Symposium 75, Canton, Mass: Science History Publications, 1990.
7 Merton, R. K., 'Singletons and Multiples in Science', p. 349.

Select bibliography

Abramovitz, M., 'Resource and Output Trends in the United States since 1870', *American Economic Review, Papers and Proceedings*, May 1956, pp. 5–23.

Abramovitz, M., *Thinking About Growth*, New York: Cambridge University Press, 1989.

Alderson, W., *Dynamic Marketing Behavior*, Homewood, Ill.: Richard D. Irwin Inc., 1965.

Arrow, K. J., 'Economic Welfare and the Allocation of Resources for Invention', in Universities – National Bureau Committee for Economic Research, *The Rate and Direction of Inventive Activity*, Princeton, NJ: Princeton University Press, 1962, pp. 609–25.

Arthur, W. B., 'Competing Technologies and Economic Prediction', IIASA, *Options* 2: 10–13, 1984.

Arthur, W. B., 'Competing Technologies: An Overview', in Dosi, G., Freeman, C., Nelson, R., Silverberg, G. and Soete, L. (eds) *Technical Change and Economic Theory*, London: Pinter, 1988, pp. 590–607.

Arthur, W. B., *Industry Location and the Importance of History*, Center for Economic Policy Research, No. 84, Stanford University, 1986.

Aspray, W., *John von Neumann and the Origins of Modern Computing*, Cambridge, Mass: MIT University Press, 1990.

Axelsson, B. and Easton, G. (eds) *Industrial Networks: A New View of Reality*, London: Routledge, 1992.

Bacon, F., 'Essays', in Robertson, J. M. (ed.) *The Philosophical Works of Francis Bacon, Ellis and Spedding*, London: George Routledge and Sons, 1905, pp. 733–814.

Bacon, F., 'New Atlantis', in Robertson, J. M. (ed.) *The Philosophical Works of Francis Bacon, Ellis and Spedding*, London: George Routledge and Sons, 1905, pp. 710–32.

Bain, J. S., *Industrial Organization*, New York: Wiley, 1959.

Basalla, G., *The Evolution of Technology*, Cambridge: Cambridge University Press, 1988.

Beninger, J. R., *The Control Revolution: Technological and Economic Origins of the Information Society*, Cambridge, Mass.: Harvard University Press, 1986.

Benndorf, H., *Marknadsföringsplanering och samordning mellan företag i industriella system* (Market Planning and Coordination between Firms in Industrial Systems), Doctoral Dissertation, Stockholm: Stockholm School of Economics, 1987.

Bernal, J., D., *Science and Industry in the Nineteenth Century*, Bloomington: Indiana University Press, 1970.

Biemans, W.G., *Developing Innovations within Networks: With Application to the Dutch Medical Equipment Industry*, Doctoral Dissertation, University of Groningen, Groningen, 1989.

Blauwhof, G., Rossum, van, W., and Zeldenrust, S., 'The Development of Technologies/Towards a Network Analysis', Paper prepared for the Dutch Workshop on Technology Research, Groningen, 31 May – 1 June 1990.

Blichner, L., *Competency Traps and Successful Experimentation*, Working paper, LOS–Senteret, Bergen, Norway, 1990.

Bloch, M., *The Historian's Craft* [1954], Manchester: Manchester University Press, 1992.

Braggins, D. W., 'The Evolution of Quantitative Image Analysers 1963–1981', in Proceedings of the Indian Statistical Institute Golden Jubilee International Conference, *Advances in Information Science and Technology, 1: Pattern Recognition and Digital Technique*, Calcutta, January, 1982, pp. 298–315.

Braudel, F., *Civilization and Capitalism 15th – 18th Century, 1: The Structures of Everyday Life*, London: Collins, 1981.

Brodin, B., *Produktutvecklingsprocesser* (Product Development Processes), Doctoral Dissertation, Stockholm: Stockholm School of Economics, 1976.

Burke, P., *The French Historical Revolution: The Annales School 1929–1989*, Cambridge: Polity Press, 1990.

Cantwell, J., 'The Technological Competence Theory of International Production and its Implications', Paper presented at the European International Business Association, 16th Annual Conference, Madrid, 12–15 December 1990.

Carlson, B. and Jacobsson, S., 'What Makes the Automation Industry Strategic?', Paper presented at the European Association for Research in Industrial Economics, 17th Annual Conference, Lisbon, Portugal, 2–4 September 1991.

Carlsson, B. (ed.) *Industrial Dynamics*, Boston: Kluwer Academic Publishers, 1989.

Chamberlin, E. H., *The Theory of Monopolistic Competition*, 3rd edn, Cambridge, Mass: Harvard University Press, 1938.

Cipolla, C. M., *Between History and Economics: An Introduction to Economic History*, Oxford: Basil Blackwell, 1991.

Clewett, R. L., 'Integrating Science, Technology, and Marketing: an Overview', in Haas, R. M. (ed.) *Science, Technology and Marketing*, American Marketing Association, 1966 Fall Conference Proceedings, Indiana University, Bloomington, Indiana, pp. 3–20.

Commons J. R., *Institutional Economics: Its Place in Political Economy* [1934], New Brunswick: Transaction Books, 1990.

Cox, R. and Alderson, W. (eds) *Theory in Marketing*, Chicago, Ill: Richard D. Irwin, 1950.

Cyert, R. M. and March, J. G., *A Behavioral Theory of the Firm*, Englewood Cliffs, NJ: Prentice-Hall, 1963.

Dahmén, E., 'Development Blocks in Industrial Economics', *Scandinavian Economic History Review* 1988(1): 3–14.

Dahmén, E., *Entrepreneurial Activity and the Development of Swedish Industry 1919–1939*, American Economic Translation Series, Homewood, Ill: Richard D. Irwin, 1970.

Darwin, C., *The Origin of the Species* [1859], London: Penguin Books, 1968.

David, P. A., 'Clio and the Economics of QWERTY', *American Economic Review* 75: 332–7 (1985).

David, P. A., 'Computer and Dynamo: The Modern Productivity Paradox in a Not-Too-Distant Mirror', Paper presented at the OECD International Seminar on Science, Technology and Economic Growth, Paris, France, 5–8 June 1989.

David, P. A., 'Learning by Doing and Tariff Protection: A Reconsideration of the Case of the Ante-bellum United States Cotton Textile Industry', in David, P., *Technical Choice, Innovation, and Economic Growth*, Cambridge: Cambridge University Press, 1975, pp. 95–168.

David, P. A., *Path-Dependence: Putting the Past into the Future*, Stanford University, Institute for Mathematical Studies in the Social Sciences, Economic Series, Technical Report 533, November 1988.

David, P. A., 'Some New Standards for the Economics of Standardization in the Information Age', in Dasgupta, P. and Stoneman P. (eds) *Economic Policy and Technological Performance*, New York: Cambridge University Press, 1987, pp. 206–39.

David P. A., 'The Hero and the Herd in Technological History: Reflections on Thomas Edison and the "Battle of Systems"', Center for Economic Policy Research, Technical Paper 100, Stanford University, 1987.

David P. A. and Bunn, J. A., '"The Battle of the Systems" and the Evolutionary Dynamics of Network Technology Rivalries', High Technology Impact Program, Center for Economic Policy Research, Working Paper 15, Stanford University, 1987.

Davies, D., Bathurst, D. and Bathurst, R., *The Telling Image: The Changing Balance Between Pictures and Words in a Technological Age*, Oxford: Clarendon Press, 1990.

Dawkins, R., *The Blind Watchmaker*, London: Penguin Books, 1986.

Dawkins, R., *The Selfish Gene*, Oxford: Oxford University Press, 1978.

Dosi, G., 'Technological Paradigms and Technological Trajectories', *Research Policy* 11(3): 147–62 (1982).

Dosi, G., 'The Nature of the Innovative Process', in Dosi, G., Freeman, C., Nelson, R., Silverberg, G. and Soete, L. (eds) *Technical Change and Economic Theory*, London: Pinters, 1988, pp. 221–38.

Dosi, G., Freeman, C., Nelson, R., Silverberg, G. and Soete, L. (eds) *Technical Change and Economic Theory*, London: Pinters, 1988.

Duijn, van, J. J., *The Long Wave in Economic Life*, London: George Allen & Unwin, 1983.

Dyring, E., *Nolla etta bild: Den nya bildrevolutionen* (Zero One Image: The New Image Revolution), Stockholm: Prisma, 1984.

Easton, G. and Lundgren, A., 'Changes in Industrial Networks as Flow Through Nodes', in Axelsson, B. and Easton, G. (eds) *Industrial Networks: A New View of Reality*, London: Routledge, 1992, pp. 88–104.

Easton G. and Smith, P., 'The Formation of Interorganizational Relationships in a Major Gasfield Development', *Proceedings of the International Research Seminar on Industrial Marketing*, Stockholm School of Economics, 29–31 August 1984.

Elster, J., *Nuts and Bolts for the Social Sciences*, Cambridge: Cambridge University Press, 1989.

Enos, J., *Petroleum, Progress and Profits*, Cambridge, Mass: MIT University Press, 1967.

Everett, M., 'EBLOC: A Graph-Theoretic Blocking Algorithm', *Social Networks* 5: 323–46 (1983).

Federation of Swedish Industry, Stockholm, *Industry in Sweden*, Uppsala: Almqvist & Wicksell Boktryckeri AB, 1928.

Feyerabend, P., *Against Method*, rev. edn, London: Verso, 1988.

Fischler, M. A. and Firschein, O., *Intelligence: The Eye, The Brain and The Computer*, Reading, Mass: Addison Wesley, 1987.

Flamm, K., *Creating the Computer: Government Industry and High Technology*, Washington DC: The Brookings Institution, 1988.

Foray, D., *Exploitation of Networks Externalities vs. Evolution of Standards: Markets, Committees and the Dilemma of Efficiency*, Paper presented at the ITS-conference, Venice, Italy, March 1990.

Ford, D., *Understanding Business Markets: Interaction, Relationships and Networks*, London: Academic Press, 1990.

Forester, T., *High-Tech Society*, Cambridge, Mass: MIT Press, 1987.

Frängsmyr, T. (ed.) *Science in Sweden: the Royal Swedish Academy of Sciences, 1739–1989*, Canton, Mass: Science History Publications, 1989.

Frängsmyr, T. (ed.) *Solomon's House Revisited: The Organization and Institutionalization of Science*, Nobel Symposium 75, Canton, Mass: Science History Publications, 1990.

Freeman, C., 'Networks of Innovators: A Synthesis of Research Issues', *Research Policy* 20(5): pp. 499–514 (1990).

Freeman, C. and Perez, C., 'Structural Crises of Adjustment, Business Cycles and Investment Behaviour', in Dosi, G., Freeman, C., Nelson, R., Silverberg, G. and Soete, L. (eds) *Technical Change and Economic Theory*, London: Pinter, 1988, pp. 38–66.

Garud, R. and Van de Ven A. H., 'Technological Innovation and Industry Emergence: The Case of Cochlear Implant', in Van de Ven A., Angle, H. and Poole, S. P. (eds) *Research on the Management of Innovation: The Minnesota Studies*, New York: Harper & Row, 1989, pp. 473–516.

Gherardi, S., *Development and Decline in Organizational Analogies: A Critical Review*, Working Paper, Dipartimento di Politica Sociale, Universita' Degli Studi Di Trento, undated.

Giddens, A., *The Constitution of Society*, Cambridge: Polity Press, 1984.

Giedion, S., *Mechanization Takes Command: A Contribution to Anonymous History* [1948], New York: Norton, 1969.

Gilfillan, S. C., *Inventing the Ship*, Chicago, Ill: Follet, 1935.

Gilfillan, S. C., *The Sociology of Invention*, Chicago, Ill: Follet, 1935.

Glete, J., *ASEA under hundra År 1883–1983: En studie i ett storföretags organisatoriska, tekniska och ekonomiska utveckling* (ASEA Hundred Years 1883–1983: A study of a Large Corporation's Organizational, Technological and Economic Development), Stockholm: Economic History Research Institute, Stockholm School of Economics, 1983.

Gould, S. J., 'The Panda's Thumb of Technology', in Tushman, M. L. and Moore, W. L., (eds) *Readings in the Management of Innovation*, 2nd edn, Cambridge, Mass: Ballinger Publishing, 1988, pp. 37–44.

Grahn, S., and Borg, C-G., *The Sky is Not the Limit: SSC and the Swedish Space Effort*, Swedish Space Corporation: Stockholm, 1982.

Greenstein, S. and Ramey, G., *Product Inertia and the Incentive to Innovate*, Centre for Economic Policy Research, No. 149, Stanford University, 1988.

Grether, E. T., 'A Theoretical Approach to the Analysis of Marketing', in Cox, R. and Alderson, W. (eds) *Theory in Marketing*, Chicago, Ill: Richard D. Irwin, 1950, pp. 113–24.

Grether, E. T., 'Pioneers in Marketing: Edwin Griswold Nourse', *Journal of Marketing* 22 (1958).

Hagedoorn, J. and Schot, J., *Co-operation between Companies and Technological Development*, Working Paper, University of Groningen, Groningen, 1988.

Hägg, I. and Johanson, J. (eds) *Företag i nätverk*, (Firms in Networks) Stockholm: SNS, 1982.

Håkansson, H., *Corporate Technological Behaviour: Cooperation and Networks*, London: Routledge, 1989.

Håkansson, H., 'Evolution Processes in Industrial Networks', in Axelsson, B. and Easton, G. (eds) *Industrial Networks: A New View of Reality*, London: Routledge, 1991.

Håkansson, H., 'Product Development in Networks', in Håkansson, H. (ed.) *Industrial Technological Development: A Network Approach*, London: Croom Helm, 1987, pp. 84–127.

Håkansson, H. (ed.) *Industrial Technological Development: A Network Approach*, London: Croom Helm, 1987.

Håkansson, H., and Snehota, I., 'No Business is an Island: The Network Concept of Business Strategy', *Scandinavian Journal of Management* 5(3): 187–200 (1989).

Hammarkvist, K-O., *Köpprocessen för nya produkter på byggmarknaden* (The Buying Process for New Products in the Construction Industry), Doctoral Dissertation, Stockholm: Stockholm School of Economics, 1976.

Hammarkvist, K-O., Håkansson, H. and Mattsson, L-G., *Marknadsföring för konkurrenskraft* (Marketing for Competitiveness), Malmö: Liber Förlag, 1982.

Hannan, M. T. and Freeman, J., 'The Population Ecology of Organizations', *American Journal of Sociology* 82(5): 929–64 (1977).

Harrod, R. F. and Hobson, J. A., *The Science of Wealth* [4th edn 1911], London: Oxford University Press, 1950.

Hayek, F. A., von, 'The Use of Knowledge in Society', *American Economic Review* 35: 519–30 (1945).

Hertz, S., 'Towards More Integrated Industrial Systems', in Axelsson, B. and Easton, G. (eds) *Industrial Networks: A New View of Reality*, London: Routledge, 1991, pp. 105–28.

Hicks, E. K. and Rossum, van, W., 'The Developmental Process of Technologies: Combined Insights from Network and Systems Theory', Paper prepared for the Dutch Workshop on Technology Research, Groningen, 31 May – 1 June 1990.

Hindle, B. and Lubar, S., *Engines of Change: The American Industrial Revolution*, Washington, DC: Smithsonian Institution Press, 1986.

Hippel, E., von, *The Sources of Innovation*, New York: Oxford University Press, 1988.

Hollander, S., *The Sources of Increased Efficiency: A Study of Du Pont Rayon Plants*, Cambridge, Mass: MIT University Press, 1965.

Hounshell, D. A., *From the American System to Mass Production: The Development of Manufacturing Technology in the United States*, Baltimore, Md: Johns Hopkins University Press, 1984.

Hughes, T. P., *American Genesis*, New York: Viking Penguin, 1989.

Hughes, T. P., *Networks of Power: Electrification in Western Society, 1880–1930*, Baltimore, Md: Johns Hopkins University Press, 1983.

Hughes, T. P., 'The Evolution of Large Technological Systems', in Bijker, W. B., Hughes, T. P. and Pinch, T. J. (eds) *The Social Construction of Technological Systems*, Cambridge, Mass: MIT Press, pp. 51–82 (1987).

Hult, J., Lindkvist, S., Odelberg, W. and Rydberg, S., *Svensk teknikhistoria* (Swedish History of Technology), Hedemora: Gidlunds Bokförlag, 1989.

Hultén, S., 'On Network Externalities and the Evolution of Networks', Paper presented at the 8th IMP Conference, Lyon, France, September 1992.

Hultén, S., *Vad bestämmer de svenska exportmarknadsandelarnas utveckling* (What Determines the Development of the Swedish Market Shares), Doctoral Dissertation, Stockholm: Stockholm School of Economics, 1988.

Hunter, L., *Steamboats on the Western Rivers: An Economic and Technological History*, Cambridge, Mass: Harvard University Press, 1949.

Jantsch, E., *The Self-Organizing Universe*, Oxford: Pergamon Press, 1980.

Johanson, J. and Mattsson, L-G., 'Internationalization in Industrial Systems: A Network Approach', in Hood, N. and Vahlne, J-E. (eds) *Strategies in Global Competition*, London: Croom Helm, 1988, pp. 287–314.

Johanson, J. and Mattsson, L-G. 'Network Positions and Strategic Action: An Analytical Framework', in Axelsson, B. and Easton, G. (ed.) *Industrial Networks: A New View of Reality*, London: Routledge, 1991, pp. 205–17.

Kamien, M. I. and Schwartz, N. L., *Market Structure and Innovation*, Cambridge: Cambridge University Press, 1982.

Katz, M. and Shapiro, C., 'Network Externalities, Competition, and Compatibility', *American Economic Review* 75: 424–40 (1985).

Kelly, P., Kranzberg, M., Rossini,. F., Baker, N., Tarpley, F. and Mitzner, M. 'The Individual Inventor: Entrepreneur', in Roy, R. and Wield, D. (eds) *Product Design and Technological Innovation*, Milton Keynes, UK: Open University Press, 1986, pp. 76–85.

Klass, P. J., *Secret Sentries in Space*, New York: Random House, 1971.

Knoke, D. and Kuklinski, J. H., *Network Analysis*, Beverly Hills, Ca: Sage, 1982.

Knorr-Cetina, K. D., *The Manufacture of Knowledge: An Essay on the Constructivist and Contextual Nature of Science*, Oxford: Pergamon Press, 1981.

Kotler, P., *Marketing Management: Analysis, Planning and Control*, 5th edn, London: Prentice/Hall International, 1984.

Kuznets, S., *Economic Development, the Family, and Income Distribution*, Cambridge: Cambridge University Press, 1989.

Kuznets, S., *Modern Economic Growth*, New Haven, Conn: Yale University Press, 1966.

Laage-Hellman, J., *Technological Development in Industrial Networks*, Doctoral Dissertation, Department of Business Studies, Uppsala University, 1989.

Laage-Hellman, J. and Axelsson, B., *Biotechnological R&D in Sweden – Research Volume, Direction of Research, Pattern of Cooperation: A Study of the Biotechnological R&D Network 1970–1985*, STU–Information 563–1986, Stockholm: Styrelsen för Teknisk Utveckling, 1986.

Landes, D. S., 'Introduction: On Technology and Growth', in Higonnet, P., Landes, D. S. and Rosovsky, H. (eds) *Favourites of Fortune: Technology, Growth, and Economic Development since the Industrial Revolution*, Cambridge, Mass: Harvard University Press, 1991, pp. 1–29.

Latour, B., 'The Powers of Association', in Law, J. (ed.) *Power, Action and Belief: A New Sociology of Knowledge?*, London: Routledge, 1986, pp. 264–79.

Law, J. and Bijker, W. E. (eds) *Shaping Technology/Building Society: Studies in Sociotechnical Change*, Cambridge, Mass: MIT Press, 1992.

Levitt, B. and March, J. G., 'Organizational Learning', *Annual Review of Sociology* 14: 319–40 (1988).

Lewis, B., *History: Remembered, Recovered, Invented*, New York: Touchstone Books, 1975.

Liljegren, G., *Interdependens och dynamik i långsiktiga kundrelationer: Industriell försäljning i ett nätverksperspektiv*, (Interdependence and Dynamics in Customer Relationships) Doctoral Dissertation, Stockholm: Stockholm School of Economics, 1988.

Lindgren, H., 'Business History, Historical Economics and Economic Theory: The Bridge-Building Function of Business History', in *The Network of Financial Capital: Essays in Honour of Ragnhild Lundström*, Uppsala Papers in Economic History, Working Paper 9, Uppsala University, 1990, pp. 45–64.

Lindqvist, S., 'Changes in the Technological Landscape: The Temporal Dimension in the Growth and Decline of Large Technological Systems', Paper presented at the conference, The Development of Large Technical Systems, at the Max Planck Institut für Gesellschaftforschung, Cologne FRG, 25–28 November 1987.

Lindqvist, S., *Technology on Trial*, Stockholm: Almqvist & Wiksell International, 1984.

Lindqvist, S., 'Vad är teknik?' (What is Technology?), in Sundin, B. (ed.) *I teknikens backspegel* (In the Mirror of Technology), Stockholm: Carlsons Bokförlag, 1987, pp. 11–33.

Lund, J., *Från kula till data* (From Abacus to Computer), Värnamo: Gidlunds Förlag, 1988.

Lundgren, A., 'Coordination and Mobilization Processes in Industrial Networks', in Axelsson, B. and Easton, G. (eds) *Industrial Networks: A New View of Reality*, London: Routledge, 1992, pp. 144–165.

Lundgren, A., *Datoriserad bildbehandling: Analys av framväxten av ett nytt teknikområde*, (Computerized Image Processing: Analysis of the Development of a New Technology), Thesis Proposal, Stockholm: Stockholm School of Economics, 1986.

Lundgren, A., *Datoriserad bildbehandling i Sverige: En fallstudie* (Computerized Image Processing in Sweden: A Case Report), Working Paper, Stockholm: Stockholm School of Economics, 1985.

Lundgren, A., *Technology and Marketing Theory*, Working Paper, Stockholm: Stockholm School of Economics, 1990.

Lundvall, B-Å., 'Innovation as an Interactive Process: From User–Producer Interaction to the National System of Innovation', in Dosi, G., Freeman, C., Nelson, R., Silverberg, G. and Soete, L. (eds) *Technical Change and Economic Theory*, London: Pinter, 1988, pp. 348–69.

March, J. G., Footnotes to Organizational Change, *Administrative Science Quarterly*, 26: 563–577 (1981).

Mattsson, L-G., 'Management of Strategic Change in a "Market – as – Networks" Perspective', in Pettigrew, A. (ed.) *The Management of Strategic Change*, Oxford: Basil Blackwell, 1987, pp. 234–56.

Merton, R. K., 'Singletons and Multiples in Science', in Merton, R. K., *The Sociology of Science*, Chicago, Ill: Chicago University Press, 1973, pp. 343–70.

Merton, T., *No Man is an Island*, Turnbridge Wells, UK: Burns & Oates, 1955.

Morison, E., *Men, Machines and Modern Times*, Cambridge, Mass: MIT University Press, 1966.

Mowery, D. C. and Rosenberg, N., *Technology and the Pursuit of Economic Growth*, Cambridge: Cambridge University Press, 1989.

Mumford, L., *Teknik och civilisation* (Technics and Civilization; 1934), Göteborg: Vinga Press, 1984.

Myhrman, J., *The Process of Economic Growth*, Working Paper: Stockholm School of Economics, January 1990.

Nelson, R. R., *High-Technology Policies: A Five Nation Comparison, Washington, DC: American Enterprise Institute for Public Policy Research, 1984.*

Nelson, R. R., 'The Simple Economics of Basic Scientific Research', *Journal of Political Economy* 65: 297–306 (June 1959).

Nelson, R. R. and Winter, S. G., *An Evolutionary Theory of Economic Change*, Cambridge, Mass: Harvard University Press, 1982.

OECD, Information Computer Communications Policy: 20, *Major R&D Programmes for Information Technology*, Paris, 1989.

OECD, Science and Technology Indicators, Report 3, *R&D, Production and Diffusion of Technology*, OECD, Paris, 1989.

Ohlsson, L. and Vinell, L., *Tillväxtens drivkrafter: En studie av industriers framtidsvillkor* (The Forces of Growth: A Study of the Future of Industries), Stockholm: Industriförbundets Förlag, 1987.

Pantzar, M. *A Replicative Perspective on Evolutionary Dynamics: The Organizing Process of the US Elaborated through Biological Metaphor*, Research Report 37, Helsinki: Labour Institute for Economic Research, 1991.

Pettigrew, A. M., *The Awakening Giant: Continuity and Change in ICI*, Oxford: Basil Blackwell, 1985.

Pevsner, N., *Pioneers of Modern Design: from William Morris to Walter Gropius*, Harmondsworth, UK: Penguin Books, 1960.

Pfeffer, J. and Salancik, G. R., *The External Control of Organizations: A Resource Dependence Perspective*, New York: Harper & Row, 1978.

Piore, M. J. and Sabel, C. F., *The Second Industrial Divide: Possibilities for Prosperity*, New York: Basic Books, 1984.

Popper, K., *The Poverty of Historicism* [1957], London: Ark Paperbacks, 1986.

Robinson, J., *The Economics of Imperfect Competition*, London: Macmillan, 1933.

Rogers, E. M. and Larsen J. K., *Silicon Valley Fever: Growth of High Technology Culture*, London: George Allen & Unwin, 1984.

Rosenberg, N., 'Learning by Using', in Rosenberg, N., *Inside the Black Box: Technology and Economics*, Cambridge: Cambridge University Press, 1982, pp. 120–40.

Rosenberg, N., *Perspectives on Technology*, Armonk, NY: M. E. Sharpe, 1976.

Rosenberg, N., 'Scientific Instrumentation and University Research', Paper presented at the annual meeting of the American Economic Association, New York City, 30 December 1988.

Rosenberg, N., 'Technological Change in the Machine Tool Industry, 1840–1910', in Rosenberg, N., *Perspectives on Technology*, Armonk, NY: M. E. Sharpe, 1976, pp. 9–31.

Rosenberg, N., 'Technological Interdependence in the American Economy', in Rosenberg, N., *Inside the Black Box: Technology and Economics*, Cambridge: Cambridge University Press, 1982, pp. 55–80.

Rosenberg, N., 'The Historiography of Technical Progress', in Rosenberg, N., *Inside the Black Box: Technology and Economics*, Cambridge: Cambridge University Press, 1982, pp. 3–33.

Rosenberg, N., 'Why Do Firms Do Basic Research (With Their Own Money)?', *Research Policy* 19(2), 1990.

Rosenberg, N. and Birdzell, L. E. jun., 'Science, Technology and the Western Miracle', *Scientific American* 263(5): 18–25 (November 1990).

Rostow, W. W., *The Stages of Economic Growth: A Non-Communist Manifesto*, 3rd edn, Cambridge Mass: Cambridge University Press, 1990.

Sahlin-Andersson, K., *Forskningsparker and företagsrelationer* (Research Parks and Relationships between Firms), Stockholm: RTK, 1990.

Scherer, F. M., *Industrial Market Structure and Economic Performance*, 2nd edn, Boston, Mass: Houghton Mifflin, 1980.

Schumpeter, J. A., *Capitalism, Socialism and Democracy* [1942], New York: Harper Torchbooks, 1975.

Schumpeter, J. A., *The Theory of Economic Development* [1934], New Brunswick: Transaction Books, 1983.

Scott, J., *Social Network Analysis: A Handbook*, London: Sage, 1991.

Sellstedt, B., *Samhällsteorier: Vad har Giddens, Habermas m fl att säga ekonomer?*, (Social Theories: What Have Giddens, Habermas and Others to Tell Economists?), Lund: Studentlitteratur, 1992.

Solow, R., 'Technical Change and the Aggregate Production Function', *Review of Economics and Statistics*, August 1957, pp. 312–20.

SOU 1991:82, Produktivitetsdelegationens betänkande, Stockholm: Allmänna förlaget, 1991.

Sprenger, C. A. J. and Stokman, F. N. (eds) *GRADAP, Manual, version 2.0*, Groningen: iec ProGAMMA, 1989.

Sraffa, P., 'The Laws of Returns under Competitive Conditions', *Economic Journal* 39: 41–57 (1929).

Staudenmaier, J. M., S.J., *Technology's Storyteller: Reweaving the Human Fabric*, Cambridge, Mass: MIT Press, 1985.

Swedberg, R., *Schumpeter: A Biography*, Princeton, NJ: Princeton University Press, 1991.

Swedberg, R., and Granovetter, M. (eds) *The Sociology of Economic Life*, Boulder, Col: Westview Press, 1992.

Sölvell, Ö., Zander, I. and Porter, M. E., *Advantage Sweden*, Stockholm: Norsteds Bokförlag, 1991.

Thompson, J. D., *Organizations in Action*, New York: Mcgraw-Hill, 1967.

Tucker, J. B., 'Business Outlook: Robot Applications Enhance Vision Sales', *High Technology*, June 1984, p. 61.

Usher, A. P., *A History of Mechanical Inventions* [rev. edn 1954], New York: Dover, 1982.

Utterback, J. M., 'The Dynamics of Product and Process Innovation in Industry', in Hill, C. T. and Utterback, J. M. (eds) *Technological Innovation for a Dynamic Economy*, New York: Pergamon Press, 1979, pp. 40–65.

Valdelin, J., *Produktutveckling och marknadsföring* (Product Development and Marketing), Doctoral Dissertation, Stockholm: Stockholm School of Economics, 1974.

Van de Ven, A. H. and Garud R., *A Framework for Understanding the Emergence of New Industries*, Discussion paper 66, Strategic Management Research Centre, University of Minnesota, February 1987.

Veblen, T., *Imperial Germany and the Industrial Revolution* [1949], New Brunswick: Transaction Books, 1990.

Veblen, T., *The Engineers and the Price System* [1921], New Brunswick: Transaction Books, 1983.

Waluszewski, A., *Framväxten av en ny massateknik: En utvecklingshistoria*, (The Emergence of a New Mechanical Pulp Technology: A Development Story), Doctoral Dissertation, Department of Business Studies, Uppsala University, 1989.

Weick, K. E., *The Social Psychology of Organizing*, 2nd edn, New York: Random House, 1979.

Wibe, S., 'Change of Technology and Day-to-Day Improvements', *Umeå Economic Studies,* 78, Umeå University, 1978.

Williamson, O. E., *Markets and Hierarchies: Analysis and Antitrust Implications*, New York: Free Press, 1975.

Winter, S. G., 'Knowledge and Competence as Strategic Assets', in Teece, D. J. (ed.) *The Competitive Challenge: Strategies for Industrial Innovation and Renewal*, New York: Harper & Row, 1987, pp. 159–84.

Yoxen, E., 'Seeing with Sound: A study of the Development of Medical Images', in Bijker, W. B., Hughes, T. P. and Pinch, T. J. (ed.) *The Social Construction of Technological Systems*, Cambridge, Mass: MIT Press, 1987, pp. 281–303.

Zuech, N. and Miller, R. K., *Machine Vision*, New York: van Nostrand Reinhold, 1989.

Index

Silicon Valley (California) 145–7,
148; preconditions for 145–6
Smith, A. 30, 52, 81
social evolution 53
social progress: context of
technological change 53–7; and
history 61, 68–74; inquiries into
68–74; and mechanization 53–4;
and technological development
36–40
social structure, and digital image
industry, Sweden 117, 121
Solow, R. 31
Sony Corporation 7, 136
space, networks in 157–67; and
cartography 164–5; competitors in
162; and complementary
technologies 167; and image
processing systems 162–3; internal
needs of Swedish Space
Corporation 158–9; and map
production 164; new technology in
161–2; and newspaper systems
159–61; spin-off effects 165–7
special initiative of STU 131–4; actors
outside 148–50; printed circuit
board inspection 171–2
specialization, in industrial networks
81, 87
specific knowledge 45
spectrography, research into 109
Spot Image (company) 163
Spotimage (company) 151
SPOT-satellite 163
SRB AB: in computer industry 22
Stanford University 145–6
Stanford University Research Park 145
Staudenmair, J.M. 54
steam-engine, Newcomen's, to
Sweden 46–7, 58–9
steel, non-metallic inclusions in,
digital image analysis in 171, 174
Stenkvist, B. 104
Strings (cartographic software) 158
Struers Vision 183
SUAB (development company) 159–60
Summer Olympics, 1984 (Los
Angeles) 153
Sweden: automobile industry in 82;
computer industry 21–2; defence

industry 117; digital image industry
see digital image industry, Sweden;
image processing networks as
special case 189–90; industrial basis
20–2; Newcomen steam-engine to
46–7, 58–9; productivity 21; R&D
expenditure 20; research parks in
147; technical ability in 19–20;
technological persistence in
railways 62
Swedish Association for Automatic
Image Processing 131, 133, 202
Swedish Coast Guard 157
Swedish Industrial Development Fund
176, 204
Swedish Meteorological and
Hydrological Institute 166
Swedish National Board for Technical
Development (STU) 115–16; bias
towards computer systems 134–5;
bridging gaps in technology 144–5;
legitimating activities of digital
processing 131; legitimating digital
image processing 150–2; new
support program (1987) 177–8; in
1983 139–40; and public policy
203–5; research and industrial
innovation, gap between 135–7;
special initiative of 131–4, 148–50,
171–2, 205
Swedish Space Corporation 114; and
cartographic systems 162–4, 202; in
development constellation 168, 200;
internal needs of and space
networks 158–9; legitimating digital
image processing 151; networks in
space 157–9, 202; in 1983 139–40;
on OSIRIS project 133, 152–3;
producer-user chains with 168; and
public policy 203–5; research and
development by 131, 134–5, 137,
162; and satellite systems 165,
166–7, 202
Swedish Space Program 148–9, 157
Swedish Space Technology Group 114
Swedish Telecom 108
Swedsurvey 167
Sydat Automation AB 137
system building in network
technologies 201–3